Beholders of Divine Secrets

Beholders of Divine Secrets

Mysticism and Myth in the Hekhalot and Merkavah Literature

Vita Daphna Arbel

State University of New York Press

Published by
State University of New York Press, Albany

Printed in the United States of America

For information, address State University of New York Press, 194 Washington Avenue, Suite 305, Albany, NY 12210-2384

Production by Kelli Williams
Marketing by Patrick Durocher

Library of Congress Cataloging-in-Publication Data

Arbel, Vita Daphna.
Beholders of divine secrets : mysticism and myth in Hekhalot and merkavah literature / Vita Daphna Arbel.
p. cm.
Based on a doctoral thesis submitted to the Hebrew University, Jerusalem in 1997.
Includes bibliographical references and index.
ISBN 0-7914-5723-0 (alk. paper) — ISBN 0-7914-5724-9 (pbk. : alk. paper)
1. Mysticism—Judaism. 2. Hekhalot literature—History and criticism. 3. Merkava. 4. Mythology, Jewish. I. Title.

BM723 .A68 2003
296.7'12—dc21 2002042638

10 9 8 7 6 5 4 3 2 1

I dedicate this book to my grandparents Ester and Alter-Avner
and to my parents Hanna and Micha with love.

Contents

Preface

This book emerged from a doctoral thesis, written in Hebrew, which I submitted to the Hebrew University in Jerusalem in 1997. In the course of further research, revision and translation, however, the book has taken on a new form. In it I examine mystical notions present in the enigmatic Hekhalot and Merkavah literature, the manner in which these are expressed through mythological imagery, as well as the possible social-cultural and ideological affiliation of members of the Hekhalot and Merkavah mystical circle.

In Jerusalem I had the great fortune to study with Professors Rachel Elior and R. J. Zvi Werblowsky as my thesis advisers. They introduced me to the exciting field of Jewish mysticism and its research. I have greatly benefited from their profound insights and perspectives and am deeply thankful for their wisdom and scholarship. Many later conversations with Rachel Elior throughout the years have continued to be an ongoing source of encouragement and inspiration and I thank her with all my heart for an insightful and stimulating continuous dialogue. I also wish to express my most sincere gratitude to Professor Haim Tadmor who promoted my interest in the ancient Near Eastern world and its intriguing legends.

My thanks to the University of British Columbia for the Humanities Research Grants that generously supported this project. I am very grateful for encouragement and support from my friends and colleagues in the department of Classical, Near Eastern, and Religious Studies. My deep thanks to Shirley Sullivan who graciously read the manuscript throughout its stages. To her friendship, attentive reading, and skillful touch of clarity I owe much gratitude. A special word of thanks goes to Omer's intriguing observations and design eye. Sincere thanks are also due to Nancy Ellegate, Kelli Williams, and the rest of the editorial staff at SUNY Press.

Finally, I would like to mention the people who immensely enrich my life and my work in so many ways—Efrat, Omer, and Menashé. My love and thanks go far beyond words.

Abbreviations

AASOR	Annual of the American School of Oriental Research
AJSR	Association for Jewish Studies Review
ANET	Ancient Near Eastern Texts. J. B. Pritchard, ed., 3d. ed. Princeton 1969.
ANEP	Ancient Near East in Pictures. J. B. Pritchard, ed., 3d ed. Princeton 1965.
AnOr	Analecta Orientalia (Rome)
AUSS	Andrews University Seminar Studies
BASOR	Bulletin of the American Schools of Oriental Research
CAD	I. J. Gelb et al., Chicago Assyrian Dictionary (1956–)
CBA	Catholic Biblical Association of America
CBQ	Catholic Biblical Quarterly
ConB OT	Coniectanea Biblica Old Testament Series
CTA	Corpus des tablettes en cunéiformes alphabétiques déscouvertes à Ras Shamra-Ugarit de 1929 à 1939. A. Herdner. Paris 1963.
HTR	Harvard Theological Review
HTS	Harvard Theological Studies
HUCA	Hebrew Union College Annual
JAOS	Journal of The American Oriental Society
JBL	Journal of Biblical Literature
JCS	Journal of Cuneiform Studies
JJS	Journal of Jewish Studies

JNES	Journal of Near Eastern Studies
JQR	Jewish Quarterly Review
JSJ	Journal for the Study of Judaism
JSNT	Journal for the Study of the New Testament
JSOT	Journal for the Study of the Old Testament
JSS	Journal of Semitic Studies
JTS	Journal of Theological Studies
KTU	Die keilaphabetischen Texte aus Ugarit einschliesslich der keilaphabetischen Texts ausserhalb Ugarit 1: Transkription: M. Dietrich, O. Loretz, and J. Samartin. Neukirchen-Vluyn 1976.
PEQ	Palestine Exploration Quarterly
Or	Orientalia
SBT	Studies in Biblical Theology
VT	Vetus Testamentum
VTSup	Vetus Testamentum Supplements

Biblical citations are from the *New Revised Standard Version* (Oxford: Oxford University Press, 1989). Citations of the Hekhalot and Merkavah literature refer to paragraph numbers in *Synopse zur Hekhalot Literatur* published by P. Schäfer in collaboration with M. Schlüter and H. G. von Mutius (Tübingen: Mohr-Siebeck, 1981). Traditional titles of texts ("macroforms") will be indicated as well. *Genizah* passages are cited from *Geniza Fragmente zur Hekhalot Literatur* published by P. Schäfer (Tübingen: Mohr-Siebeck, 1984). English translations of passages from the Hekhalot and Merkavah literature are my own unless otherwise stated.

Introduction

> Rabbi Akiva said:
> Who is able to contemplate the seven palaces
> and behold the heaven of heavens
> and see the chambers of chambers
> and say: "I saw the chamber of YH?"
>
> —*Ma'aseh Merkavah, Synopse,* 554.

This question is posed by Rabbi Akiva, a central figure of the Hekhalot and Merkavah literature of late antiquity. In it we find mentioned several claims and aspects which distinguish the mysticism found in this literature. We hear of "contemplation," "ascent to heaven," and "vision of divine palaces." We learn that a human being can cross traditional boundaries between the phenomenological and the transcendent realms, make a contemplative ascent to heaven, behold the chambers of God in a personal manner, and communicate these experiences and visions to others. We also encounter an enigma: Who is this qualified person?

The first part of the question: "Who is able to contemplate the seven palaces?," seems to describe a spiritual introspective process, taking place on an internal level, in which a visionary reflects and meditates upon the seven palaces of God, placing them in the center of his contemplation, imagination, and thought. The second part: "and to ascend and behold the heaven of heavens, and to see the chambers of chambers," pertains to beliefs, practices, and revelations. It claims the existence of a different reality, beyond the phenomenological world, envisioned as a celestial realm of God, in which his divine palace is situated in the heaven of heavens. It also appears to introduce the possibility of divine-human encounters outside traditional norms of historical revelation. These words seem likewise to affirm a specific religious consciousness, which enables a human being to exceed parameters of traditional norms, time, and space, and to initiate a direct encounter with the divine, in a meditative process, visualized as a personal, otherworldly voyage to heaven.

The third part of the question: "and say I saw the chamber of YH," may refer to the manner in which contemplative experiences and their attendant, interpreted divine visions and revelations, are formulated and conveyed through verbal expressions, and sayings. Rabbi Akiva's query also seeks to discern "Who" can take part in such quests which, in fact, offer an alternative to the traditional concept of divinely initiated communication between God and his people. It also, perhaps, indicates an attempt to distinguish the identity of the ones who are involved in these endeavors, and to situate them in an historical and cultural context.

This study concentrates on the facets of Rabbi Akiva's question as a framework for the discussion. It explores the nature of the mystical tradition found in the enigmatic Hekhalot and Merkavah literature and the manner in which its mystical notions are molded and communicated. The social and cultural contexts of its writers will be considered as well.

The Hekhalot and Merkavah literature includes various manuscripts and literary traditions written and edited over a long period of time, arguably between the third and seventh centuries C.E., in Palestine and Babylonia. They contain overlapping mystical, cosmological, messianic, and magical traditions, presented in several literary forms. With a full awareness of the complexity of this literature and the intricacy of its traditions, this study focuses on the mystical dimensions of the literature. It examines several treatises in which these mystical notions principally find expression. These include textual units known *Hekhalot Rabbati* (The Greater Book of Hekhalot), *Hekhalot Zutarti* (The Lesser Book of Hekhalot), *Ma'aseh Merkavah* (The Works of the Chariot), *Sefer Hekhalot* (The Book of Hekhalot) also entitled the *Hebrew Book of Enoch* or *3 Enoch*, the *Shi'ur Komah* traditions (Measurements of the Divine Body), various fragments known as *Shivhei Metatron*, and several texts found in the Cairo *Genizah*.

The discussion treats these topics in six chapters. The first chapter of this study presents a brief overview of the Hekhalot and Merkavah literature as it was composed, edited, and integrated over a substantial period of time. It introduces debated historical questions of origin and dating, as well as the complex nature of its manuscripts, literary traditions, and conceptual notions. Maintaining the view that scholarly analysis of mystical phenomena is primarily textually based, the chapter then discusses aspects of the mystical tradition found in the Hekhalot and Merkavah literature, in light of current observations and methodological premises in the study of mysticism.

The second chapter distinguishes specific mystical characteristics to be found in the Hekhalot and Merkavah literature, in light of methodological premises in the study of mysticism. Applying a literary-phenomenological approach, the discussion first classifies significant mystical aspects present in several Hekhalot and Merkavah literary units and accounts, both theoretical and practical. It then demonstrates the ways in which these notions interact as they create a distinctive mystical tradition. In particular, attention will be paid to the interplay between mystical techniques, ritualistic practices, inner perceptions, and spiritual transformation on the one hand, and the ability to decode divine visions and revelations, which these entail, on the other hand.

The second topic which this study addresses is the presence of mythology in Hekhalot and Merkavah mysticism. Scholars have demonstrated connections between the Hekhalot and Merkavah literature and similar notions in priestly traditions, rabbinical writings, the Dead Sea Scrolls, apocalyptic texts, early Christian literature, Gnostic sources, and magical theurgical traditions and practices. The present investigations calls attention to additional mythological echoes which resonate in various mystical narrations of the Hekhalot and Merkavah literature. This aspect has not yet been thoroughly investigated in scholarly literature. This study seeks to demonstrates its importance. It suggests that mythological patterns of expressions, as well as themes, and models rooted in Near Eastern mythological sources, are evoked in the Hekhalot and Merkavah literature, in a spiritualized fashion, as the principal way of presenting its mystical content.

Chapter 3 provides background to a close literary-phenomenological analysis of the relationship of myth and mysticism to be found in chapters 4 and 5. It distinguishes the nature of mystical discourse in Hekhalot and Merkavah mysticism, suggesting that this tradition conceptualizes and conveys many of its mystical notions by evoking a variety of mythological frameworks. It then introduces dominant characteristics of the three prevalent mythological frameworks, presumed to be employed in Hekhalot and Merkavah mysticism. These include mythological forms of thought and expression in general, as well as biblical, and Mesopotamian mythology in particular. The chapter concludes with an assessment of the pertinence and possible applicability of these three mythological forms in Hekhalot and Merkavah mysticism. It demonstrates that this tradition employs specific patterns, often characterized as mythological, such as prose narrative style, pictorial imagery, tangible metaphors, and figurative language, in order to construct and articulate abstract, mystical concepts. The discussion further treats the apparent probability that mythological traditions contained in the Hebrew bible have bestowed some degree of inspiration on several Hekhalot and Merkavah mystical presentations. Finally, in light of the view that traditions within a given cultural-religious group, or within neighboring cultures, interact with one another in an ongoing process of absorption, transformation and interchange, the discussion demonstrates the presence and prominence of Mesopotamian mythological traditions in the syncretistic Hellenistic Roman world of late antiquity, in which the Hekhalot and Merkavah literature was compiled. These are treated as plausible sources, which could have inspired the Hekhalot and Merkavah imagery, directly or indirectly.

The fourth and the fifth chapters demonstrate, by a close literary-phenomenological analysis, the manner in which various mystical aspects are presented in the Hekhalot and Merkavah descriptions. Chapter 4 focuses on the spiritual voyage, outlined in a dialectical way in the Hekhalot and Merkavah literature. It discusses the manner in which the spiritual-contemplative processes are described in a mythological fashion as actual corporal ascents to heaven, taking place in a mythological cosmos. The discussion examines, in particular, three main topics: (a) the image of the visionary, (b) the inner journey, and (c) the spiritual transformations at its end.

Chapter 5 concentrates on the concept of a figurative and abstract God, revealed at the height of the mystical-visionary ascent. It examines depictions which treat God's spiritual character, infinite transcendent nature, and his inconceivable qualities, and demonstrates how they are expressed by traditional themes and imagery rooted in specific mythological traditions. These include, for example, enormous physical size, exceptional beauty, exclusive kingship, and a tangible supremacy.

Both chapters 4 and 5 examine mythological patterns present in various Hekhalot and Merkavah mystical accounts from a phenomelological perspective. They also trace the possible origin of several Hekhalot and Merkavah themes to specific mythological, ancient Near Eastern sources, both biblical and Mesopotamian. They conclude with an analysis of the manner in which ancient mythological images and themes are interiorized, spiritualized, and reinterpreted in order to convey new mystical notions in the Hekhalot and Merkavah literature.

Embracing the approach that mystical literature and cultural social realities are bound together, chapter 6 concludes the discussion by considering possible cultural and ideological implications of the previous literary and phenomenological observations regarding the context of Hekhalot and Merkavah mysticism and its authors. Based on distinct similarity in self-perception and ideological interests, the chapter proposes that the enigmatic Hekhalot and Merkavah mysticism could be considered a product of Jewish intellectuals of late antiquity, possibly scribes and sages associated with classes of priests and with temple traditions, who, in keeping with Near Eastern scribal traditions of "the wise," reapply several of their principles and concepts to mystical teachings.

1

The Hekhalot and Merkavah Literature and Its Mystical Tradition

> Those who define mysticism in terms of a certain type of experience of God often seem to forget that there can be no direct access to evidence for the historian. Experience as such is not a part of the historical record. The only thing directly available to the historian or historical theologian is the evidence, largely in the form of written records . . .
>
> —McGinn, *The Foundations of Mysticism,* xiv.

INTRODUCTION

The title of this chapter associates mysticism with the Hekhalot and Merkavah literature, suggesting that this literature includes records of a mystical tradition. Before attempting an examination of this proposal, it is important to clarify the following. What is the Hekhalot and Merkavah literature? What is meant when applying the debated and ambiguous term mysticism in this context? Which parts of the Hekhalot and Merkavah literature exhibit notions and outlooks which could be characterized as mystical? These topics will be addressed in this chapter. Its first section will present an overview of the Hekhalot and Merkavah literature, its nature, origins, traditions, themes, and the development of its research. The second section will introduce principle issues and methodological approaches to the study of mysticism, relevant to the present investigation. It will then discuss broad characteristic features of Hekhalot and Merkavah mysticism present primarily in several literary sources. None of these writings reveal a coherent mystical doctrine conveyed in a methodical fashion. Yet, despite some inconsistency, parallel accounts complement each other, disclosing interconnected experimental and theoretical aspects of one tradition, which endured over a long period of time, despite its noncanonical status. Its goals, religio-spiritual attitudes, practices, revelations, and exegetical perceptions demonstrate specific traits which, from a phenomenological perspective, can be characterized as mystical.

THE HEKHALOT AND MERKAVAH LITERATURE

The anonymous corpus known as the Hekhalot and Merkavah literature derives its name from two of its principal themes. The first theme involves descriptions of visionary heavenly ascents through the seven divine palaces (Hebrew: Hekhalot **היכלות**). The second theme features meditations and interpretations of the chariot vision (Hebrew: Merkavah **מרכבה**).[1] The collective title, "Hekhalot and Merkavah literature," may give the impression of a cohesive corpus of writings with a specific homogeneous tradition or a consistent religious outlook. This literature, however, is not a unified body of work having one spiritual approach. On the contrary, the Hekhalot and Merkavah literature consists of several anonymous and enigmatic manuscripts, each of which includes various literary genres and diverse traditions.[2]

The Hekhalot and Merkavah manuscripts are written in Hebrew and Aramaic with several borrowings from Greek.[3] They came into existence over an extensive period of time. According to several scholars, they took shape in Palestine and Babylonia during the Mishnaic and Talmudic periods of the second and fifth centuries. Others date this literature to the sixth and the eighth centuries, C.E., the late phase of the Geonic period.[4] These texts involved a long process of writing, editing, and redacting. They have not been preserved in their original and complete form but are found instead as fragmented manuscripts and literary units in later sources. A major body of the manuscripts has been found in medieval Europe, among the writings of the *Hasidei Ashkenaz* movement. These manuscripts were edited by members of this school at the end of the twelfth and the beginning of the thirteenth century C.E.[5] Hekhalot and Merkavah material has been preserved as well in the work of early Jewish philosophers from the tenth century and in polemic *Karaite* literature.[6] Additional fragments, the authorship of which is attributed to the ninth century, have been found in the Cairo *Genizah.*[7] Short segments of the Hekhalot and Merkavah texts were also included in various *Midrashim* and in the Babylonian and Jerusalem Talmuds.[8]

The Hekhalot and Merkavah literature is distinctively multifaceted, presenting complex and sometimes contradictory notions of God, angels, and human beings.[9] Each manuscript, in fact, may be seen as an anthology of different traditions and subject matters. Cosmological concepts, magical and theurgical traditions, accounts of visionary ascensions to the celestial world, descriptions of the angelic realm, rituals of adjurations, messianic contemplation, theosophical speculations concerning the nature of God, his appearance and the dimensions of his divine figure (*shi'ur komah,* שיעור קומה), are several of the central topics which the Hekhalot and Merkavah treatises introduce simultaneously.[10]

The diversity of the Hekhalot and Merkavah literature as well as the complexity of its texts make difficult any attempt to reach clear, solid conclusions regarding the scope of the corpus, the relationships among its various parts, the time and social climate of its composition, and its dominant characteristics. Questions concerning the literature have therefore been disputed in the scholarly literature and many speculations have not been definitively proven.[11] The following is a brief overview of the Hekhalot and Merkavah literature; its origins, literary traditions, and prevalent themes.

Historical and Social Background

The first attempts to anchor the Hekhalot and Merkavah literature in a specific Jewish tradition and to set the historical and chronological date of its compilation were made in the nineteenth century. Several scholars of that period considered texts of this literature as obscure late manuscripts which stand outside the normative Judaism of late antiquity and early Middle Ages. The historian H. H. Graez, for example, attributed the Hekhalot and Merkavah literature to the post-Talmudic and Midrashic periods. In Graetz's opinion the literature's exceptional and irrational themes, such as descriptions of angels, magical formulas, ascents to heaven, and descriptions of the body of the divine, could not correctly be seen as the product of legalistic rabbinical Judaism, but rather reflect the presence of Islamic influence from sources of the eighth and ninth centuries.[12] Other scholars, in contrast, viewed the Hekhalot and Merkavah texts as authentic Jewish writings from a much earlier date. M. Gaster, considered the Hekhalot and Merkavah literature as a remnant of an ancient school of thought dating from the Second Temple period. A. Jellinek regarded the manuscripts as late homilies, which had not been included in the classical collections. He issued several of the treatises in his edition *Bet ha-Midrash.* S. A. Wertheimer shared a similar attitude and included several Hekhalot and Merkavah texts in his collection, *Batei Midrashot,* as did S. Musajoff, who included Hekhalot and Merkavah texts in his edition, *Merkavah Shelemah.*[13] In the twenties, H. Odeberg published a critical edition of *Sefer Hekhalot,* also labeled by him as *The Hebrew Book of Enoch* or *3 Enoch.* As the title reflects, Odeberg considered the text to be a part of the ancient apocalyptic Enochic literature from the first centuries B.C.E. and the first century C.E.[14]

G. Scholem's writings mark the beginning of contemporary academic study of the Hekhalot and Merkavah literature. Scholem and several other scholars dated the Hekhalot and Merkavah literature to a much earlier time than had previously been suggested.[15] The literature, according to this view, was attributed to mainstream orthodox Rabbinic circles in the Tannaim period, around the turn of the first century C.E., and then developed in various ways during the following six or seven centuries.[16] These conclusions have been challenged by several scholars. E. E. Urbach and D. J. Halperin have shown differences between the Hekhalot and Merkavah tradition and that of Rabbinic Judaism, in which they have not found any trace of mystical activity but rather that of a homilitical midrashic study of Ezekiel's chariot.[17] M. S. Cohen, P. S. Alexander, and M. D. Swartz have argued that different Hekhalot and Merkavah texts and literary units cannot be dated to the first centuries C.E. Instead, they contend these texts took shape over several centuries in Palestine between the early Amoraic period and the post-Talmudic time in Babylonia.[18]

Not only the chronological dating of the Hekhalot and Merkavah literature remains unclear, but also the identity and the social-historical background of its authors or compilers. No clear answers can be deduced from the literature itself.[19] Well-known Tannaitic figures such as Rabbi Ishmael, Rabbi Akiva, and Rabbi Nehunia ben Ha-Kanah are presented in the various narratives as main speakers, yet the information they communicate often conflicts with documented historical data. Their descriptions relate primarily to an imaginary reality, and their views frequently contradict the accepted traditional norms of the Mishnaic and Talmudic periods of the second and fifth centuries C.E.[20]

Diverse theories have been suggested to determine the writers' identities. Members of a mystical school, originating in Palestine in Tannaitic and Talmudic times, were considered by Scholem to be the early authors of the Hekhalot and Merkavah literature, which later extended to Babylonia and subsequently to Europe. P. Schäfer sees this literature as an expression of an elite post-rabbinic group of scholars, originating in Babylonia. "People of the land," including uneducated lower class rebels from a younger generation, were the writers of this literature, according to Halperin. This group challenged the old rabbinic authorities, making theurgic use of the *Sar Torah* traditions of the Hekhalot and Merkavah in order to gain a higher social status and authority. Associating the Hekhalot and Merkavah literature with magical literature J. R. Davila considered professional scribes as the composers of the literature. Lacking formal rabbinic training and venerable social status, they challenged the Rabbis with magic. In a recent study he has identified the people behind the Hekhalot and Merkavah literature as practitioners of ritual power, compared to shamans and shamans/healers. Swartz sees the authors as educated groups who lacked formal rabbinic training. These groups, placed between the elite and the common lower classes, were found in circles of synagogue functionaries, liturgical poets and professional scribes. R. Elior situates the Hekhalot and Merkavah literature in the context of priestly-angelic lore. She attributes it to members of priestly circles, whose concern was to preserve and reconstruct Temple traditions after its destruction as well as to transform the imperceptible divinity into a perceivable order.[21]

The cultural-historical background of Hekhalot and Merkavah literature has also been studied from various angles. As scholars have demonstrated, the literature shares many characteristics with several major religious movements which flourished in the same cultural climate both within Judaism and outside of it. Similarities have been drawn on the level of the general structure of ideas and as well on the level of detailed literary motifs and themes. In addition to the connection of this literature with the Talmudic and Midrashic literature,[22] interdependence between Hekhalot and Merkavah hymnology and Jewish traditional prayers has been documented, and significant impact of priestly-angelic traditions from the First and Second Temple periods on the Hekhalot and Merkavah literature has been demonstrated.[23] The Hekhalot and Merkavah literature has also been linked to several other traditions and texts from a similar cultural environment. These include apocryphal and apocalyptic literature,[24] the Qumran texts,[25] Gnostic traditions,[26] and early Christian literature.[27] Connections between several Hekhalot and Merkavah traditions and various Jewish and Greco-Roman magical traditions of late antiquity have been studied as well.[28]

Scholarly Editions and Methodological Approaches

From the middle of the nineteenth century several Hekhalot and Merkavah manuscripts were published by Jellinek, Wertheimer, and Musajoff.[29] In the twenties, the first critical edition of a Hekhalot and Merkavah manuscript, *Sefer Hekhalot,* was published by H. Odeberg, who also labeled it *The Hebrew Book of Enoch* or *3 Enoch.*[30] Critical editions of specific manuscripts and literary units were published later by scholars such as P. S. Alexander, M. S. Cohen, R. Elior, I. Gruenwald, K. Hermann, and G. Scholem.[31] In the late 1970's P. Schäfer suggested a different approach to the study of the manuscripts. Questioning the convention of separating the Hekhalot and Merkavah literature into fixed, defined, and independent textual units and books, Schäfer and his colleagues published a synoptic edition of the Hekhalot and Merkavah literature. This edition is composed of seven manuscripts from medieval European sources, presented in one sequence and divided into nine hundred and thirty orderly, consecutive paragraphs. A later edition of the Hekhalot and Merkavah texts, also published by Schäfer, comprises twenty-three fragments from the Cairo *Genizah*. Photographs of the texts, comments, explanations and references to other related Hekhalot and Merkavah sources are also part of this edition.[32]

In several discussions, Schäfer has promoted the historical-textual approach to the study of the Hekhalot and Merkavah literature. In these, he has emphasized the greater importance of clarifying questions regarding the relationships among the manuscripts and various textual units over the lesser importance of the study of their particular characteristics.[33] Other scholars, in contrast, have suggested employing an overall contextual-phenomenological perspective in order to explore the unique attributes of the literature. This second approach treats the literature as a corpus with a common spiritual outlook and a shared literary heritage, reflected in the various texts, despite obvious differences and contradictions. Scholars have appropriately adopted thematic, contextual, phenomenological, and historical approaches as fruitful methods for analyzing the manuscripts. These methods allow major conceptual themes and outlooks found in the literature to be distinguished and assessed.[34]

Among the various conceptual themes and phenomenological features of this literature, its mystical teachings, principles, and ideas have been the topic of much discussion in significant studies. This study, as well, focuses on the Hekhalot and Merkavah mystical tradition. Recognizing mysticism as one of many notions of this multilayered literature, it seeks to explore its specific features. As an introduction, it is thus pertinent to discuss two topics, the nature of mystical literature in general, and of the Hekhalot and Merkavah mystical literature in particular.

MYSTICISM IN THE HEKHALOT AND MERKAVAH LITERATURE

Recent scholarship presents two primary approaches to the study of mysticism in the Hekhalot and Merkavah literature. On the one hand, several scholars claim that this literature contains records of genuine otherworldly experiences, preparatory techniques, and revelations, all seen as its mystical core. In Scholem's opinion, for example, the soul's ascent to heaven and its attainment of God is the dominant mystical concept of this literature. It reveals evidence of ecstatic visionary experiences which later degenerated into magical writings. I. Gruenwald likewise associates mysticism in this literature exclusively with ascent traditions. J. Dan identifies three types of mystical elements in the literature, among which the ascent to the Merkavah is the most significant. In Elior's view, the mystical aspects of this literature are represented by a new concept of divinity as well as by the practice of ascent to heaven. K. E. Grözinger highlights the mystical ascent as well as mystical preparatory techniques and stages.[35]

On the other hand, some scholars assert that the Hekhalot and Merkavah literature includes merely literary constructions, which do not reveal authentic mystical experiences and practices. Urbach and Halperin, for instance, maintain this view, arguing that the ascent theme should not be regarded as the primary aspect of this literature, which reflects mostly literary developments. Schäfer argues that the literature does not provide any indication of how the heavenly ascent was carried out, or even if it was practiced at all. M. Himmelfarb assets that the literature includes stories to be repeated and not descriptions of tenable experiences and rites.[36]

This dichotomy between the experimental and the exegetical aspects of the Hekhalot and Merkavah mystical tradition has been challenged recently in several studies. Alexander discusses the interdependency of these two aspects in any study of Hekhalot and Merkavah mysticism and asserts: "from early on in the movement both 'theoretical' (i.e. exegetical) and 'practical' (i.e. experimental) approaches to the Merkabah were followed."[37] Rejecting any distinction between the two E. R. Wolfson states: "Such a distinction is predicated on the ability to isolate phenomenologically an experience separated from its literal context—a questionable presumption, inasmuch as all such experiences occur within a literary framework.[38]

This approach parallels a prevalent view according to which the academic access to mystical teachings, experiences, revelations, and doctrines of any mystical school is available mainly through its literary writings. Scholars have argued in support of this claim, maintaining that only the literary records give expression to mystical notions and enable students of mysticism to explore their meaning, thus, the analysis of mysticism is primarily textually based. S. T. Katz makes this observation very clearly, asserting that the key to understanding mystical phenomena in general is through analysis of its literary evidence:

> There are no pure (i.e., unmediated) experiences. Neither mystical experience nor more ordinary forms of experience give any indication, or any grounds for believing, that they are unmediated. That is to say *all* experience is processed through, organized by, and makes itself available to us in extremely complex epistemological ways.[39]

Sharing this perspective, scholars such as R. M. Gimello, P. Moore, and C. A. Keller assert that mystical writings form the only data for any analysis of mysticism. The study of mysticism appears, therefore, to be primarily literary, philological, and exegetical.[40] In his investigation of mystical phenomena, B. McGinn's perception accords with this perspective: "The only thing directly available to the historian or historical theologian is the evidence, largely in the form of written records."[41]

This approach to the study of mysticism seems to be particularly valid in the case of the Hekhalot and Merkavah mystical tradition. In its enigmatic and fractured collection of literary texts, we do not find records of pure, unmediated mystical experiences or revelations, presented as verified, firsthand, personal testimony. Instead, the many Hekhalot and Merkavah passages provide a rich tapestry of theoretical literary descriptions and of first, second, or third hand pseudepigraphical testimonies of visionary experiences and revelations, which demonstrate certain mystical characteristics. These writings may present records of authentic experiences translated into words. They may also be bound up with accepted traditional norms, or based on literary conventions shared by a specific group.[42] Since the literary texts, in their present form, constitute our only link to Hekhalot and Merkavah mysticism of late antiquity, the pure nature of authentic mystical experiences, their validity, or the accuracy and correctness of reported mystical claims are topics which stand beyond the scope of our investigation. Instead, through a careful analysis of the written data, substantial insights into the nature of the Hekhalot and Merkavah mystical tradition and its special traits can be achieved.[43]

What is Meant by Mysticism

As we approach Hekhalot and Merkavah mysticism through a study of its literature, we need to discern the term mysticism, as well as to specify which parts of the Hekhalot and Merkavah literature exhibit notions and outlooks which could be characterized as mystical. The many studies of mysticism make clear that every examination of this wide phenomenon defies any clear-cut attempt at its definition. Mysticism is a phenomenological concept, coined by Western scholars, which refers to various types of teachings, experiences, and goals of varied spiritual trends.[44] Deeply influenced by the perspectives, backgrounds, and interests of its scholars, the definitions and classifications of mysticism are numerous and diverse. Rather than distinguishing what mysticism is, this study focuses on several of its characteristic qualities, denoted from a phenomenological perspective, which are of particular interest for this investigation of the Hekhalot and Merkavah tradition. Beneficial observations on these aspects are offered by McGinn in his discussion of the heuristic nature of mysticism:

> When I speak of mysticism as involving an immediate consciousness of the presence of God, I am trying to highlight a central claim that appears in almost all mystical texts. Mystics continue to affirm that their mode of access to God is radically different from that found in ordinary consciousness, even from the awareness of God gained through the usual religious activities. . . . As believers, they affirm that God does become present in these activities, but not in any direct or immediate fashion. Mystical religious texts are those that witness to another form of divine presence, one that can, indeed, sometimes be attained within the context of ordinary religious observances, but which need not be. What differentiates it from another form of religious consciousness is its presentation as both subjectively and objectively more direct, even at times as immediate.[45]

McGinn's observation highlights several distinctive principles, which are significant for the study of Hekhalot and Merkavah mysticism. This observation expands the notion of mysticism, recognizing that the *unio mystica* model is not its only characteristic feature, and the principle of union with God does not embody its sole essence. Acknowledging alternative mystical models McGinn perceives a state of an immediate consciousness of the presence of God as pivotal and further contends:

> . . . union is only one of the host of models, metaphors, or symbols that mystics have employed in their accounts. Many have used it, but few have restricted themselves to it. Among the other major mystical categories are those of contemplation and the vision of God, deification . . . ecstasy. All of these can be conceived of as different but complementary ways of presenting the consciousness of direct presence.[46]

Several additional conceptual and ideological traits are suggested by McGinn's observation presented above. References to specific consciousness of the presence of God demonstrate a claim that there is an alternative realm of absolute divine entity, or ultimate reality, beyond the phenomenological world, which can be attained by human seekers. The mystical awareness is different from the awareness of God gained through the usual religious activities and thus, the attainment of the divine, according to this view, often occurs outside the framework of established, traditional religious life. In his discussion of the nature of mysticism, Dan similarly observes: "There is an alternative, nonsensual, and nonlogical way of achieving truth, the *via mystica,* which can lead the mystic . . . to embrace some aspects of the hidden truth."[47]

McGinn's account also emphasizes the internal mental realm of human consciousness, on which both the spiritual quest and its attained revelations occur. It highlights unique spiritual perception, awareness, and state of mind, radically different from that found in ordinary states of being, that influence the ways in which the ultimate divine reality is attained. J. E. Collins' observation, presented from a phenomenological-psycological perspective, further elucidates this aspect:

> One who subjects himself/herself to the discipline required of the mystic path, either by self effort or by submission to a spiritual guide, experience, as a result of his/her dedication to this discipline, radical change within his/her consciousness. This transformation of consciousness may be manifested in a new epistemology, cosmology, ontology, soteriology, and so forth.[48]

The significance of such human's states of consciousness, indirectly, also indicates another characteristic of the mystical phenomena—the private, introspective nature of the mystical process, which seems to be, primarily, of personal concern. D. Merkur's view of mysticism advances this aspect:

> What, in my opinion, finally distinguishes mystics from other types of religious ecstatic is their standing in society. Shamans, mediums, and prophets are public social functionaries who act on behalf of their coreligionists in contacting their gods or spirits. Coreligionists may perform similar practices for personal or private reasons. Mystics tend to seek experiences of exclusively private concern. Private orientations may be achieved through religious experiences of many different type, mystical union is merely one example. In all cases, it is the inward turn, due to the impossibility of possessing public religious authority, that I think characterizes mysticism wherever it is found.

Finally, McGinn's observation denotes the significance of religious texts, through which mystical notions are conveyed. Recognizing literature as a source in which mystical concepts are described, expressed, and communicated verbally, this assertion denies a previous, commonly received view about the absolute nature of mystical ineffability. In a similar vein C. A. Keller notes: "Mystical writings are . . . texts which discuss the path towards realization of the ultimate knowledge . . . and which contain statements about the nature of such knowledge."[50]

McGinn's reference to religious texts also indicates, it seems, the significance of an exclusive religious perspective, from which experiences and revelations are decoded and presented in the textual sources. Spiritual awareness of other realities is thus related as a mystical consciousness of the presence of God. Merkur's observation, directs attention to the specific nature of mystical states of mind:

> Mystical experiences are religious uses of otherwise secular alternate states of consciousness—or more precisely, alternate psychic states. What makes an alternate state experience a religious one is its personal or cultural valuation.[51]

The subsequent chapters of this study examine in detail the intricate manner in which these notions, characterized as mystical, are presented in the distinct context and terminology of the Hekhalot and Merkavah mysticism. The following discussion of this chapter, as an introduction, briefly describes the presence of such notions in specific sources of the Hekhalot and Merkavah literature. It intends to demarcate its mystical writings and to outline their prominent features.

The Hekhalot and Merkavah Mystical Literature

Several of the Hekhalot and Merkavah literary texts are regarded as forming the main mystical core of the literature: *Hekhalot Rabbati* (The Greater Book of Hekhalot), *Hekhalot Zutarti* (The Lesser Book of Hekhalot), *Ma'aseh Merkavah* (The Works of the Chariot), *Sefer Hekhalot* (The Book of Hekhalot), also known as the *Hebrew Book of Enoch* or *3 Enoch, the Shi'ur Komah* texts (Measurements of the Divine Body), various fragments relating to Metatron known as *Shivah Metatron* and several *Genizah* fragments.[52]

Descriptions in *Hekhalot Rabbati* present an account of Rabbi Ishmael's journey to heaven in order to find out if the death decree of ten prominent Jewish sages was decided by God.[53] Rabbi Nehunia ben Ha-Kanah's ecstatic ascent is similarly recorded. The text also outlines various stages of the visionary ascent, paradoxically designated in the texts as the "descent to the Merkavah," including its goals, techniques, and revelations.[54] Depiction of the upper worlds, the divine chariot, and the angelic rituals are provided.

Hekhalot Zutarti relates Rabbi Akiva's ascent to the upper heavens, delineated in a version of the story of "four who entered the *Pardes*," found also in the Tosefta, the Talmud, and the Midrash. Rabbi Akiva's accomplishments are highlighted as he is compared to the other three sages who "entered the *Pardes*."[55] Their harsh fate illustrates indirectly the risks of the journey as well as the ways in which to avoid them. Rabbi Akiva also describes his vision of ascending to heaven, and instructs members of Merkavah group who wish to ascend. This literary tradition also makes references to Moses, portrayed as an ancient mystic who ascended on high to behold God.[56] The text also offers details concerning spiritual goals and specific methods and practices designed, it seems, to influence the adept's awareness and to induce ecstasies. It narrates the stages of the visionary ecstatic journey, including its dangers and challenges. Divine revelations are also disclosed.[57]

Ma'aseh Merkavah provides information concerning spiritual goals, techniques, visionary ascents to the chariot, and spiritual achievements.[58] It includes general descriptions, songs, hymns, and prayers, recited by the Merkavah seekers before God, as well as a few accounts presented as their personal testaments.

Sefer Hekhalot, known as *3 Enoch* or *The Hebrew Book of Enoch,* reports Rabbi Ishmael 's ascent to the highest seventh heaven and recounts his encounter with the Prince of the Countenance, Metatron, who shows him the structure and secrets of the divine world. The account details the personal experiences and spiritual transformation which Rabbi Ishmael undergoes before he enters the divine realm. The story of Enoch, son of Jared, the human being who was transformed into the divine archangel Metatron, echoes Rabbi Ishmael's account. It offers additional data concerning the voyage from the phenomenological to the transcendent world, the final transformation at the end of the path, and the nature of divine revelations.[59]

The *Shi'ur Komah* traditions consist largely of visions of the manifested, anthropomorphic image of God.[60] They also incorporate subtle exegetical interpretations of these revelations, presented from a specific spiritual viewpoint as will be demonstrated. Finally, several *Genizah* fragments from Cairo add various details, mainly about the visionary journey and its entailed revelations.

All these Hekhalot and Merkavah accounts present, in a distinctive language and vocabulary, several particular features, which reach a level of explicit literary formulation. These are closely related to the mystical notions discussed above. The Hekhalot and Merkavah mystical accounts claim the existence of an alternative realm of ultimate reality which stands beyond the physical phenomenological world. Seen from a specific religious perspective, this sphere is classified in terms such as the Heaven of Heavens, the King's palaces, or God's Merkavah (chariot). These traditions, likewise, acknowledge an inner contemplative process of attaining the absolute achieved by human seekers. This experience is depicted as visionary contemplative journeys out of this world to celestial realms. The members of the Merkavah circle undergo a series of mental inner stages, through which several qualified individuals acquire a unique spiritual perception, awareness, and consciousness. This state enables them to attain the divine reality in a personal direct manner, which seems to be of private concerns. They see God's celestial palaces, behold the King at his beauty, and gaze at the Merkavah.

As mentioned earlier, in these Hekhalot and Merkavah diverse literary accounts, we find no consistent information regarding mystical concepts. In none of the writings can we find an attempt to convey mystical ideas in a methodical fashion, or to introduce a coherent and systematic mystical doctrine. On the contrary, complex references to various mystical teachings, practices, visions, revelations, and exegesis are present in the nonhomogeneous Hekhalot and Merkavah literary genres. They are transcribed in multiple modes of expression and composed from diverse perspectives as records of inner experiences and visions, as well as theoretical information, general descriptions, narratives, and instructions.

We read reports revealed as the mystics' testaments during the experience.[61] Likewise, the mystics' later reflections of their experiences are recorded, as well as reports and explanations from a third person's perspective.[62] Theoretical teachings or what seem to be narrations of exemplary mystical principles are also found in the Hekhalot and Merkavah literature.[63] Narratives, such as the "*Pardes* story" or the "account of the ten martyrs," also provide references to mystical concepts, as well as direct dialogues between teacher and disciple, and general instructions, directed to the people who aspire to engage in specific spiritual quests.[64] Poetic forms, expressive prayers, exegetical interpretations of mystical visions are additional literary genres which manifest mystical concepts in the Hekhalot and Merkavah literature.[65]

Both the variety of sources and the lack of consistency clearly challenge attempts to draw precise and decisive conclusions regarding the nature of Hekhalot and Merkavah mysticism. It is important, however, to note the advantages of such a broad and richly layered literature. Consideration of the many-sided mystical literature of any tradition, followed by an analysis of its significant literary genres, can contribute to a wide understanding of this specific mystical tradition. The broad range of significant literary texts, genres, and forms do not obscure the investigation. Rather, they reveal its many aspects, phases, and outlooks, and can be of great value for comprehending the complexity of any specific mystical tradition. In his discussion of mystical literature, Keller observes diverse literary genres which are often included in mystical sources. Often, according to Keller, these different literary categories do not present unbroken and direct accounts of the pure experience. Nevertheless, when seen holistically, they provide access to prominent aspects and characteristics of the specific mystical tradition in which they were compiled.[66]

The advantages of this approach in the study of the Hekhalot and Merkavah literature becomes evident. Its wide scope in structure, genre, and content, allows an extensive examination of the mystical tradition. It provides rich material from various sources and angles, which manifest many characteristics and parallel aspects. Furthermore, the breadth of this literature exhibits corresponding notions found in several of its literary accounts. These similar aspects, which occur in various composite texts and redactions, demonstrate the shared conceptual and spiritual heritage of Hekhalot and Merkavah mysticism. It is meaningful to note that the Hekhalot and Merkavah literature was never granted any official canonical rank. Nevertheless, common mystical notions prevailed over long periods of time in its diverse textual components. The lasting nature of these ideas attest to the vitality, respected status, and continuity of the Hekhalot and Merkavah mystical tradition.

2

Hekhalot and Merkavah Mysticism

> Some elements found in mystical awareness include: (i) the apprehension of ultimate reality, (ii) attainment of perfection through mental, emotional and volitional purification, (iii) an attitude of serenity and total (transcendent) awareness, (iv) a sense of freedom from time-space conditions and (v) expansion of consciousness and spontaneity through self discipline.
>
> —F. J. Streng, "Language and Mystical Awareness," in *Mysticism and Philosophical Analysis,* 142.

INTRODUCTION

The current chapter will examine mystical notions of the Hekhalot and Merkavah literature. From a literary-penomenological perspective, it will seek to distinguish the specific mystical characteristics of this tradition, in light of current observations and methodological premises in the study of mysticism. The discussion will first classify significant aspects present in Hekhalot and Merkavah mysticism, both theoretical and practical. It will then demonstrate the ways in which these notions interact as they create a distinct mystical tradition. In particular, attention will be paid to the interplay between mystical techniques, ritualistic practices, spiritual transformation, and inner perceptions on the one hand, and divine revelations and the interpretations, which they entail, on the other hand.

A COMMON MODEL

> Visions appear . . . as interior projections or visualizations of the respective community's myth-dream which the subject has chosen, consciously or unconsciously, as his own personal myth-dream.[1]

> . . . for the people of the world, for you, and for everyone who wishes to descend and gaze at the King in His beauty. He should take this path and descend, and he will not be harmed.[2]

In the Hekhalot and Merkavah literature many descriptions overlap or correspond in content. At the same time accounts and details in various treatises diverge and vary. Yet, with regard to the mystical aspects of this literature, it is possible to assert with confidence that the diverse voices do not contradict each other. Despite some inconsistency, the different references to mystical notions do not create a controversial tension within the various texts and redactions of this manifold literature. Rather they complement each other presenting various angles of one common tradition. In this tradition we can discern a multilevel model, reflecting both theoretical and experimental aspects.[3]

Parallel Hekhalot and Merkavah accounts present collective mystical assumptions, goals, religio-spiritual attitudes and practices. These are shared by righteous heroes of the remote legendary-mythological past, such as Moses and Enoch. These same teachings may also be embraced by worthy visionaries of a more recent past, such as Rabbi Ishmael, Rabbi Akiva, and Rabbi Nehunia ben Ha-Kanah, as well as by deserving visionaries of the circle of Yordei Merkavah (descenders to the chariot) in the present and future. It is clear that adepts of any age may follow the same path, undergo parallel prescribed experiences, and gain corresponding experiences of encountering the divine in the context of their own historical conditions, geographical locations, and chronological time.

The different literary traditions, moreover, seem to portray a similar "ideal type" or role model who represents an image of a exemplary mystic of this specific circle. Such models represent, in a variety of ways, several categorical norms for their community. Since models often manifest the proper religious attitude and moral-spiritual disposition, their conduct becomes heuristic. They assert a practical way of following the theoretical teaching; they provide an authoritative confirmation of the possibility that human beings, under special circumstances, can experience divine reality in a personal, direct manner. They also disclose a specific interpretation to the revealed divine reality.[4]

Although several different individuals are depicted in the Hekhalot and Merkavah accounts as ideal mystics, they all seem to mirror each other and to play corresponding roles. Enoch is introduced in *3 Enoch* as a model for Rabbi Ishmael as well as for all the descenders to the chariot. Moses is delineated in *Hekhalot Zutarti* as the prototype for

Rabbi Akiva and all future visionaries. Rabbi Ishmael, Rabbi Akiva, and Rabbi Nehunia ben Ha-Kanah are presented throughout this literature as models for all worthy and qualified mystics who are expected to follow their pattern.[5] These models demonstrate a clear standard of perfection, acknowledged by members of the Hekhalot and Merkavah circle. They embody as well an example of the suitable attitude and practice, to be followed by dedicated adepts. As both temporal and trans-temporal figures, these individuals are introduced not only as historical but also as contemporary models, whose teachings endure and remain valid and heuristic for committed adepts in each succeeding generation.

A description in the *Genizah* illustrates this notion of a shared system. It refers to a common and established mystical path which leads to an optimal destination, as well as to an ideal type of a seeker, who wishes to reach such a destination, to experience the divine realm, and to behold celestial visions in a proper manner:

> You should write and set the Seal of the Descent to the Merkavah for the people of the world, for you, and for everyone who wishes to descend and gaze at the king in His beauty. He should take this path and descend, and see, and he will not be harmed.[6]

The discussion below will examine the mystical tradition of the Hekhalot and Merkavah literature and its particular features. The thesis we will examine is as follows. Several different accounts, in themselves often ambiguous and fragmentary, include a variety of references to mystical notions. These references, when considered together, complete each other and present a distinct shared mystical tradition. According to this tradition, the highest aim is that of gaining direct experience of God and the divine reality. This goal appears to be dependent upon the visionaries' inner awareness and spiritual development on the one hand, and on their perception and exegetical ability on the other.

More specifically, according to several Hekhalot and Merkavah accounts, the ultimate goal of the seekers' spiritual journey is to "behold the king in his beauty" and to "gaze at the visions of the Merkavah." These goals seem to express a mystical aspiration to encounter God and to perceive the nature of concealed divine reality. Such objectives are not achieved easily. Before divine visions and revelations are granted, adepts undergo a complex process of an ethical, spiritual, and mental metamorphosis. They expand their perception beyond its ordinary limits and in so doing gain a new awareness.

Crossing of conceptual boundaries lead them into the divine realm. They behold visions and revelations from a mystical perspective and can recognize and interpret their concealed meanings. In this way, for a short period of time, human perception and divine reality correspond and become one. During such mystical encounters visionaries can offer an exegesis of hidden truths, know God directly, and correspondingly share the divine perspective.[7] From this viewpoint it seems that the complex notion of "beholding divine visions" is, in fact, the core of the Hekhalot and Merkavah mysticism.

The discussion below will demonstrate this observation. It will explore parallel accounts of Hekhalot and Merkavah mysticism which present aspects such as its goal, methods, stages, spiritual transformation, divine revelation, and their exegetical interpretation, as interconnected components of one spiritual path.

THE MYSTICAL GOAL

> Basic to mystic awareness is the claim that attitudinal
> purification is necessary for right perception.
> *What* one knows is closely related to *how* one knows.
> To see beyond the apparent, or superficial world means
> a change in the mechanism of apprehension.[8]

> When will he descend, he who descends to the Merkavah?
> When will he see the heavenly majesty? . . .
> When will he see what no eye has ever seen?[9]

Distinct biblical and rabbinical views often presuppose the existence of boundaries between celestial and terrestrial domains, as well as between human beings and the divine. These boundaries are not to be crossed. Human attempts to push the limits, encounter God's realm, and see his visible appearance are often heavily restricted or prohibited altogether. These views are expressed, for example, in Psalm 115: 16: "The heavens are the Lord's heaven but the earth he has given to human beings." So, too, we hear God say in Exodus 33:20: "You will not see my face, for no man can see me and live." According to prevalent biblical and later post-biblical and rabbinical sources, likewise significant encounters between God and his people were divinely initiated. They occurred on the terrestial, historical realm, in specific occasions, in which God revealed his words to messengers, such as angelic figures, or prophets. The most famous event is the revelation at Mt. Sinai. Then, on one unique occasion, God communicated to Moses and the community his ultimate teachings, which were embodied into the Torah and the commandments.[10]

In several of the Hekhalot and Merkavah writings a different spiritual outlook finds expression. The communication between God and human beings is not limited to a unique divine revelation and its continuous manifestation in the Torah. Likewise, human encounters with God are no longer divinely initiated and proclaimed to people merely through prophetic or angelic mediators. Instead, Hekhalot and Merkavah mysticism emphasizes a personal visionary praxis of attaining God, constituted by humans. According to this tradition a human being, under certain conditions, can experience a visionary—ecstatic encounter with God, see concealed celestial visions, and understand, independently, the meaning of such revelations.[11] Contrary to predominant views, such an occurrence is not presented as an outcome of the divine's initiative. Instead, it is the visionary's own decisions, spiritual exercises, personal deeds, and inner awareness which lead to this encounter. This experience is often expressed in many of the Hekhalot and Merkavah passages by expressions such as "beholding the king in his beauty," and "gazing at the visions of the Merkavah."

In its presentation of such ventures, the Hekhalot and Merkavah mysticism parallels other ancient Mediterranean religions. In these too diverse forms of encounter with the divine, especially through heavenly journeys, are prominent.[12] Although it is beyond the scope of this study to compare the complex traditions of celestial journeys, nonetheless it is important to emphasize their distinct presentation in the Hekhalot and Merkavah literature, before we develop this analysis further. Journeys to heaven, according to many Hekhalot and Merkavah accounts, are not dependent upon the divine's will. Instead, human beings, under certain conditions, can initiate a voyage out of this world. Not only do the visionaries' own decisions constitute the heavenly ascents, but also their personal deeds, perception, and inner awareness affect the outcome of such journeys. Seekers who ascend to heaven are concerned with eschatological revelations, and deterministic plans of future history to a degree. Personal encounters with God and the divine realm, however, seem to be their principal aspiration. Adepts primarily long to behold God and the Merkavah, in a visionary journey to heaven which takes place during their lifetimes.

Repeated statements in *Hekhalot Zutarti, Hekhalot Rabbati, Ma'aseh Merkavah, 3 Enoch, Shi'ur Komah,* and in the *Genizah* fragments announce this foremost goal of the seekers in a similar fashion. The visionaries, Rabbi Ishmael, Rabbi Akiva, and Rabbi Nehunia ben Ha-Kanah, wish to "ascend to heaven and behold the king in his palace," "gaze upon the vision of the Merkavah," "look at the Merkavah," "catch sight of the heaven of heavens," "view a glimpse of the chariot," "catch sight of the Mighty One," or "behold the King in his beauty."[13] The various drafted parallel terms and images introduce a basic mystical premise of the Hekhalot and Merkavah tradition. The divine reality, denoted metaphorically as "the Merkavah," the "Chambers of God," "Heaven of Heavens," and the "Divine Palaces," is perceived as an incomprehensible transcendent realm, the perception of which is normally beyond human capacity.

The ultimate aspiration of the Hekhalot seekers is restated by analogous verbs such as "gazing," "beholding," "seeing," or "watching." These corresponding verbs apparently function as technical terms in the literature. They convey, in similar terminology, the adepts' desire to be able to access the divine realm. For example, Rabbi Akiva describes his elevated divine revelation, referring to the time when he "caught sight of the Mighty One."[14] Rabbi Ishmael, in a similar manner, asks about the process which leads one to be able to "behold the vision of the Merkavah."[15] He also recounts his highest spiritual experience using similar terminology: "I saw the King of the Kings sitting on a high and exalted throne, and his servants were attending him on his right and on his left."[16]

Many statements in various Hekhalot literary texts suggest that this ultimate aim, namely attaining the divine by beholding his vision, is a conceivable and permissible goal.[17] Not only is it the final aspiration of the mystics' quest, but also God himself, as confirmed in several accounts, wishes to be seen. He longs for the exceptional, qualified adept who can cross the boundaries between the phenomenological and the transcendent realms, ascend to heaven and see divine revelations, which are concealed from both mortal and angelic eyes:

> TWTRWSY'Y YHWH, God of Israel, yearns and waits . . .
> When will he descend, he who descends to the Merkavah?
> When will he see the pride of high?
> When will he see the end of salvation?
> When will he hear the end of wonders?
> When will he see what no eye has ever seen?
> When will he ascend and attest before
> the seed of Abraham, His beloved . . . [18]

Those, moreover, who gain visions of the Merkavah are required to report to their confidants and describe the awesome and glorious divine sights:

> A heavenly punishment on you, descenders to the Merkavah, if you do not tell and say what you have heard; and if you do not testify what you have seen about the countenance of exaltation, might, pride and glory.[19]

According to these Hekhalot and Merkavah perceptions, attaining God's realm and experiencing his presence by beholding his visions seem to be the ultimate desire of both God and the descenders to the chariot. Yet conflicting statements in several sources deny this option. Narrations in certain passages maintain an alternative, more traditional view, namely that God and human beings are forever separate. Although a few exceptional people are capable of crossing the boundaries, the act of passing from one realm to another is seen in these accounts as problematic and dangerous to both human and divine creatures. Angelic beings must undergo vigorous preparations such as purifying themselves in a river of fire before they return from what seems to be the profane Earth to the pure heavens.[20] Likewise, human beings are generally prevented from approaching God by fierce celestial guards, who stand at every heavenly gate in order to block access to the divine sphere:

> At the entrance to the seventh palace stand and rage all mighty ones, ruthless, powerful, and hard, terrible, and frightening, higher than mountains and sharper than hills. Their bows are strung before the countenance; their swords polished in their hands. Bolts of lightning emanate from their eyeballs, channels of fire from their noses, and torches of coal from their mouths. They are adorned (with) helmets and armors; lances and spears hanging on their arms adorn them.[21]

Not only is the act of crossing the boundaries very harmful, but also the attempt of beholding the divine is itself particularly dangerous. Human beings and angels alike are restricted from seeing God. Destructive consequences and terrifying effects are anticipated for those who dare:

> Of no creature are the eyes able to gaze at Him, not the eyes of flesh and blood, and not the eyes of his servants, and the one who does gaze at Him, and peers and sees, his eyeballs are seized and turned, and his eyeballs emit and shoot forth torches of fire, and they scorch him and they burn him.[22]

These conflicting attitudes suggest two different approaches. Beholding God and the Merkavah is at once a supreme goal, which is encouraged and desired, and an option which is absolutely prohibited and denied.

This paradox has been the topic of much study by scholars. G. Scholem makes a distinction between the transcendent God and his visible appearance. He argues that God's glory, the *"kavod"* (כבוד) is only the revealed aspect of the divine, which becomes visible to the Merkavah mystics.[23] This observation gained support from other scholars such as I. Gruenwald, who claims: "Despite the daring modes of expression, one can find in that literature about the contents of the mystical experience, that the possibility of a direct visual encounter with God is generally ruled out."[24] R. Elior pays particular attention to the unusual quality of the vision and the uniqueness of the human perception during the experience. She states: "The vision described is not a human vision, which is forbidden, but rather a momentary glimpse of enlightenment through super-sensory perception."[25] The human possibility, however, of beholding and understanding divine visions is limited, according to Elior. She argues further that the Hekhalot and Merkavah literature establishes clear boundaries that limit or prohibit human exegesis of divine visions, and contends that the traveler actually sees the Merkavah, and not God himself.[26] P. Schäfer examines this issue in light of dialectical hidden and manifest aspects of God, and interprets God's names as his revealed aspect.[27] According to I. Chernus, the vision of God is restricted in order to avoid its destructive effects on the visionary.[28] E. R. Wolfson associates the vision of God with the adepts' quasi-deification or angelification, expressed through the image of enthronement in heaven: "it is by virtue of the enthronement that the mystic can see which is ordinarily concealed from both human and angelic eyes."[29]

These and other suggestions have been advanced by scholars to explain the seeming contradiction between a transcendent or immanent vision of the divine. From a different perspective this contradiction can be resolved by regarding the imperceptibility or inaccessibility of God as a stage in the adepts' awareness. God cannot be seen or understood by most human beings in their normal mortal state. For some he becomes accessible when they reach a certain level of awareness, which is different from ordinary consciousness. The ability "to behold," however, is gained during a long spiritual voyage. Seeing visions of God and experiencing the presence of the divine is thus the ultimate aspiration and the outcome of the journey.

In his discourse on the nature of mystical awareness of the divine, mentioned above, B. McGinn makes an insightful observation which is relevant in context of the Hekhalot and Merkavah mysticism:

> When I speak of mysticism as involving an immediate consciousness of the presence of God, I am trying to highlight a central claim that appears in almost all mystical texts. Mystics continue to affirm that their mode of access to God is radically different from that found in ordinary consciousness. [30]

It seems that various Hekhalot and Merkavah accounts refer to the act of beholding in these terms. Distinct statements introduce a perception of God which is "radically different from that found in ordinary human consciousness," suggesting that it is possible to see the vision of God as the culminating stage of the voyage to the Merkavah. This option is limited, however, and dependent on the mystics. The desire to behold a vision of the divine can be achieved only if they expand their human perspective and develop their spiritual ability "to see" visions, as well as to comprehend their concealed meaning. When adepts reach this stage, they can grasp divine truths hidden behind appearances, perceive God's abstract qualities through his manifested vision, and interpret the meaning of such revelations, as Rabbi Akiva's statement at the opening of *Hekhalot Zutarti* suggests:

> If you want to single yourself out in the world so that the secrets of the world and the mysteries of wisdom will be revealed to you, study this teaching and be careful with it until the day of departure. Do not try to understand what lies behind you and do not investigate the words of your lips. You will understand what is in your heart and keep silent, so that you will attain the beauty of the Merkavah.[31]

This statement pronounces the privilege of seeing divine revelations as a process involving specific internal attitudes, spiritual perception, and proper comprehension, in addition to traditional religious proficiencies. "Understanding of the heart" appears to be associated with a more than logical investigation and intellectual comprehension. Spiritual awareness, insight, and inner understanding are perceived also to be necessary prerequisites for enabling one to see "what no eye has ever seen" and to "behold God and the Merkavah." Before visions are granted and attained, adepts are expected to expand their perception beyond an ordinary human perspective and to gain a new awareness. In this way capable adepts are able to access the divine realm, obtain revelations, and realize their veiled meanings, as human perception and divine reality correspond and become one, for a temporary period of time. Relevant to this suggestion is F. J. Streng's observation of the nature of mystical awareness:

> Basic to mystic awareness is the claim that attitudinal purification is necessary for right perception. *What* one knows is closely related to *how* one knows. To see beyond the apparent, or superficial world means a change in the mechanism of apprehension.[32]

METHODS AND TECHNIQUES

> In all known periods . . . Jewish mystics were in possession of, and apparently practiced, a wide variety of mystical techniques. Some of these bore obvious magical color, whereas

> in a few this aspect was overcome; all of them included a deep involvement of the mystic, who was expected to invest considerable effort in order to attain his religious goal.[33]

> Rabbi Nehunia ben Ha-Kanah sat and arranged before them
> all the matters of the Merkavah: descent and ascent;
> how one who descends descends,
> and how one who ascends ascends.[34]

Full spiritual awareness is not instantly granted by God as a gift of inspiration to the devoted disciples. Nor can it be attained automatically by faithful believers. The Hekhalot and Merkavah seekers acquire such a spiritual level in a gradual manner. McGinn treats the nature of a progressive process of gaining inner awareness, which leads to encounters between God and humans:

> It is important to remember that mysticism is always a process or a way of life. Although the essential note—or better, goal—of mysticism may be conceived of as a particular kind of encounter between God and human, between the Infinite Spirit and the finite human spirit, everything that leads up to and prepares for this encounter as well as all that flows from it for the life of the individual in the belief community, is also mystical. [35]

Several Hekhalot and Merkavah accounts include references to a specific mystical path or *"via mystica"* which leads adepts to reach their objectives. According to J. Dan the stages of this path can be learned and followed.[36] A pivotal report in *Hekhalot Rabbati* illustrates this process. It depicts Rabbi Nehunia ben Ha-Kanah as a master sitting among his disciples in a "mystical assembly" amid torches of fire and light. He reveals to them the nature of the mystical path and explains both aspects of the spiritual practice—how to reach the Merkavah and how to come back:

> . . . and he [Rabbi Nehunia ben Ha-Kanah] sat on a bench of pure marble. . . . We all came and sat before him and there were friends who stood on their feet because they saw torches of fire and light dividing them and us. . . . Rabbi Nehunia ben Ha-Kanah sat and arranged before them all the matters of the Merkavah: descent and ascent; how one who descends descends, and how one who ascends should ascend . . . [37]

The *"via mystica"* involves, among other components, various techniques and methods, intended both to induce visions and to influence the adept's perception. These include ascetic practices, bodily posture, fasts and special diets,[38] rituals of cleansing the body, and repetitions of special hymns, prayers, and incantations.[39] They include as well repeated utterance of divine names and letters,[40] active visualization and meditation techniques,[41] and recitation of adjurations and incantations.[42] The Merkavah seekers are required to adapt such methods in a dynamic process. Thus, from a phenomenological perspective Hekhalot and Merkavah mysticism corresponds to an non-passive mystical model, which P. Moore classifies:

> Mystical experience not only comprises static and constant features, in regard to which the mystic remains passive; it has also a dynamic and developing character, sometimes carrying the subject along with it (as in the case of ecstasy properly so-called), but often inviting his active response and co-operation.[43]

Different hypotheses have been suggested in order to explain the mental effect of various methods, and the nature of the experiences described in the Hekhalot and Merkavah accounts. These include ecstatic trance, ascents of the soul, deep meditation, dream vision, psychological contemplation, hallucination, para-hypnotic states of mind, shamanistic practices, and auto-suggestive dreams.[44] As mentioned earlier, it is beyond the scope of this present study to investigate the genuineness of the experiences and their authentic historical or psychological validity. Instead, we shall treat the literary testimony of these revelations as our evidence. This testimony appears to describe a spiritual-mental process which affects the visionaries' consciousness, beliefs, and perception.

The following examples reflect this observation. In *Ma'aseh Merkavah*, Rabbi Ishmael, inspired by his teacher Rabbi Nehunia ben Ha-Kanah, recites the necessary names of angels and ascends to the Merkavah. While sitting next to his master on Earth, in his mind he travels in heaven, experiences visions of divine reality, and unfolds them to his master.[45] *Hekhalot Zutarti* recounts a similar contemplative process, when speaking of the divine Name which "was revealed to Rabbi Akiva when he was contemplating and beholding the Merkavah; and he descended and taught it to his students."[46] This narrative suggests that while Rabbi Akiva was meditating the Merkavah in the terrestrial world, he attained, spiritually, the celestial realm and received the secret Name of God. *Hekhalot Rabbati* relates how Rabbi Ishmael ascends to the chariot, in order to learn information about the ten martyrs, while participating in a gathering with his companions on Earth.[47] The same account describes Rabbi Nehunia ben Ha-Kanah's inner spiritual journey, depicting him among his disciples in the earthly realm, and at the same time gazing at heavenly sights and sharing his visions.[48]

There is no doubt, as P. Schäfer, D. J. Halperin, M. M. Swartz, and R. M. Lesses have demonstrated, that some of the methods and practices reflect strong magical interests and aim at magico-theurgic goals.[49] In addition to such methods, directed to influence divine powers or to provoke safe ascents, yet other methods are designed to alter human perception and in so doing they affect the adepts' ability to attain the divine.

The Babylonian rabbinic leader of the eleventh century, Hai Gaon, first discussed the effects of various preparational practices on the adepts' ability to behold divine visions. According to his understanding:

> Perhaps you know that many of the sages believed that whoever is worthy, [possessing] several [moral] attributes which are mentioned and specified, when he wants to see the Merkavah and glimpse the Hekhalot of the angels on high, there are ways of doing so. He is to sit in fasting a certain number of days, and lay his head between his knees, and whisper many songs and praises, which are specified, to the ground. And so you can glimpse inside it and its chambers as one who sees with his eyes the seventh Hekhalot and sees as if he is entering from one Hekhal to another and sees what is in it.[50]

As Halperin shows, Hai Gaon's observation was based on one passage in *Hekhalot Zutarti* which, in fact, is related to the *Sar Torah* tradition and not to the mystical tradition of the Hekhalot literature.[51] Nevertheless, Hai Gaon's general conclusions regarding the mystical path seem to be valid, despite his probable reliance on an inappropriate passage. "The supernal palaces [Hekhalot] can be gazed at and contemplated not only by referring to an external event," asserts M. Idel, "but by concentrating upon one's own 'chambers'. The scene of revelation is thus no longer supermundane hierarchy of palaces, but the human consciousness. . . "[52] An examination of other passages of the Hekhalot and Merkavah literature discloses that the terminology applied conveys details regarding the effect of various methods and practices on the adept's inner perception. These lead the participants from an ordinary human state of mind into an altered state of mind in which they can obtain divine visions.[53] Concepts such as consciousness, perception, or inner insight are not explicitly mentioned. They are nonetheless recognized in the narratives as the capability to behold God, to observe the Merkavah, and to see divine visions, which is the main objective of the various techniques.

For example, Rabbi Ishmael speaks of a technique of praying which leads to seeing God:

> Rabbi Ishmael said: Rabbi Nehunia ben Ha-Kanah said to me: "Everyone who prays this prayer in all his power is able to

> look at the splendor of the *Shekhina*
> and the *Shekhina* is beloved to him."[54]

Rabbi Ishmael mentions the repetition of names as a technical tool which enables the Merkavah seekers to catch sight of the divine:

> Rabbi Ishmael said: "I asked Rabbi Nehunia
> ben Ha-Kanah my teacher:
> When one recited twelve words,
> how can one look at the splendor of the *Shekhina*"?[55]

The influence of songs on the ability to attain heavenly visions is also made clear:

> Rabbi Akiva said: "Happy is the man
> who stands in all his power
> and brings songs before the cherubim of YHWH
> God of Israel and who looks at the chariot and sees all
> things that they do before the throne of glory."[56]

Emphasizing the link between technical methods and the mystical goal of seeing the divine, the question in the opening of *Hekhalot Rabbati* affirms the effect of reciting songs on the adept's vision and perception of the Merkavah:

> What are the songs that one utters
> when he wishes to gaze into the vision of the Merkavah,
> to descend in peace and to ascend in peace?[57]

A statement in *Ma'aseh Merkavah* speaks of the method of contemplative meditation and its effects on the visionaries' awareness of God's realm:

> Rabbi Akiva said: "Who is able to contemplate
> the seven palaces and behold the heaven of heavens
> and see the chambers of chambers
> and say: 'I saw the chamber of YH?'"[58]

Rabbi Akiva relates how adepts reflect about the seven palaces of God and in so doing make them the center of their mental meditation. They are then able, in their visions, to ascend to the celestial spheres, catch sight of the inner, heavenly chambers and experience the presence of the divine.

ETHICAL AND SPIRITUAL ALTERATION

> Any adequate account of mystical practices
> would have to include the whole programme
> of ethical, ascetical, and technical practices
> typically followed by mystics.[59]

> When I ascended to the first palace, I was righteous;
> in the second palace, I was pure; in the third palace,
> I was upright; in the fourth palace, I was perfect;
> in the fifth palace, I brought holiness before the
> King of Kings, blessed be His name.
> In the sixth palace, I said the sanctification before Him.[60]

Several Hekhalot passages assert that only the most accomplished individuals, who can evidently exhibit their traditional religious knowledge, ethical behavior, and sometimes their distinguished family and racial lineage, can initiate an ascent to the Merkavah.[61] Other statements claim that theoretically all Jewish people can follow the "matter of the Merkavah," and attempt to embark on the heavenly voyage.[62] According to both patterns success is not promised. The mystical path involves stages of spiritual development, and failure is a definite possibility.

Moore, in his assessment of mystical experiences, doctrines and techniques, has specified the nature of such a gradual process, which includes practices of a special kind : "Any adequate account of mystical practices would have to include the whole programme of ethical, ascetical, and technical practices typically followed by mystics within religious traditions."[63] Several mentions in the Hekhalot and Merkavah literature clearly reflect a similar attitude. The mystical path involved an inner process of perfecting oneself and gaining high spiritual and ethical virtues such as purity, righteousness, and holiness:

> I asked of Rabbi Akiva for a prayer that a man prays when ascending to the Merkavah and requested from him the praise of RWZYH YHWH, God of Israel. Who knows what it is? And he said to me: "Holiness and purity are in his heart and he prays a prayer."[64]

The process of accomplishing ethical and moral integrity is sequential and gradual. Several accounts reflect "the tendency to set the stages of ascent in parallel with the degree of perfection," as Scholem has observed.[65] During their journeys out of this world adepts acquire moral qualities, inner strength, and spiritual capacity. They become able to experience divine reality as they proceed toward the seventh divine palace. In his report to Rabbi Ishmael, Rabbi Akiva relates how levels of spiritual wholeness correspond to explicit stages of the celestial journey:

> When I ascended to the first palace, I was righteous; in the second palace, I was pure; in the third palace, I was truthful; in the fourth palace, I was perfect; in the fifth palace, I brought holiness before the King of Kings, blessed be His

> name. In the sixth palace, I said the sanctification before Him who spoke and fashioned and commanded all living beings, so that the angel would not destroy me. In the seventh palace, I stood in all my power. I trembled in all my limbs.[66]

As the journey unfolds, adepts are challenged with physical and spiritual ordeals. They are required to prove themselves in several stages, which progressively lead them to the upper seventh palace.[67] It is significant to note that the ascent does not culminate instantly in an encounter with God, nor does it lead to an immediate acceptance and participation in the divine realm. It appears that even upon reaching the final destination, the travelers are not yet considered "qualified" or "deserving" to take part in the Merkavah realm and to see the King in his beauty. A clear reference is made in the literatures to two categories of people: those who are worthy to behold the divine and those who have not yet reached this stage.[68] This distinction could be related to the adept's spiritual ability to make the transition from an ordinary level of awareness to a deeper level of understanding and perception, which enables an attainment of divine truth.

In his discussion of the practical aspects of Jewish Kabblistic mysticism, Idel observes an important trend, appearing relevant to the Hekhalot and Merkavah mysticism:

> From its beginning. ecstatic Kabbalah was an elite lore . . . pointing the way that very few may follow for their own spiritual perfection rather than the means for the restoration of divine harmony.[79]

This observation sheds light on Hekhalot and Merkavah's demand for the spiritual perfection, accomplished only by several qualified individuals, who can make the transition from limited awareness to levels of transcendent perception. It seems that before adepts are granted permission to participate in the highest realm, they are obligated to demonstrate their newly acquired spiritual awareness and consciousness, described metaphorically as their ability to decipher manifested visions with "the eyes of the heart." The nature of such mystical ability is clarified by Dan:

> The mystic denies that . . . human faculties are related to divine truth in any way; the more they are developed and followed, the farther one is led away from the truth. The only avenue to truth is the forsaking of these human faculties and the adherence to a completely different quest for truth, in non-sensual and supralogical means.[70]

The famous "water test" at the entrance to the sixth palace can be seen in this light as a procedure which tests the adepts' capability to perceive divine truth, not through the common avenues of knowledge based on human logic or the senses. Instead, in order to be recognized as "qualified" to enter the seventh palace of God and to behold his presence, adepts are called to approach divine visions in a different fashion.[71]

As recorded in *Hekhalot Zutarti* and *Hekhalot Rabbati*, at the entrance to the sixth palace, a vision of "thousands upon thousands of waves of water" is revealed to the travelers. Yet, "there is not a single drop of water there, only the radiance of the marble stones with which the palace is furnished."[82] Unworthy or unqualified individuals are deceived by their human conception of the vision. They rely on sensual observations and logical conclusions, accept the validity of the manifested vision, and thus inquire: "what is the nature of the water?" Deserving mystics, being able to rely on spiritual, nonsensual and supralogical methods of perception, are capable of beholding the vision and of decoding its meaning. They discern its concealed essence and therefore see the marble behind the illusion of water. In the context of Hekhalot and Merkavah mysticism, it seems, the vision of the water/marbel is not presented as an allegory but as a transcendent reality which is suitable to the visionary stage of spiritual and exegetical perception. Eligible adepts are capable of interpreting the vision correctly and thus are qualified to enter the seventh heaven and to see God.

Passages in *Hekhalot Zutarti* delineate the details of this test, which was forced upon the four sages who entered the *Pardes,* Ben Azai, Ben Zoma, Aher, and Rabbi Akiva. The emphasis appears to be on the act of beholding and on a profound understanding, which allows comprehension of the concealed depth of apparent revelation:

> And these are those who entered the *Pardes:* Ben Azai, and Ben Zoma, and the Other, and Rabbi Akiva. Ben Azai peered into the sixth palace and saw the brilliance of the air of the marble stones that were paved in the palace. And his body could not endure and he opened his mouth and asked them: "These waters, what are their nature?" And he died . . . Ben Zoma peered at the brightness of the marble stones and perceived it as water. His body could endure not to ask them, yet his mind could not endure it. And he was harmed. He went out of his mind . . . [73]

> Rabbi Akiva said: "Ben Azai gained and stood at the gate of the sixth palace. And he saw the brilliance of the air of the pure marble stones. And he opened his mouth twice and said: 'Water, Water'. In a wind of an eye they cut his head off and threw upon him eleven thousand iron cutters." This sign will be for generations, that a person should not err at the gate of the sixth palace.[74]

The account describes the sages who were expected to unravel the disclosed sight. Of the four, only Rabbi Akiva was able to see the marble stones behind the misleading facade of waves of water. Thus, only he was considered by God to be "worthy of beholding my glory."[75]

SPIRITUAL TRANSFORMATIONS

> The shift from conventional to mystical awareness . . . expresses a new attitude or temperament which is more than, but inclusive of, intellect or ideas. The nature of the total awareness can be defined in terms of its comprehensiveness and its total purity.[76]

> I saw a light in my heart like the days of heaven . . . since I stood on my feet and saw my face shining from my wisdom, I began to explain each and every angel in each and every palace. [77]

The climax of the journey is a stage of inner transformation. This transformation enables qualified adepts to transcend their ordinary human perspective and to obtain an elevated awareness and spiritual perception. Thus, they are able to observe the true meaning of veiled divine visions and achieve their mystical goals at the end of their ecstatic ascent.[78]

Several Hekhalot and Merkavah accounts present this stage as a threefold pattern of self-transformation, using a familiar pattern of death and rebirth.[79] This pattern has very much in common, it seems, with a pattern of initiatory rite of passage which is typically discussed in the contexts of both myths and rituals. A. van Gennep, followed by C. Bell, speaks of the rite of passage as one type of ritual which includes three stages: a stage of separation, followed by a transitional state (termed liminal), and concluded by a reincorporation into a social group with a different status.[80] This rite, often displayed in patterns of symbolic death and rebirth, "enables the individual to pass from one defined position to another, which is equally well defined."[81] As a result, the process leads to "a new way of seeing and acting."[82] In Hekhalot and Merkavah mysticism, the social objective is not prominent. Instead, a process of symbolic death and rebirth, which seems analogous in structure to the tripartite pattern described by van Gennep, leads the visionaries to cross conceptual boundaries between the terrestrial and the celestial realms.

In the first stage, often illustrated metaphorically by images of a ritual death, the Hekhalot adepts collapse, faint or fall down as they let go of their human disposition. In the second stage, illustrated by images of rebirth, awakening, or illumination, adepts surpass their previous ordinary human perception. They are granted a new and wider awareness, and reach an exceptional spiritual understanding. A heavenly ceremony sometimes follows this stage, granting it an official and formal seal. In the third stage, the visionaries gain a god-like insight and a new status. They are no longer limited by their human, logical, or sensual perception. Instead, their ability "to see" is unrestricted. They rely on their spiritual potential and can therefore see and comprehend divine visions with their own "understanding of the heart." The following discussion will examine the significance of the transformation process and the way it leads the Merkavah seekers to accomplish their mystical goal and to behold divine revelations and visions. Several Hekhalot and Merkavah literary traditions, especially *3 Enoch, Hekhalot Rabbati, Hekhalot Zutarti, Ma'aseh Merkavah,* and *Shi'ur Komah,* demonstrate this aspect.

Rabbi Ishmael, in the beginning of *3 Enoch,* recounts his ecstatic experience. Having passed from palace to palace, attempting to gain sight of the celestial realm, he stands finally at the gates of the seventh palace, receives permission to enter, and is immediately overwhelmed by God's closeness. Before he sees visions of the chariot, he falls down and faints, only to be revived and restored by Metatron, "the heavenly Prince of the Divine Presence."[83] God then enlightens Rabbi Ishmael's eyes and heart so that he will be capable of participating in the new heavenly reality:

> Then I entered the seventh palace and he led me to the camp of the Shekhinah and presented me before the throne of glory so I might behold the chariot. But as soon as the princes of the chariot looked at me and the fiery seraphim fixed their gaze on me, I shrank back trembling and fell down . . . until the Holy One, blessed be he, rebuked them . . . At once Metatron, Prince of the Divine Presence, came and revived me and raised me to my feet, but still I did not have strength enough to sing a hymn before the glorious throne of the glorious King. . . . But after an hour the Holy One, blessed be he, opened to me the gates of the Chariot . . . He enlightened my eyes and my heart to utter psalms, praise, jubilation, thanksgiving, song, glory, majesty, laud and strength.[84]

Following the stage of inner transformation, Rabbi Ishmael is led on a tour through the celestial realm by the angel Metatron. The angel uncovers to him divine sights, which he is now able to behold. Metatron constantly uses the same sentence before itemizing the concealed divine mysteries: "Come and I will show you."[85] Consequently he introduces abstract visions which are normally beyond recognition, emphasizing Rabbi Ishmael's new mystical ability to see amorphous visions such as the souls of the righteous, the spirits of the stars, the "hand of God which no creature can see."[86] Among the spectacles he sees are the following:

> . . . letters by which the heaven and earth were created . . .
> fire burns in the midst of hail . . .
> lightning flashes in the midst of mountains of snow . . .
> thunder rumbles in the highest heights . . .
> the souls of the righteous who have already been created
> and have returned, and the souls of the righteous
> who have not yet been created . . . the spirits of the stars
> which stands in the "Raqia" . . . the souls of the angels
> and the spirits of the ministers . . .
> the right hand of the Omnipresent One . . .
> that even the seraphim and the ophanim
> are not allowed to look on."[87]

When observing these wonders, Rabbi Ishmael is an active participant. He observes directly, acknowledging his own new proficiency to behold astonishing and extraordinary, intangible sights:

> I saw fire, snow and hailstones enclosed one within the other,
> without one destroying the other . . .
> I saw lightning flashing in the midst of mountains of snow,
> without being quenched . . .
> I saw thunders and voices roaring
> in the midst of flames of fire . . .
> I saw rivers of fire in the midst of rivers of water,
> and rivers of water in the midst of river of fire . . . [88]

Metatron goes on to display before Rabbi Ishmael the secret heavenly curtain (pargod, **פרגוד**), on which all the deeds and thoughts of all the generations of the world are recorded, past and future:[89]

> Metatron said to me: Come and I will show you
> the curtain of the Omnipresent One,
> which is spread before the Holy One, blessed be He,
> and on which are printed all the generations
> of the world, and all their deeds
> whether done or to be done, till the last generation . . .
> and I saw each generation and its potentates. . . .
> Adam and his generation, their deeds and their thoughts;
> I saw Noah and his generation of the Flood,
> their deeds and their thoughts;
> Nimrod . . . Abraham . . . Isaac . . . Ishmael . . .
> Jacob . . . the twelve tribes . . . Amram . . . Moses . . .
> Aaron and Miriam . . . Joshua . . . the Judges . . .

Eli . . . Phineas . . . Elkanah . . . .Samuel . . .
the Kings of Judah . . . the Kings of Israel . . .
the Kings of the gentiles . . .
their deeds and their thoughts . . . [90]

His new sentient state allows Rabbi Ishmael to be free of human limitations, historical situations, and the circumstances of passing time. He can gaze not only at the remote past, but also at the far future. He sees and understands the manifest deeds and unseen thoughts of all the generations of the world from Adam to the Messiah:

. . . and I saw the Messiah, the son of Joseph,
and his generation and all they will do . . .
the Messiah, the son of David, and his generation
and all the battles and wars and all they will do to Israel
whether for good or bad.[92]

The triple pattern of transformation is clearly present in the above description, emphasizing the link between the mental-spiritual awareness of the adepts and their potential of seeing divine visions. Rabbi Ishmael faints and surrenders his human consciousness in a stage that can be understood as symbolic death. A stage of rebirth follows. Rabbi Ishmael is revived, elevated to a higher spiritual level by the heavenly prince Metatron, and enlightened by God himself. He gains a special spiritual perspective and an "understanding of the eyes and the heart." Following a transition to an even higher level, Rabbi Ishmael is initiated into the divine realm. He then partakes in the heavenly liturgy, praises God with the angels, and sings hymns before the glorious throne. He is capable of exceeding the limits of human perception and thus beholds elusive and inconceivable visions, normally beyond mortal eyes. With this new "understanding of the heart," Rabbi Ishmael can look at metaphysical, abstract sights in the divine realm. He sees the amorphous spirits of the stars, or the souls of angels. He watches the formless thunders and the voices roaring, and gazes at miraculous sights of fire, snow, and hailstones enclosed one within the other. From this divine-like viewpoint, Rabbi Ishmael transcends time and place as he observes events and mighty individuals in the far off past or the distant future.

Hekhalot Rabbati presents a similar process. Rabbi Ishmael is asked by Rabbi Nehunia ben Ha-Kanah to ascend into the Merkavah and there to find out in heaven the destiny of the ten martyr-sages. He goes up and is devastated to discover the future calamities awaiting the Jewish people. He is then comforted by the heavenly guardian Hadari'el, who exposes various heavenly eschatological secrets before him and permits him to experience the divine realm. This event is preceded by a stage of transformation, which clearly refers to the same pattern discussed above:

> . . . when I heard this loud voice I trembled and I was silent and I fell back until Hadari'el the prince came and bestowed upon me a spirit and soul; and raised me on my feet . . . and he led me into the archives of comfort, archives of salvation, and I saw groups of serving angels sitting and weaving garments of salvation and making crowns of life for the righteous persons . . . He sat me down in his lap and asked me: "what do you see?" I told him: "I see seven bolts of lightning running as one."[93]

After Rabbi Ishmael undergoes a stage of separation from his common human disposition, he is given spirit and soul, reincorporated into a new state, and thus becomes capable of seeing concealed visions beyond phenomenological reality:

> . . . I heard the sound of great noise coming from Eden . . .
> and there was David, king of Israel, leading, and
> I saw all the kings of the house of David following . . .
> David stood and uttered songs and praises
> which no ear has ever heard before. [94]

The model of self-transformation is likewise evident in this report. Initially Rabbi Ishmael loses his consciousness. He is then revived by an angelic figure who elevates him and grants him a new life. After his transformation Rabbi Ishmael, unrestricted by human capacities, gains an independent divine-like outlook. He sees the interior of celestial archives, exhibited before him, and witnesses heavenly sights. He is evidently qualified to participate in the divine reality which does not conform to conventional laws of chronological time and historical place. Rabbi Ishmael hears voices from Eden, sees King David accompanied by the kings of Israel and listens to them praising God in extraordinary acclamations that no one has heard before.

From a phenomenological perspective, it is significant to note that all parallel Hekhalot and Merkavah accounts of the transformation process acknowledge both the physical aspects of the experience—described in images such as trembling, fainting, falling down, standing—and its mental, spiritual components—often depicted as the ability of beholding divine visions. It seems, thus, that in this tradition the mystical experience is seen as total and integral, involving the physical body, sensation, emotion, and perception. Moore's observation asserts this aspect of the mystical phenomenon, which he discerns as:

> not only "mental" phenomena or "disembodied" states of mind, but as involving tactile, substantial and corporeal dimensions also . . . mystical doctrines and theories include a good deal about subtle bodies, psychic organs, and higher forms of existence interpreting (though sometimes reacting with) the ordinary world of things and persons.[95]

A third narrative in *Hekhalot Rabbati* gives formal details of this integrated transformational process. In this account, the information is provided as an objective, general report, directed at all determined adepts, not as a personal testament of a single visionary:

> . . . and whenever one wishes to descend to the Merkavah, Anafi'el, the prince, opens the doors of the gate of the seventh palace for him. This man enters and stands at the threshold of the gate to the seventh palace. The holy living creatures raise to him five hundred and twelve eyes . . . and that man then trembles, shakes, and shudders. He is stricken and faints and he falls backwards. And the prince Anafi'el supports him, and sixty-three other gatekeepers of the seventh palaces. They support him and say: "fear not, son of the beloved seed, enter and behold the King in his beauty and you will not be destroyed and you will not be burned." . . . They give him strength and immediately a horn is sounded above the firmament over their heads and the holy living creatures cover their faces and the Cherubim and Ophanim turn their faces around. And he enters and stands before the throne of His glory. . . . As soon as he stands before the throne of glory, he opens and says songs that the throne of glory chants every day.[96]

This presentation relates a paradigmatic tripartite model of symbolic death and rebirth for everyone who requests to descend to the Merkavah. In the first stage, adepts faint and fall back. They are then revived by the angel Anafi'el and other divine beings (corresponding to the figures of Metatron and Hadari'el of the previous narratives), who assist them and grant them new strength. A blast of the heavenly horn proclaims this phase officially. Consequently, they enter divine chambers, stand before God, and join the throne of glory in the celestial rituals.

Once again, it is possible to note a repetitive version of this pattern in *Ma'aseh Merkavah.* Rabbi Ishmael, inspired by his teacher, Rabbi Nehunia ben Ha-Kanah, learns from him details concerning the methods of ascent by uttering names:

> Rabbi Ishmael said: "Since I heard from Rabbi Nehunia ben Ha-Kanah my teacher this report . . . I stood on my feet and asked him all the names of the princes of wisdom, and from the question that I asked I saw a light in my heart like the days of heaven . . . since I stood on my feet and saw my face shining from my wisdom . . . I began to explain every angel in each and every palace."[97]

In this passage, the first stage of the transformation is not mentioned directly. It can, nonetheless, be inferred from statements relating the second stage, in which Rabbi Ishmael stands up and is fused with light. This report leads to the assumption that he was not standing, but was perhaps in a state of unconsciousness before he was granted divine wisdom and enlightened understanding. As soon as Rabbi Ishmael gains "light in his heart," he himself is able to recognize and to distinguish every angel in each of the heavenly palaces. He comprehends the vision and describes the "details of the heavenly realm." This elevated stage is recognized by his teacher, Rabbi Nehunia ben Ha-Kanah, who questions his disciple, expressing astonishment at his independent, extraordinary ability.[98]

Enoch's elevation from a terrestrial being into the supreme celestial angel Metatron is recorded in *3 Enoch* in a similar manner, but on a cosmic scale:[99]

> Before the Holy One, blessed be he, set me to serve the throne of glory, he opened for me 300,000 gates of understanding, 300,000 gates of prudence, 300,000 gates of life, 300,000 gates of grace and favor, 300,000 gates of love, 300,000 gates of Torah, 300,000 gates of sustenance, 300,000 gates of mercy . . .[100]

> I was enlarged and increased in size until I matched the world in height and breadth. He made to grow on me 72 wings, 36 on one side and 36 on the other . . . He fixed in me 365,000 eyes. . . . There was no sort of splendor, brilliance, brightness, or beauty in the luminaries of the world that he failed to fix in me. [101]

During the metamorphosis, which occurs on a physical, mental, and spiritual level, Enoch sheds his human form and becomes a divine figure. The transition from one level of existence to another is followed by a stage of enlightenment, during which Enoch is granted divine wisdom and gains an exceptional spiritual and mental understanding. He then crosses the boundaries between the finite and infinite realms in a non-temporary way. He sees and decodes veiled levels of reality and obtains unseen visions and enigmatic secrets. Like the Creator, he himself looks and beholds the mysteries of divine wisdom, the order of nature, the depth of the Torah, and the hidden thoughts of the human heart:

> The Holy One, blessed be he, revealed to me from that time onward all the mysteries of wisdom, all the depths of the perfect Torah and all the thoughts of human hearts. All mysteries of the world and all the orders of nature stand revealed before me as they stand revealed before the Creator.

> From that time onward I looked and beheld deep secrets and wonderful mysteries. Before anyone thinks in secret, I see his thought; before he acts I see his act. There is nothing in heaven above or deep within the earth concealed from me. [102]

In Hekhalot and Merkavah mysticism, we have seen that the process of transformation leads the mystic to experience a change in consciousness, gain an enlightened perspective, and understand the innermost truths of revealed visions. Rabbi Akiva, Rabbi Ishmael, and Enoch reach this stage, as well as other members of the "descenders to the Merkavah" circle. Though most accounts do not specify explicitly the nature of such a state, descriptions of the divine-like perception, which accomplished mystics gain, demonstrates its quality. *Hekhalot Rabbati* proclaims this state in the well-known *gedulla* passage, which seems to emphasize the independent ability of mystics to behold and see all, like God himself:

> The greatest thing of all is the fact that he sees and recognizes all the deeds of human beings, even in the chamber of chambers, whether they are fine or corrupt deeds . . .

> The greatest thing of all is the fact that all creatures will be before him like silver before the silversmith, who perceives which silver is refined, which silver is unfit, and which silver is pure.[103]

PARALLEL PATTERNS OF SPIRITUAL TRANSFORMATION

> In the history of religion the objective representation is typically in the form of myth, and it generally precedes the mystical stage, which may appear as an internalized version of the same motif.[104]

The previous section examined the process of transformation in Hekhalot and Merkavah mysticism. This tradition, as we have seen, incorporates a common mythological-ritualistic pattern of transformational death and rebirth, in a spiritual manner, in order to convey an inner shift of perception, consciousness, and awareness. It is relevant, in this context, to consider H. Jonas' seminal analysis of mystical movements of late antiquity, which seems to disclose what appears to be an apparent parallel notion.[105] Although the scope of this analysis does not allow a full treatment of this topic, several observations are worth noting.

Exploring the development of early Western mysticism, Jonas has suggested that several traditions employ in their mystical teaching mythological-ritualistic structures, in an interiorized and spiritualized manner. Myth, according to Jonas, is the objective representation of the "way of being in the world" and is usually prior in time to mystical realizations, "which may appear as an internalized version of the same motif."[106] Examining one basic notion of ancient religion, the ascent and descent of the soul, Jonas has followed the alterations of this theme, originating in mythology, into mystical systems, in particular the late pagan mystery cults, Gnostic mysticism, and eventually the mystical philosophies found in the teachings of Origen and Plotinus. These mystical traditions, demonstrate the "transposition of a mythological scheme into the inwardness of a person, with the translation of its objective stages into subjective phases of self-performable experience."[107] In Jonas' view, the late mystery cults play an important mediating role in this transformation of perspective, since their ritualistic performance of the death and rebirth myth, introduces the basic categories and images later used in mystical thoughts.

This observation becomes clear upon examination of several aspects related to the mystery cults of the Graeco-Roman world.[108] The mysteries were widely influential from the first century C.E., and reached a peak of popularity in the second century onward, when they fell under the influence of late Greek religious thought and were transformed from imported cults into universal mystery cults.[109] Despite the diverse origin and the different cultic myths and views of individual mysteries, certain collective features or even a unified theological framework, common to most mysteries, especially in the late period, have been discerned.[110] Moreover, despite the vow of secrecy by which participants were initiated into the cults, some information about the mysteries' traditions, goals, rites, and beliefs did filter through to the general public.[111] As scholars have shown, in addition to esoteric teachings restricted to inner groups, the mystery cults had a public facade and some of their views were apparently meant to be known by the general community.[112]

Several external characteristics of mystery cults have been noted: organization of the members into communities, certain ethical or ascetic obligations, mutual support, the obligation of obedience to the leader of the cult, and the preservation of specific traditions guarded in secrecy.[113] In addition to these external similarities, various cults shared a common set of beliefs and doctrines. Initiation into the great mysteries of the gods, introduced through a prevalent process of symbolic death and rebirth, was one of these shared and widespread doctrines.[114] This procedure enabled initiated adepts to enter into the mysteries of various gods, to become like them and be involved in their fate, and to be filled with their divine power. The terminology of "rebirth" *(palingenesia)* "reformation," "transfiguration," was coined in the context of these rituals. "Purification" and "seeing" *(epopteia)* were official steps of these initiation rites in antiquity.

One passage quoted by Stobaeus and attributed by him to Plutarch, is often cited to demonstrate several significant aspects of the death and rebirth process. According to this account, the stage of rebirth is preceded by an hazardous journey in which the seekers wander in fear, face dangers, tremble, and shudder, before they experience an illumination and enter a new, higher stage of divine existence:

> At first there is wandering, and wearisome roaming, and fearful traveling through darkness with no end to be found. Then, just before the consummation, there is every sort of terror, shuddering and trembling and perspiring and being alarmed. But after this, a marvelous light appears, and open places and meadows await, with voices and dancing and the solemnities of sacred utterances and holy visions. In that place one walks about at will, now perfect and fully initiated.[115]

In Jonas' view, the emphasis on the death and rebirth model, related in this account among other sources, was not so much on ritualistic external aspects, but more on internalized spiritual experience.[116] In the late mystery cults traditional ascetic or cathartic preparations, which the devotees underwent, became an autonomous system of self-transformation. In Jonas' words, "sanctifications and ascetic preparations of all kinds exchange their ritualistic for a more directly personal function in the life of the self."[117] Jonas has directed attention to the proximity of the term *teleisthai* (to be initiated and perfected) to the verb *teleutan* (dying), and emphasized the inner significance of the symbolic death and rebirth experience which led devotees to be transformed, initiated into the mysteries, and be united with the gods.[118] The experience of ecstasy, thus, was associated not only with a formal concept of cultic union with the gods, but also with an interiorized version of the process, associated with the individual's inner spiritual achievements: "Ecstasy, instead of merely certifying that apotheosis has taken place, can, in its own right and experimental quality, be taken to represent perfection itself."[119]

As Jonas has contended, the spiritualized interpretation of the mythical- ritualistic theme of death and rebirth, found in late mystery cults, created the basic categories for later mystical tradition found in Gnostic and early Christian sources. Clearly there are many differences between these traditions and the mysticism of the Hekhalot and Merkavah. Jonas' observations are relevant, however, since they elucidate an important shared phenomenon, namely, the tendency to apply a ritualistic theme of symbolic death and rebirth, in a spiritualized, internalized fashion, in order to depict an inner change of perception and awareness which enable adepts to be conscious of the divine.

EXEGESIS OF DIVINE VISIONS

> A recognition of the interdependence of experience and interpretation can help avoid some of the false problems evident in scholarship of mysticism.The emphasis on mystical experience has led not only to the neglect of mystical hermeneutics, but also to an emphasis on first person, autobiographical accounts of specific visionary or unitive experiences of God.[120]

> He is, so to say, like us . . . and this is His glory
> which is concealed from us.[121]

As we have seen, several Hekhalot and Merkavah accounts present a dialectic approach to the prospect of seeing divine visions. Beholding God and the Merkavah is at once the ultimate mystical goal, desired by God and human beings, but also a practice which is strongly denounced and prohibited. Moreover, God, the object of the adept's vision, is depicted as both accessible and, at the same time, as totally imperceptible.

These contradictions may be reconciled by the notion of the enhanced perception and vision gained by mystics. Revelations of divine reality, it seems, are dependent upon the visionaries' subjective state of spiritual perception. Following a change of consciousness, the descenders to the Merkavah experience the effect of the inner transformation on a cognitive-spiritual level. They acquire additional inner understanding and a greater capacity of comprehending visions. This enlightened mode enables qualified mystics to behold visions of the divine, which are normally concealed from all eyes. They understand masked truths and interpret revelations correctly.

Thus, it appears that Hekhalot and Merkavah mysticism ascribes a great significance to hermeneutical insights and exegetical perception which are mystical in essence. The ones who seek visions of the King and his chariot can actually gaze at these manifested visions when they are capable of interpreting their authentic meaning. They are then able to respond to God's request, to see "what no eye has ever seen,"[122] to penetrate divine mysteries, to decode revelations, and thus to reach deep theosophical truths. In this way, the exegetical process becomes an integral part of the mystical encounter with God.

This practice of "mystical exegesis," however, is unique in Hekhalot and Merkavah mysticism. As M. Fishbane, J. J. Collins, and others have discerned, the primary method of decoding visions and revelations, in both biblical-prophetic literature and apocalyptic sources, is through a divine revealed inspiration or through an angelic interpretation.[123] Hekhalot and Merkavah mysticism, in contrast, seems to emphasize, primarily, a humanly attained mystical perception. Divine revelations and visions are not elucidated by an angelic messenger or by divine inspiration. Instead, they are deciphered by human descenders to the chariots who complete their journey, gain "an understanding of the heart," transcend limited human apprehension, and acquire an enlightened perspective. Then, for a short time, their human perception and divine reality correspond.

In several accounts, this notion surfaces, as we have seen. An example from *Hekhalot Zutarti* denotes clearly both the paradoxical concept of the divine, and the distinctive mystical awareness to perceive it. It opens with a theoretical question regarding human ability to behold visions of God:

> Who is able to explain, who is able to see?
> First, it is written (Exodus 33:20):
> For no one shall see me and live.
> And secondly, it is written (Deuteronomy 5:21–24):
> that God speaks with a human and he lives.
> And thirdly it is written (Isaiah 6:1):
> I saw YHWH seated on a throne.[124]

Different contradictory views are offered further in the passage, but none of them appears to be adequate. The account then ends with Rabbi Akiva's explanation, which sheds light on the complexity of seeing the divine, and seems to be acceptable and most suitable:

> He is, so to say, like us
> and He is greater than all
> and this is His glory
> which is concealed from us.[125]

Rabbi Akiva recognizes God's transcendent supremacy: "He is greater than everything." He also perceives God's manifested qualities in an anthropomorphic figurative way: "He is, so to say, as we are." At the same time, Rabbi Akiva acknowledges the hidden essence of the vision, normally lying beyond human observation: "His glory consists in this that he is concealed from us." We see then that for an adept such as Rabbi Akiva, who has reached the ability to "behold" and "gaze" from a mystical perspective, the two aspects of God, the visible and the abstract, or the concrete and transcendent, are acknowledged as one. Through exegesis of ambiguous figurative and concrete visions, Rabbi Akiva reveals the transcendent supremacy of God.

An additional manifestation of this exegetical enlightened perspective is present in a *Shi'ur Komah* passage, in which Rabbi Akiva decodes God's image as it was revealed to him in a vision:[126]

> The countenance of His face is like the image of a spirit,
> like the form of a soul that no creature can recognize.
> His body is like chrysolite, filling the entire world.
> Neither the near nor the far can look at Him.[127]

This observation is highly significant. Rabbi Akiva beholds God's manifested, figurative image. He perceives corporeal attributes such as body, form, limbs, and the other specific features. At the same time he also sees beyond the visible surface, and recognizes God's spiritual qualities and transcendent nature, presented metaphorically as of soul and spirit. Rabbi Akiva, a worthy mystic, goes far in his exegesis of divine visions. He beholds and deciphers their hidden meaning and thus reaches a profound divine truth.

CONCLUSION

With this example of Rabbi Akiva we conclude this chapter. As we have seen the case of Rabbi Akiva is not isolated. It exhibits a characteristic outlook of Hekhalot and Merkavah mysticism, found in corresponding accounts, and investigates the links between inner spiritual transformation on the one hand and divine revelations and spiritual exegesis on the other hand. According to the Hekhalot and Merkavah mystical tradition, therefore, we can discern that human beings can develop an immediate consciousness of the unperceived God and behold veiled meaning of divine visions.

This ability is dependent ultimately upon single individuals and their spiritual accomplishments, gained gradually through following a prescribed mystical path of self-discipline. Alternation of a common sensual and logical human perception, attainment of spiritual perception, and proper comprehension are some elements introduced in these traditions as leading to an inner transformation. The transformation in turn enables the Merkavah seekers to gain a transcendent awareness of divine reality. The option of seeing visions of the divine, impossible for most human beings, is thus achieved temporarily by a small number of visionaries who can perceive, decode, and interpret them. Seen as valid in both historical and legendary times for spiritual seekers of the past, present, and future, such an outlook is present in parallel Hekhalot and Merkavah accounts and thus exhibits a shared spiritual-mystical approach, reflected in a continuing literary tradition.

3

Mythical Language of Hekhalot and Merkavah Mysticism

> In the post-biblical world . . . Jews and various competing versions of Judaism were important repositories for the mythic imagination: sometimes figures from the archaic pre-biblical world reappeared with new vigor . . . at other times new motifs, including some borrowed from the surrounding cultures of the Hellenistic world.
>
> —A. Green, *Keter,* ix.

INTRODUCTION

As many studies of mysticism have observed, mystical phenomena are often distinct from concrete situations of everyday life. Moreover, they frequently evolve outside the conventional realms of normative religions. Thus, by their very nature, specific mystical notions of various traditions often stand beyond common verbal expression and familiar vocabulary. Nonetheless, even mystical notions which are not clearly conveyed by conventional language still find expression. P. Moore makes the following observation:

> Even those aspects or stages of mystical experience acknowledged as difficult or impossible to describe, are not necessarily beyond all possibility of communication. For if mystics are using language at all responsibly, then even what they say about the indescribable types or aspects of experience may at least serve to define them . . . [1]

A variety of vocabularies and verbal discourses are exercised by different mystical schools in order to mold and to transmit their teachings. Through a rich tapestry of writings groups and traditions convey their mystical conception in diverse styles, forms, and manners of expressions. Mystical rhetoric is often contingent on symbols and paradoxes. Frequently it breaks linguistic conventions, and employs philosophical terms and metaphors in a complex fashion. Each tradition develops a common vocabulary, imagery, and style according to its unique nature, as S. T. Katz discerns:

> Mystical literature comes in many forms, and the modality chosen as the means of communication in any instance is not incidental or tangential to its content.[2]

What kind of verbal discourse and patterns of expression articulate the essence of mystical teachings, revelations, experiences and spiritual interpretations found in the Hekhalot and Merkavah literature? One notable feature of this tradition is the manner in which it introduces many of its mystical notions through presentations ranging from the extremely intangible to the concrete and particular. As we have seen, in a large number of descriptions the spiritual dimensions of an inner voyage and its metaphysical goals are stated. The literature presents a mental contemplative or ecstatic path of crossing conceptual-spiritual boundaries, which leads to an awareness of transcendent truths. It is most significant to note that this process and its obtained goals are externalized. Various accounts describe it, in concrete and tangible images, as a dangerous corporeal journey out of this world, which leads the Merkavah-seekers to a tactile heavenly sphere in which God resides in his palaces and reigns from his celestial throne.

Such presentation, I suggest, reveals the distinctive manner in which Hekhalot and Merkavah mysticism conceptualizes and conveys many of its mystical notions, by evoking a variety of mythological themes and patterns. A clarification is needed when we refer to "mythology" in relation of Hekhalot and Merkavah mysticism. What exactly is meant when we use this term? In this mystical school we find several mythological frameworks through which mystical teachings, experiences, visions and revelations are expressed and formalized. We find mystical notions presented through the applications of patterns such as figurative language, pictorial images, and visual metaphors, which appear to be mythological in nature. We also encounter echoes from particular mythological traditions, rooted in ancient Near Eastern sources, including primarily biblical and Mesopotamian imagery and themes. These, however, not only resurface, but are also reformulated and reinterpreted to assume additional characteristics in the new mystical context of the Hekhalot and Merkavah literature. In many ways, it is possible to assert that the language of mythology plays a major generative and expressive role in Hekhalot and Merkavah mysticism.

Chapters 4 and 5 will demonstrate this observation by presenting a concise phenomenological and literary examination of the manner in which Hekhalot and Merkavah mysticism integrates diverse mythological patterns. This chapter, as an introduction, will establish the basic methodological groundwork for the perspective on mythology and its application in Hekhalot and Merkavah mysticism taken in this study. It will treat the following: the nature of mythological thought and expression in general, features of biblical mythology, and aspects of Mesopotamian mythology as well as its lasting presence and influence in late antiquity.

MYTHOLOGICAL PATTERNS AND TRADITIONS

Mythological Patterns of Thought and Expression

Theories of myth vary greatly. Focusing on distinct fields of study, as well as on diverse methodologies, scholars have interpreted myth differently. Since an exploration of the multiple meanings of myth is beyond the scope of our inquiry, the following discussion avoids plunging into the vast sea of myth-definition and classification. Rather, it introduces selected observations, reflecting varied academic perspectives, intended to shed light on specific features of mythological patterns of thought and expression. These features seem to be present in certain Hekhalot and Merkavah mystical narrations, as will be demonstrated further.

Contemporary studies of myth, originating in varying disciplines, have moved away from a narrow understanding of myth which associates the genre with archaic, polytheistic modes of thought. Despite obvious differences between theories, departing from perspectives such as anthropology, linguistics, folklore, psychology, religious studies and sociology, it is possible to affirm that they all share the view that myth reflects a distinct mode of thought, comprehension, and expression. S. Ackerman advances this observation: "Historians of religion, while often deferring on how to interpret any specific myth, tend to agree that all myths, through the use of symbolic language, communicate transcendent meaning within a culture . . ."[3]

Myths reveal spiritual truths, ethical concepts, collective dreams, and the traditional beliefs of a specific group or community. They are often distinguished by particular modes of expression which include prose narrative style, dramatic action, pictorial imagery, and the use of figurative language. Through the narration of stories, the incorporation of visual images, personified metaphors, concrete examples, tangible illustrations and dramatic plots, myths transmit the significant concepts, views and values of the tradition from which they emerge. Such notion of mythical language, asserted by H. Frankfort and H. A. Frankfort, is still valid:

> The imagery of myth is therefore by no means allegory. It is nothing less than a careful chosen cloak for abstract thought. It represents the form in which the experience become conscious.[4]

W. Doniger's observations also shed light on the nature of the mythological expression:

> The major part of the impact of any myth lies not in its argument or logos (true or false) but in its imagery, its metaphors. The power of a myth is as much visual as verbal. The myth confines the function of philosophy . . . with the symbolism of ritual or cosmology. . . . Myths are both events and images, both verbs and nouns.[5]

In a similar vein W. Burkert asserts the power of myth to state profound conceptual notions using specific modes of expression. In myth, according to Burkert "significant human situations are united with fantastic combinations to form a polyvalent semiotic system which is used in multifarious ways to illuminate reality."[6]

Biblical Mythology and Hekhalot and Merkavah Mysticism

A consensus that the Hebrew bible reflects a primary break with the world of mythology has often been claimed in diverse earlier works of biblical scholarship. Based on a narrow conception of myth, as an expression of a polytheistic viewpoint, the biblical monotheistic accounts were set apart repeatedly as non-mythological, historical documents.[7] In the last few decades, however, scholars have acknowledged the presence of myths within the monotheistic context of the bible, and the prevailing view that 'there are no myths in the Bible' has been disputed. Since a thorough survey of this scholarly development would be too vast in this context, the following observations represent this perspective.[8]

G. H. Davies, for instance, contends: "Mythology is a way of thinking and of imagining about the divine rather than thinking and imagining about the gods . . . myth is a way of thinking, independent of a polytheistic setting."[9] Studying the origins of biblical monotheism, M. S. Smith questions several earlier scholarly definitions of myth, classified by him as narrow and formal, and concludes: "A minimum view may begin, therefore, with the circumscribed definition of myth as narratives about divine beings, but without excluding narratives with only one deity such as Yahweh." Investigating the pervasive mythological elements in the Hebrew bible and attempting to explain why such a prominent material has been disregarded, N. Wyatt speculates: "Attempts to emancipate the bible from myth arise from the inevitability of eisegesis within a committed readership, and the mistaken view that myth has nothing to teach us and somehow misrepresents the message."[10]

In the context of Jewish studies, F. Rozenzweig and M. Buber have examined the notion of monotheistic myth.[11] Judaism as a living religion, they assert, has a conception of myth which does not contradict the monotheistic idea of God. It is in a similar spirit that other scholars have confirmed the existence of myth in biblical and post-biblical Jewish literature. A. Green points out the key place of the Hebrew Bible as a source for ancient mythology:

> As we move beyond the one time scholarly assumption that the Bible knew myth only to refute it, or as we come to soften the overly sharp distinctions scholars once made between sacred myth and sacred history, we come to understand that Hebrew Scripture itself is among the most important sources for the recovery of this ancient human legacy.[12]

In a similar vein, Y. Liebes, in a study on the ongoing evolution of myths from biblical to Jewish mystical literature, affirms:

> Myths are shared by all religions, but are also the source of each religion's uniqueness, as they are concerned with the particular and concrete rather than with generalization. . . . Each religion has its own myth into which it absorbs and incorporates influences from other religions, and this is also true for the Jewish religion. Even Judaism's monotheistic essence is not contradictory to myth, and monotheism itself has its own far-reaching myth.[13]

No doubt, a number of different traditions played a part in the formation of the Hekhalot and Merkavah mystical discourse. Among these, material contained in the Hebrew bible, including its mythological lore and conceptions, has a great potential as a significant source of inspiration. Statements in the Hekhalot and Merkavah literature attest that the biblical corpus was regarded as pivotal in the circle of the chariot seekers and its members were obligated to master it, as part of their preliminary, preparatory education. As has been asserted earlier, only the one "who has read the Torah, Prophets, and Writings," among other Jewish traditional teachings, was distinguished as qualified to ascend to the chariot. It is possible, therefore, to consider the Hebrew bible and several of its varied mythological traditions as a possible source which may have given rise to or shaped several mystical narrations of Hekhalot and Merkavah literature. This is not to claim that the Hekhalot and Merkavah authors and compilers adopted all facets of the incorporated biblical mythological themes, stories, and imagery. Nonetheless, old mythical material from several biblical texts seem to have been elicited, and altered eventually, in order to embody and to articulate certain, novel Hekhalot and Merkavah mystical notions.

Mesopotamian Mythology and Its Presence in Late Antiquity

The suggestion that Hekhalot mystical descriptions may have evoked and reapplied Mesopotamian mythological themes is contingent on acknowledging the enormous distance which separates the ancient Near East and its vast diversity of mythical traditions from the reality of the Jewish mystics of late antiquity. Not only the historical, chronological inconsistency, but also distinctions in evolving conceptual patterns, religious beliefs, personal behavior, and social codes create an apparently unbridgeable gap between the two cultures.[14] Difficulties in establishing, with full certainty, linear transmission of the Mesopotamian contents as well as modes of contact between literary traditions also hinder an examination which goes beyond listing similarities and differences. At first glance such a conceptual and historical chasm seems to suggests that there are no proper grounds for linking or even associating Hekhalot and Merkavah accounts and the extensive ancient Mesopotamian mythological tradition.

It is important, however, not to confuse issues such as tracing influence, studying borrowed motifs, examining literary-cultural linkage, or constructing comparisons, with the phenomenological assertion suggested in this study. This investigation does not announce the Mesopotamian mythological background as the origin of the Hekhalot and Merkavah literature. Nor does it suggest that this literature derives its mystical content from Mesopotamian mythology or its variations. Instead, the study proposes that mythological themes and patterns, rooted in ancient Mesopotamian traditions, and accessible in late antiquity among other sources, were reapplied in the new evolving context of the Hekhalot and Merkavah literature and thus acquired new mystical meanings.

The study, therefore, does not intend to examine the transformation and transmission of specific Mesopotamian mythological accounts, or of selected themes from the Bronze Age to Assyrian, Babylonian, Persian, and Hellenistic cultures in general, and Jewish circles in particular. In fact, an avoidance of being tied to any particular evolutionary model seems beneficial in this context. Yet, prior to an investigation of how selected ancient mythological themes were re-evoked, and re-embraced, it is important to consider their historical and literal availability in the cultural world of late antiquity, in which Hekhalot and Merkavah mysticism emerged.

Let us first consider biblical, post-biblical, and classical literatures as mediating sources through which ancient themes could have reached the writers and compilers of the Hekhalot and Merkavah literature. Presence of ancient Near Eastern mythological traditions in biblical sources have long been recognized. Explicit traditions in books such as Genesis, Exodus, and Deuteronomy, as well as in prophetic literature, Psalms, Lamentations, the Song of Songs and other texts demonstrate such a presence clearly. An effective example, as we shall see, is that of the chariot vision of the prophet Ezekiel.[15] Mythical images in that vision correspond to Mesopotamian traditions, and in turn resonate as well in many of the Hekhalot descriptions, where they are framed in a mystical context.

Various apocalyptic writings, such as the books of Daniel and Enoch, among other sources, also apply Near Eastern themes and traditions, as early and more recent scholars have established.[16] One compelling example is the Mesopotamian account of the antediluvian king of Sippar, Enmeduranki, to whom the gods had revealed the secrets of divination. Versions of the Enoch traditions were partly modeled on this account. As we shall see in chapter 4, echoes of this story occur also in the Hekhalot and Merkavah mystical narrations.[17] As mentioned earlier, explicit conceptual and literary connections link Hekhalot literature to both biblical and apocalyptic literature. Thus, it is conceivable that ancient mythological notions could have reached the Hekhalot and Merkavah mystical literature, albeit indirectly, through these biblical and apocalyptic sources.

Indirect links between Mesopotamian traditions and the Hekhalot writings may have occurred through other Jewish sources as well. Imprints from Mesopotamian sources are found in rabbinical texts, particularly in the fields of language, law, and agadic literature. The Talmud and the Mishnah reflect such echoes, as do other folk lore and several Jewish ceremonies, apparently related to Babylonian religious myths. Further examples demonstrate the effect of Mesopotamian concepts in rabbinical hermeneutical techniques.[18]

Non-Jewish sources may also be regarded as indirect channels through which ancient Mesopotamian mythology could have reached the Hekhalot and Merkavah mysticism. The presence of Mesopotamian mythic traditions in Greek mythology have been demonstrated by classical scholars. Evidence of Mesopotamian mythical themes has been observed as well in Greco-Roman magical and astronomical writings and in the syncretistic mythology of late antiquity. These traditions, available in the cultural context in which Hekhalot literature was compiled, could have been appropriated and reintegrated into its mystical content.[19]

It is possible to consider the availability of Mesopotamian myth during Greco-Roman times. Regarding this matter, several factors are relevant. We must look at the conservative character of the Mesopotamian mythological tradition, and as well consider its persistence and lasting influence in the ancient Near East and Mediterranean worlds even up to the first few centuries of the common era.

The mythological writings of the ancient Near East are in no way homogeneous. The component parts of its civilization vary from a demographic, political, social, and theological viewpoint.[20] There are, however, common features which connect and distinguish the mythological tradition in spite of its multiple literary voices and varied religious ideologies.[25] The Sumerian and later Akkadian, Babylonian, Assyrian, Hittite (Hurrian), and Ugaritic (Canaanaite) cultures developed their own new and creative views, values, and narratives over time. In this formative process, however, old traditions were not ignored or rejected, but rather reintegrated into the new forms. It is possible to find consistency in conceptions of the pantheon, cult practices, court ceremonies and rituals, cosmological and cosmogonical concepts, royal ideologies, temple traditions, as well as theories of magic and science.

The common assumption that ancient Mesopotamian tradition and myth did not endure after the death of cuneiform writing has been largely abandoned. Instead, scholars have recognized the persistence of the Mesopotamian tradition up until the first few centuries of the common era. "Ideas do not necessarily die when the civilization that nurtured them expires," contends the assyriologist S. N. Kramer.[22] H. W. F. Saggs, in a similar manner, affirms:

> There was thus a demonstrably horizontal continuum between the religious concepts of Israel and those of Syria and Babylonia. It follows, therefore, in view of the indisputable vertical continuum between Israelite religion and modern Judaism and Christianity (and less markedly, Islam), that the conceptual barrier between ancient Mesopotamia and modern religious thought need not be as absolute. [23]

Saggs points out several specific examples to support this statement. In Syria, worship of Assyrian deities was accompanied by celebrations which corresponded exactly with the festival dates of the new Assyrian period. These festivals were celebrated at least until the beginning of the third century C.E. Isaac of Antioch, in the fifth century, was familiar with the continuing practice of the Tammuz cult, as well as with the worship of the solar and lunar deities Shamash, Sin, and Bel-Shamin. Saggs also emphasizes that during the first centuries

C.E. early Christian figures such as Paul, the apostle and Clement of Alexandria, made direct reference to pagan thought, literature, and myths. Obviously these were rejected by the early Christians as fundamentally invalid, but it is nevertheless important to note that many of the mythological traditions in question were well-known during that time.[24] A. Heidel sites the Neoplatonist Damascius of the fifth and sixth centuries C.E., who was apparently familiar with the details of the Babylonian creation story, *Enumah Elish*, and was able to explain its theogony.[25] Additional examples demonstrate the survival of the Mesopotamian mythological tradition during the early centuries C.E. Versions of the Babylonian "Akitu festival" were preserved in copies from the Seleucid period.[26] The *Lament over the City of Uruk*, a Sumerian poem from the third millennium B.C.E., was recopied at the beginning of the Hellenistic period. Translation of the *Phoenician Theology* by Philo of Biblos at the end of the first century C.E. shows the effect of Ugaritic myth, which was probably accessible at that time.[27]

Over the last decade, scholarship on ancient Mesopotamian culture has developed in significant ways. Recent findings has come to light, as well as new methodological approaches and an awareness of the lasting presence and effect of this culture. Historical, textual and archeological evidence demonstrates specific channels in which Mesopotamian traditions—embodied in literature, architecture, art, and myths—have migrated not only to immediate neighboring cultures in the Mediterranean and the Near East, but also to later cultures in late antiquity and early Islam. Presenting an abundance of proof, scholarly works have traced systematically the legacy of Mesopotamia from the third millennium B.C.E., and onwards into the Middle Ages.[28]

S. Dalley, for example, demonstrates the survival of Mesopotamian traditions in early Islamic texts.[29] A. Salvesen determines the presence of ancient Mesopotamian cults during the early centuries C.E., especially in the Aramaic and Syriac cultures in Mesopotamia[30] In the Aramaic speaking region of northern Mesopotamia, works of Syriac writers reveal the longevity of ancient Near Eastern mythological beliefs. Worship of local forms of Mesopotamian deities, such as Sin, Shamash, Nergal, Nusku, Bel, and Nebo, continued well into the Christian era in cities such as Harran, Edessa, and their surroundings.[31] T. M. Green, who has studied in particular the religious traditions of Harran, reaches similar conclusions.[32]

It is also worth noting that Akkadian cuneiform was used alongside Aramaic up to the time of the Neo-Babylonian Empire (626–539 B.C.E.). The use of Aramaic prevailed as the principal means of communication in the first centuries C.E., and probably transmitted ideas from the earlier cultures of Assyria and Babylonia. Mesopotamian astrological and astronomical traditions were absorbed into Aramaic and Syriac sources. Mesopotamian impact was also present in magical works and amulets, wisdom literature, court narratives, and dialogue poetry.[33]

In order to discern specific evidence of the lasting existence of ancient Mesopotamian mythology in late antiquity, we will examine two cases, intended to serve as models. Chapters 4 and 5 will discuss several Hekhalot and Merkavah mystical descriptions which seem to evoke themes from two Mesopotamian mythological accounts, the *Gilgamesh Epic* and *Enumah Elish*, known as the Babylonian creation story. As a study case, the discussion below seeks to demonstrate that these two traditions survived long after those in which they originated. Furthermore, they were accessible in the cultural context in which the Hekhalot and Merkavah literature developed, in several locations in Babylon and Palestine of late antiquity.

Our first example is the *Epic of Gilgamesh*. The latest Akkadian tablets of the *Epic of Gilgamesh* come from Uruk of the late Babylonian period, some time after the fall of Babylon in 539 B.C.E., and perhaps as late as the Seleucid period, after the reign of Alexander the Great.[34] Versions of this narration continued to spread long after the cuneiform system of writing lost prominence. In his book *The Evolution of the Gilgamesh Epic*, J. Tigay discusses the continually evolving oral tradition of Gilgamesh during the late third and second millennium B.C.E.[35] Other scholars show that Gilgamesh mythical traditions continued to persist even in later times. During the Parthian period (141 B.C.E.–226 C.E.) the *Epic of Gilgamesh* was copied anew at the library of the city Uruk.[36] At Qumran, for example, an Aramaic version of a *Book of Enoch* was found among the fragments of the Dead Sea scrolls, dated to the last century B.C.E. This version includes, as its second part, the *Book of Giants*, a section which was probably replaced later in the Ethiopic book of Enoch by the *Similitudes*. J. T. Milik, in his editions of these fragments of the Dead Sea Scrolls, uncovers in them many references to Gilgamesh traditions. These include especially names and features of the main characters, which betray the influences of Hittite and Akkadian versions of Gilgamesh.[37] J. C. Reeves reveals traces of the Gilgamesh tradition in the *Book of the Giants*, one of the sacred books of the Gnostic Manichaeans.[38] This analysis suggests that Mani, who died sometime in 274 or 277 C.E., probably used themes from the *Epic of Gilgamesh* in the formulation of his religious ideas. S. Dalley detects components of the *Epic of Gilgamesh* not only in the Dead Sea scrolls and the tradition of Manichaean storytelling but also in later sources. Several of the Gilgamesh themes were incorporated into the *Alexander Romance*, one of the most widely known pieces of fiction in late antiquity. They emerge later in versions of *The Tale of Buluqiya* and in the

Arabian Nights, sources which may be associated with the Islamic period and with Sufi and Jewish mystical circles, including the Hekhalot and Merkavah literature.[39]

Enumah Elish, known as the *Epic of Creation*, a Babylonian literary composition written in Akkadian, is our second example.[40] Regarding this work, historical and cultural conditions in the Near East of late antiquity are of importance. In several cities in both the north and the south of Mesopotamia, various beliefs and practices of ancient Mesopotamian origin were maintained. Among them is the cult of the god Bel. As his name and attributes indicate, Bel assimilated the characteristics and traditions of the Babylonian city god Marduk.

In Babylon Bel was the epithet for the god Marduk. This deity played a primary role in the Babylonian pantheon as the supreme god who triumphed over the forces of chaos and established the cosmos. Since the time of King Hammurabi of Babylon, in the eighteenth century B.C.E., the god Bel-Marduk became the central deity of the pantheon, playing a major role in the Babylonian story of creation, *Enumah Elish*. During the New Year festival, *akitu*, the *Epic of Creation* was recited publicly and re-enacted with the intention of consolidating the order of the cosmos with its symbolic reestablishment.[41]

For a long time it has been assumed in the scholarly literature that this tradition ceased to exist in Greco-Roman times, especially after the cuneiform writing had disappeared. As new documentation suggests, however, this was not the case. S. Dalley brings forth evidence from various places in northern and southern Mesopotamia which shows that the cult of Bel-Marduk and the celebration of the *akitu* festival continued in the Roman period. She documented the different cities in which the *akitu* New Year festival was celebrated with the public recitation of *Enumah Elish* from the early Iron Age (c. 1000–539 B.C.E.) until the Roman period.[42] Supported by archeological, textual, and iconographical indications, Dalley concludes: "Aramaic inscriptions as well as new cuneiform texts and other pieces of evidence from rabbinical, Classical and Syriac texts, show that cults of Bel continued to flourish during the Parthian period both within and outside areas controlled at times by Rome: at Palmyra, Dura-Europos, Apameaon-Orontes, and Harta, the cult, or at least its buildings, appears to be newly emerged, but at Ashore, Arbella, Harran, and Babylon powerful traditions of great antiquity have survived into the Roman period."[43]

Dalley also attests that Bel-Marduk's old ritual of the New Year was most likely performed with some kind of recitation of the *Enumah Elish*. One interesting piece of evidence regarding this matter is a text dating from an indeterminate, late Babylonian period, which has been published recently.[44] It shows that the *akitu* festival was performed not only once a year, but also on other occasions, with recitations of the *Enumah Elish*. In addition, as Dalley notes, the presence of an Aramaic loanword and an Aramaic verbal prefix is evident in this text. "This indicates that the text was not fossilized but absorbed some elements of current language. This evidence opens up the possibility that an Aramaic version of the epic was recited in second century Palmyra."[45] "The language in which the epic of creation was recited began as Babylonian, but creeping Aramanicization may have resulted eventually in an all-Aramaic version," Dalley affirms.[46]

Evidence from the city of Palmyra further indicates the endurance of *Enumah Elish* in the first centuries C.E. During the Parthian period, one of its main temples was dedicated to the god Bel. An inscription dating from 44 B.C.E. mentions priests of Bel and thus shows that, in that time, the city was associated with the cult of Bel. The temple of Bel was rebuilt from 32 C.E. onwards with partial funding from the city of Babylon. This demonstrates the existence of the cult of Bel in Babylon as well. On a five meter long frieze, sculpted in the main doorway of the temple, is an image of the god Bel in his chariot, drawing his bow and shooting at Tiamat. This scene appears to correspond to descriptions in *Enumah Elish*. Furthermore, the temple was inaugurated in 32 C.E. on the sixth day of Nisan, the date of *akitu*, the New Year festival. Many terracotta vessels, found in the temple of Bel, are thought to have been used in the banquet held during the *akitu* festival in which *Enumah Elish* was regularly recited. The cult of Bel persisted in Palmyra at least until 380 C.E., when pagan rites became forbidden by Theodosios. In Dura-Europos the cult of Bel was also known. A fragment of a wall painting dating from the late first century C.E., found in a temple in Dura-Europos, appears to present Bel as a giant, probably with a horse and a chariot. Excavations in the city Assur attest that the *akitu* house, the temple of the New Year festival restored by Sennacherib around 700 B.C.E., was rebuilt there according to its old plan. Dalley contends: ". . . it would certainly not have been restored unless rituals performed there were still current . . . we cannot suppose that the old ritual for the New Year was performed without some kind of recitation of the *Epic of Creation*."[47] Even in the fifth century C.E. some version of *Enumah Elish*, the *Epic of Creation*, probably not in cuneiform, was still known, as we learn from the writings of Damascius (born ca. 480 C.E.).

H. J. W. Drijvers, in his studies of the pagan religions in Mesopotamia of late antiquity, focuses on the city of Edessa in northern Mesopotamia as a model for registering the religious climate in other places in northern and southern Mesopotamia during Greco-Roman times.[48] Among other examples, he demonstrates clearly the persistence of the cult of Bel-Marduk and his festivals in Edessa in the first centuries C.E. Christian documents provide specific evidence. Examples of these documents include the *Doctrina Addai,* dating from the end of the fourth century or the beginning of the fifth century C.E. This document, attributed to Jesus' first apostle in Edessa, speaks of worship of the god Bel and other deities in a polemic criticism of pagan beliefs.[49] Mention of Bel, among other gods, is made also in Jacob of Sarug's *Homily on the Fall of the Idols* from the fourth century C.E. Jacob, the bishop of Sarug (451–521 C.E.), makes specific references to Bel in Edessa and various pagan gods in other places in Mesopotamia.[50] Similar references to pagan practices in Edessa are found in the polemic writings of Ephrem Syrus against pagan beliefs, especially in his *Hymni contra Haereses.*[51]

Yet another example is found in the document *The Acts of Sharbel,* dating from the same period.[52] This document which describes the martyr Sharbel, a pagan high priest of Edessa who converted to Christianity, gives evidence of the dominance of the god Bel at Edessa. The document furthermore mentions a central feast, which took place at Edessa at the beginning of Nisan [April]. During that time of festivities, the gods were brought together, in a procession, to the high altar at the center of the city. In the words of this document: "The whole population assembled near the big altar in the center of the city . . . where all the deities were gathered, adorned and got a place of honour: Nebo and Bel and other companions . . ."[53] Dancing, music, and the reciting of ancient myths accompanied this celebration. The date of this celebration matches the Babylonian tradition in which the festival of the New Year, *akitu,* took place.

Joshua the Stylite's *Chronicle,* records the celebration of pagan rites at Edessa in 497 and 498 c.e. From a disapproving Christian perspective, he recounts what appears to be the celebration of the *akitu* festival and the recitation of the *Epic of Creation*: "There come round again the time of that festival at which the pagan myths used to be recited, and the citizens took even more pain about it than usual."[54] A statement by the Jewish Rabbi, Rav, founder of the rabbinic school at Sura in central Mesopotamia, probably after 219 c.e., further attests that the cult of Bel was well known at his time: ". . . there are five permanent temples of idolatry: the Bel temple in Babylon, the Nebo temple in Borsippa. . . . "[55]

As well, several Mesopotamian mythical traditions were clearly available in late antiquity, the variety of evidence confirms. On certain occasions in both the Assyrian and the Babylonian regions of Mesopotamia of late antiquity, the *akitu* festival was performed and the Babylonian *Epic of Creation, Enumah Elish,* was recited in a form which could have been accessible. In addition, the *Gilgamesh Epic* was well known in Mesopotamia and in other areas in the first few centuries C.E. In this context, it is important to note that during the first centuries of the common era several major centers in Palestine and Mesopotamia kept in close contact with one another. Thus, various interactions were unavoidable.[56]

The data presented above allows us to acknowledge the existence and availability of Mesopotamian mythological notions in the first few centuries C.E., within the context of Near Eastern and Mediterranean cultures. The Hekhalot and Merkavah literature crystallized in this syncretistic context, which prevailed in both Babylonia and Palestine. As several scholars attest, Hekhalot and Merkavah mysticism reflects an attempt to mold new spiritual attitudes and religious views, both by conforming to existing Jewish teachings and by embracing other available traditions. Explicit affinities, as mentioned, link the Hekhalot and Merkavah literature to apocalyptic sources, Greco-Roman magical-theurgical writings, the Dead Sea scrolls, the literature of early Christianity, and to Gnostic traditions.[57] As J. Dan maintains, the Hekhalot and Merkavah literature shows a tendency to keep true to the Jewish tradition, follow the *Halachah* and the study of the Torah. Nonetheless, it also re-embraces other nontraditional themes and conceptual patterns:

> What made the world of the ancient mystics unique when compared to that of the Talmudic and Midrashic sages is especially noticeable in the fact that this literature brought about the revival of Jewish sources from the second temple era—primarily the Enoch literature and the apocalyptic literature. . . . In this fashion the authors of this literature [Hekhalot and Merkavah] expressed their independent spiritual position, which is opposed to the attitude found in the midrashim of the Sages.[58]

This attribute of the Hekhalot and Merkavah literature may also support the prospect of re-envoking available Mesopotamian mythical themes in its new mystical context. It is true that unequivocal evidence proving either specific or exclusive evidence does not exist. It nonetheless seems plausible to consider that the authors of Hekhalot and Merkavah literature could have formulated and conveyed their mystical perception by reapplying Mesopotamian mythological themes, clearly accessible in the Greco-Roman world of late antiquity.

CONCLUSION

Contemplating the nature of the mystical discourse in Hekhalot and Merkavah mysticism, the study suggests that this tradition conceptualizes and conveys many of its mystical notions by evoking a variety of mythological forms. As will be demonstrated in chapters 4 and 5 below, various Hekhalot and Merkavah mystical notions, experiences, and revelations are formulated and expressed through mythological patterns, supplemented by the re-application of specific themes rooted in biblical and Mesopotamian mythological traditions. As a methodological introduction to a detailed literary-phenomenological analysis of the mythological language in Hekhalot and Merkavah mysticism, this chapter distinguished the three prevalent mythological frameworks, presumed to be employed in it. It introduced dominant characteristics of mythological forms of thought and expression in general, and of biblical, and Mesopotamian mythology in particular.

Considering the pertinence and possible applicability of these three mythological forms in Hekhalot and Merhavah mysticism, this chapter further presented several observations. First, mythological modes of thought and expression often convey a variety of speculative or abstract notions through methods such as pictorial imagery, tangible metaphors, and figurative language. These traits, among others, characterize many mystical narrations of the Hekhalot and Merkavah literature, conveying a distinctive feature of its mythological language. Second, since proficiency in all sections of the Hebrew bible was required of all members of the Merkavah circle, evidently this group was familiar with the mythological material of the biblical corpus which, in turn, could have inspired several mystical presentations. Third, sound and absolute affiliation between Hekhalot and Merkavah mysticism and Mesopotamian mythology, or its variations, cannot be confirmed with certainty. This conclusion, however, does not exclude the probability that mythological themes and patterns, rooted in ancient Mesopotamia and available in late antiquity, were reapplied in its new evolving context and thus acquired new mystical meanings. Avoiding an evolutionary model of investigation, the discussion did not trace transformation and transmission of specific Mesopotamian mythological accounts from the Bronze Age, Assyrian, Babylonian, Persian, and Hellenistic cultures, including Jewish traditions. Instead, it determined the availability of various Mesopotamian mythological traditions in the first few centuries c.e. within the context of Near Eastern and Mediterranean traditions—the historical cultural setting in which Hekhalot and Merkavah mysticism had emerged. Based on this evidence, and in light of the view that traditions within a given cultural-religious group, or within neighboring cultures, interact with one another in an ongoing process of absorption, transformation and interchange, we established the probability that Mesopotamian mythological traditions, present in the syncretistic

Hellenistic-Roman world of late antiquity, could have inspired the Hekhalot and Merkavah imagery, directly or indirectly.

This present chapter provided the background for examining mystical transformation of various mythological forms in the context of the Hekhalot and Merkavah literary accounts, in a manner which seems to correlate to a more widespread development, which A. Green has observed:

> In the post-biblical world . . . Jews and various competing versions of Judaism were important repositories for the mythic imagination: sometimes figures from the archaic pre-biblical world reappeared with new vigor . . . at other times new motifs, including some borrowed from the surrounding cultures of the Hellenistic world.[59]

The following discussion will proceed in two parallel directions. The next two chapters will offer a literary-phenomenological analysis of the manner in which the three mythological frameworks are utilized in the new context of Hekhalot and Merkavah mysticism. Chapter 6 will conclude the discussion by considering social-cultural implications of the literary-phenomenological evidence.

4

Mystical Journeys in Mythological Language

INTRODUCTION

The mystical journey is the focus of this chapter. The discussion will examine the modes in which its various aspects are stated, with particular emphasis on two issues: use of mythological patterns of thought and expression, and adoption of biblical and Mesopotamian mythological themes. As chapter 2 has shown, many Hekhalot and Merkavah accounts depict an inner processes of crossing conceptual-spiritual boundaries, which take place in the adepts' imagination and mind. By contemplating and meditating on the Merkavah, visionaries embark on an inner-mental journey, advancing from one level to the next towards their transcendent goal. They exercise various spiritual methods and gradually expand their ordinary consciousness. At the end of the voyage, qualified "descenders to the chariot" cross the borderlines between the human and divine. Then, for a short period of time, they exceed common human perception, behold the King in his beauty, see visions of the Merkavah, and comprehend the meanings of such revelations. We find descriptions of this process in a large number of Hekhalot and Merkavah accounts.

Alongside these are other accounts, in which the process is externalized. Instead of an inner journey we find in these a voyage presented as a concrete, physical ascent to heavenly districts. The Hekhalot and Merkavah spiritual seekers are often portrayed as exceptional heroes who initiate a dangerous, corporeal venture out of this world. They travel in an upwards direction and proceed towards actual royal palaces of God, situated in physical upper heavens. On their way, they tour unknown paths of bright celestial territories in which winged sacred beasts roam, glowing angels fly, and horses of fire wander. They experience adventures, cross bridges over rivers of fire, enter blocked gates, appease angry guardians, show magical seals, and repeat secret passwords. During their journey these adepts encounter merciless ordeals, pass paradoxical tests, and overcome harsh dangers before they reach God's throne. The spiritual-mental stages of their course are frequently conveyed by the precincts of an imaginary celestial geography; their feelings of fear and awe are personified; their spiritual difficulties are made tangible; mythological patterns of a symbolic death and rebirth and of corporeal transformation are often applied to denote their shifts of consciousness.

An indirect form of mystical exegesis play a role in this presentation. The mythological components are not deciphered by any specific exegetical system in the Hekhalot and Merkavah literature. Their new mystical context, nonetheless, introduces them in a fresh light, suggesting an alternate exegetical understanding. Common, public mythological patterns as well as ancient themes from Near Eastern traditions are utilized to convey personal, inner processes of traversing spiritual realms and of attaining transcendent truth. Infused with new meanings these mythological forms express the Hekhalot and Merkavah mystical notions, as ancient threads are rewoven together to create new visions. The following analysis will establish these observations by focusing on three principal themes: the image of the visionary, the journey, and the process of transformation at its end.

THE MYSTICAL-MYTHICAL HERO

> If you want to single yourself out in the world
> so that the secrets of the world
> and the mysteries of wisdom
> should be revealed to you . . . [1]

Various types of mystics are idealized in different traditions. Each model embodies certain estimable paradigmatic traits and exemplifies attributes considered to be of ultimate value to a specific religious group. In certain traditions, for example, an ideal mystic is a self-reflective adept who considers inner-surrender to the divine as the ultimate goal. Other mystical communities introduce the model of a moral and ethical disciple who follows authoritative teachings. An emotional lover of God who strives to unite with the Source, a receptive, humble believer who is guided by the divine are likewise well-known exemplary images. If we try to characterize the "ideal mystic" of Hekhalot and Merkavah mysticism, it seems that such a figure is portrayed in the paradigmatic image of a mythological hero.

Beneficial for this discussion is S. Chatman's conceptualization of character as a "paradigm of traits."[2] In Chatman's view, characters are identified in their literary contexts by means of set traits which distinguish them. The "paradigm of traits" is a constant construct. It is not dependent on specific situations or fluctuating tones present in the literature. The characters, therefore, are continually portrayed, in a variety of accounts, by the same set of stable qualities and attributes. The discussion to follow will examine how the Hekhalot and Merkavah visionaries are depicted by explicit characteristics, or "paradigms of traits" which often portray the prototype of a mythological hero.

Mythological Patterns

The hero, a prevalent figure of world mythology, has been the subject of numerous comparative studies, which have often emphasized the commonality of all cultures and of their collective, universal construction of the hero character. Acknowledging particular ethos and unique nuances of varied cultures, such sweeping and often unfounded assertions have been challenged by contemporary scholarship. Nonetheless, as S. Niditch has contended, recent comparative work on the hero patterns indicates that in a large cross section of mythological accounts, the hero figure can be distinguished by several common characteristics. With careful attention to conceptual differences between traditions and their distinct forms of expression, scholars such as A. Dundes, A. B. Lord, and S. Niditch have asserted a number of such shared characteristics, several of which are relevant to our discussion.[3]

The hero figure is an exceptional figure of great energy, power, and courage, who often initiates a personal quest in order to achieve several seemingly unreachable goals. Convinced that he alone holds power over his progress and hence over his success or failure, the hero figure assumes responsibility over his ventures, experiences difficulties, combats both natural and supernatural forces, as well as personal limitations. Against all odds he frequently achieves his objectives which are not only of personal advantage but also of essential benefit to the community at large.

Several Mesopotamian narratives provide specific manifestations of the hero model. These include, among other sources, the Sumerian and Akkadian versions of the story of Gilgamesh;[4] the myth of Adapa found in fragmentary tablets from Tell el-Amarna in Egypt of the fifteenth or fourteenth centuries B.C.E., and from Assur of the second millennium B.C.E.;[5] and the myth of Etana, found in an old Babylonian version from Susa and Tell Harmal, a middle Assyrian version from Assur, and a standard version from Nineveh.[6] These varied accounts are obviously different in their historical and conceptual contexts, literary style, plot, and other details. An analysis of all such components is beyond the scope of this study. A phenomenological examination, nonetheless, reveals a similar "paradigm of traits" which distinguishes the hero in all these accounts.[7]

Portrayed as an exceptional being with unique characteristics and unequaled nature, Gilgamesh, the famous king of Uruk, is a prime example. "Perfect in strength" and "perfect in awesomeness," he surpasses both the attributes and accomplishments of "every man" even before he embarks on his various quests.[8] Etana, chosen by the great Anunna-gods to be the king of the city Kish, is likewise a superior human being.[9] Adapa from the city Eridu is the first of the seven antediluvian sages sent by the gods to bring civilization to humankind. He, too, is depicted in the Babylonian legend as a man of superior stature, "a sage—nobody rejects his word—clever, extra wise . . . holy, pure of hands."[10]

These figures pursue goals which cannot normally be accomplished by human beings. They all attempt to move beyond the boundaries of the human world and enter divine realms which are clearly prohibited to most mortals.[11] T. Abusch's observations of the separation between the divine and human realm give a background against which the valiant aspects of their mythical quest become clear. Abusch demonstrates the shift from an early Mesopotamian conception of a continuum of celestial and the terrestrial realms to a tripartite conception of the structure of the cosmos.[12] This tripartite arrangement establishes clearly defined boundaries that separate the three distinct districts of Earth, Heaven, and the Underworld. Each cosmic realm is understood as separate. The notion of a fluid movement between the realms was reestablished as a threat to the structure of the universe. A Sumerian text of *Gilgamesh and the Land of the Living* verifies this notion:

> A man, (even) the tallest, cannot reach heaven.
> a man (even) the widest, cannot cover the earth.[13]

In spite of this basic human condition, the mythological sources mentioned above present a hero who strives not only to reach divine realms, but also to achieve status and qualities exclusively associated with the gods. These accomplishments, if attained, can often benefit the society at large and elevate its disposition.[14]

Etana ascends to the remote heavens in order to find the plant of birth, which belongs to the gods. On the wings of an eagle, he travels the cosmic regions in search for the impossible.[15] Adapa, the wisest human being, overcomes and disables the South Wind before he is summoned to the celestial realm.[16] Refusing to consume the bread and water of life offered to him by the high god Anu, he thus fails divine tests and looses immortality forever. Gilgamesh, superior in rank, status, and qualities, voluntarily undertakes two heroic journeys. First, he travels to the pine forest, in a "journey [which] is not to be taken," wishing to create for himself "a name that endures."[17] Seeking eternal life after Enkidu's death, Gilgamesh undertakes a second journey beyond the borders of the mortal world, in order to attain other levels of existence, and to transcend both his own human condition as well as the common lot of all human beings. Both voyages are extremely dangerous. Gilgamesh, however, soberly faces opposition, trials, and obstacles which no human before him has ever encountered. His choice is determined by himself alone as he states: "I am adamant: I shall take the road . . . I shall face unknown opposition, [I shall ride along an unknown] road."[18]

Even though the storylines and themes of each of these mythological accounts are different, they all present parallel paradigmatic features of the hero figure. Several aspects are particularly emphasized: unique attributes, a personal choice which leads to heroic deeds and persistence, an effort to depart from conventional geographical and temporal restrictions, an attempt to surpass the human condition and to achieve transcendent qualities, and an intention to elevate human existence.

Hekhalot and Merkavah Mysticism

Well-known Tannaitic figures are depicted as the principal mystics in the Hekhalot and Merkavah literature. The accounts identify them as Rabbi Ishmael, Rabbi Akiva, and Rabbi Nehunia ben Ha-Kanah. Yet, as scholars have pointed out, this presentation contradicts historical and chronological evidence which is also supported by sources such as the Talmud and Midrash. Consequently, the Hekhalot and Merkavah narratives are not regarded as sources of authentic biographical information. Likewise the literary testimonies of mystics are considered pseudepigraphic by most scholars, and the historical identity of the Hekhalot and Merkavah visionaries is still dubious.[19]

Throughout the various Hekhalot and Merkavah accounts, however, a consistent paradigmatic model of an "ideal mystic" is depicted. Regardless of the adept's individual nature and literary biography, all qualified "descenders to the chariot" resemble one another in their disposition, goals, deeds, and accomplishments. They are characterized as people of superior stature, who attempt an inconceivable journey to divine domains in order to obtain celestial secrets as well as to behold God and the Merkavah in a personal manner.[20] In their distinction as exceptional individuals and in the pattern and nature of their journey, the prototype of these mystics closely corresponds the figure of the mythological hero described above.

The Hekhalot and Merkavah seeker is by no means a passive, patient believer who waits or longs for divine revelation and for spiritual enlightenment. Nor is he an obedient, responsive disciple who surrenders to God's call, or is raptured in ecstasy.[21] Rather, this visionary is portrayed as an active and determined figure, who initiates a corporeal journey beyond the borders of the phenomenal world, with the explicit purpose of reaching the divine. The visionary's physical destination is the sky, where he finds the sacred palaces of God. He is self-motivated, sets the goal for himself, and ventures forth on a highly dangerous journey to heaven in order to fulfill his aim. The opening sentence of *Hekhalot Zutarti* is a good example of this attitude. In it, the adept's own wish is clearly the primary motive for the journey:

> If you want to single yourself out in the world
> so that the secrets of the world and the mysteries of wisdom
> should be revealed to you . . . [22]

In a similar fashion, in *Hekhalot Rabbati,* Rabbi Ishmael emphasizes the seeker's own aspiration and asks:

> What are these songs which one recites
> who wishes to behold the vision of the Merkavah,
> to descend safely and to ascend safely?[23]

In an alternative Hekhalot and Merkavah pattern the visionary is chosen as an emissary to the heavens in answer to an immediate and specific social need. Thus, he leaves his safe reality and travels out of this world in order to seek a divine answer to a problem which threatens his community. Such a case is presented in *Hekhalot Rabbati.* According to the pseudo-historical background, Rabbi Nehunia ben Ha-Kanah sends his disciple, Rabbi Ishmael, up to heaven to find out why the Roman Empire was allowed to decree the execution of several Jewish sages.[24]

Both these patterns agree, however, that the journey is extremely dangerous even to the point of being beyond accomplishment. Various Hekhalot and Merkavah passages state and restate that God's realm is inaccessible to most humans. They proclaim the unpredictable danger of divine proximity and the destructiveness of a direct vision of God:

> Pleasant Presence, adorned Presence,
> Presence of beauty, Presence of flame,
> Presence of YHWH, God of Israel,
> when He sits on His throne of glory,
> and His loftiness is established in the seat of His adornment.
> His beauty is more pleasant than the beauty of mighty acts.
> His adornment is superior to the adornment of
> bridegrooms and brides in their bridal canopy.

> He who gazes at Him is instantly torn.
> He who glimpses at His beauty
> is instantly poured out like (the content of) a jug.[25]

The traveler who launches such hazardous journey is aware, from the outset, of its obstacles and complications. He recognizes the tremendous difficulties and dangers awaiting him, yet remains entirely committed to his goals. Striving to behold the vision of God and the Merkavah, he aspires to ascend and descend unharmed, knowing that he should be the one to earn this goal.

Various personal qualities, associated with the figure of the "descender to the chariot," correspond to the mythical hero model as well. The Hekhalot and Merkavah adept is certainly introduced as an exceptional individual, equipped with distinctive spiritual and intellectual characteristics. A passage in *Hekhalot Rabbati* gives a telling example. Rabbi Ishmael inquires: "What is the quality [of the Merkavah seeker] like?"[26] Rabbi Nehunia ben Ha-Kanah's answer refers to precise personal characteristics of such a figure. Every person, theoretically, can attempt the journey. Only the most accomplished individuals, however, who manifests superb moral and excellent ethical attributes, elevated spiritual stature and extensive knowledge of Jewish tradition, can complete it:

> Anyone who is pure and is emptied of idolatry, incest, bloodshed, slander, false oaths, profanation of the Name, impertinence and in valid enmity, and who keeps every positive and negative commandment.[27]

Though these qualities may be seen as the standard religious and ethical obligations of every Jewish believer, such a state of faultlessness is admitted to be virtually impossible for anyone to achieve. Rabbi Ishmael is totally overwhelmed by these requirements. Distressed and frustrated, he addresses his teacher Rabbi Nehunia ben Ha-Kanah and protests that such an ultimate perfection in a human being is impossible: "If so, there is no end to the matter, for you have no human, with soul in him, who is pure and emptied of these eight attributes."[28]

According to an alternative Hekhalot and Merkavah model, esteemed ancestry and racial lineage are additional attributes which qualify the travelers to the chariot. For example, in *3 Enoch*, Metatron, prince of the countenance, argues with opposing angels on behalf of Rabbi Ishmael. They ask:

> . . . why have you allowed one born of a woman
> to come and behold the chariot?
> From what nation is he?
> From what tribe? What is his character?[29]

Metatron contends that his virtuous genealogy and priestly lineage should allow Rabbi Ishmael to enter the divine realm:

> He is the people of Israel, which the Holy One, blessed be He, chose to be his people out of the seventy tongues. He is from the tribe of Levi, which presents the offering to His name. He is from the seed of Aaron, whom the Holy One, blessed be He, chose to be his own servant, and on whose head He Himself bound a priestly crown to Sinai.[30]

Even to the eligible individual, success is not assured. In order to reach the final destination and to enter the divine realm, the hero mystic must face dangerous trials and tests, answer perplexing questions and accomplish arduous tasks. Only his own virtues and strength eventually assure his safety and success in these. The descender to the Merkavah is neither endowed with supernatural powers by which he performs his mission, nor is he granted divine privileges which protect him. On the contrary, an adept who wishes to descend and ascend safely, must rely primarily on what wisdom, power, and determination he brings with him on the quest. Before he attains divine revelation, the seeker's worthiness must be proven by his own thoughts, perception, acts, and deeds throughout the journey.[31]

According to several instructional accounts the Hekhalot and Merkavah hero mystic also plays a role in his community. After experiencing the heavenly reality, the visionary returns to the terrestrial world. Following God's decree, he is then obligated to testify before his group and to report the content of his visions:

> . . . tell my sons what I am doing during the morning and afternoon and evening prayers . . . teach them and tell them . . . and testify to them whatever testimony you have. See what I do to the countenance of the face of Jacob, your patriarch, which is engraved for me on my throne of glory.[32]

Such a testimony can be seen as a beneficial message to the congregation, especially in times of trouble. Both the pseudo-historical setting and the historical background support this suggestion. In the times of the Roman persecution of the Jews and after the devastation of the Jewish people following the destruction of the Second Temple,[33] a confirmed report of God's existence in heaven could have greatly consoled the community. The few qualified visionaries, who ascend to God's realm, are able to witness an enduring divine order and consequently bring back to Earth consolation and hope. Through their personal experience, they relieve the distressed human community and, in some ways, elevate their reality.[34]

To summarize: mystical accounts in the Hekhalot and Merkavah literature neither outline an optimal profile of the exemplary "descender of the chariot" nor detail a uniform, standard criterion, which qualifies an aspired visionary to become one. Furthermore, although the writings recognize Rabbi Ishmael, Rabbi Akiva, and Rabbi Nehunia ben Ha-Kanah, well-known Tannaitic teachers, as the main heroes of the Merkavah mystical circle, this literary testimony is considered pseudoepigraphic by most scholars. Thus, information concerning both the historical identity of the Hekhalot and Merkavah visionaries, as well as their characteristics is still unclear.

Throughout the various Hekhalot and Merkavah accounts, however, a consistent paradigmatic model of an "ideal mystic" is depicted. Such a figure is characterized by a "paradigm of traits," which typically classified the "hero," a prevalent figure in large cross section of mythological traditions, as representative Mesopotamian accounts illustrate. Distinguished by similar traits, motivations, and goals, the descenders of the chariot emerge as mystical-mythological heroes. Equipped with exceptional qualities, extraordinary virtues, and venerable rank, they seek to separate themselves from geographical and temporal restrictions, reach the heavenly realm, encounter the divine, and achieve celestial secrets—all beyond ordinary human attainment. Recognizing that such objectives are extremely dangerous or altogether unachievable, these heroes consciously decide to pursue them, relying, it seems, on what powers and skills are within them that allow them to prevail.

THE INNER-OTHERWORLDLY JOURNEY

> . . . the path of the heavenly ladder
> with its one end on earth and one end on
> the right foot of the throne of glory.[35]

Evident in Hekhalot and Merkavah mysticism are a great number of accounts which present a contemplative, spiritual journey or an ecstatic voyage taking place in the adept's imagination, vision, and belief. Several principal passages illustrate these aspects. For example, in *Hekhalot Zutarti,* Rabbi Akiva is described as attaining the secret name in heaven during a contemplative-meditative situation, "when he was beholding the Merkavah; and he descended and taught it to his students."[36] In the same text, Rabbi Akiva recounts his vision: "I had a vision and I observed the whole universe and saw it as it is. I ascended in a wagon of fire and gazed on the palaces of hail . . ."[37] *Ma'aseh Merkavah* presents Rabbi Ishmael's introspective experience as an ascent to heaven. While he remains on Earth, seated before his teacher, he travels in his mind to celestial realms.

> Rabbi Ishmael said: "Since I heard from Rabbi Nehunia ben Ha-Kanah my teacher this report . . . I stood on my feet and asked him all the names of the princes of wisdom, and from the questions that I asked I saw a light in my heart like the days of heavens . . . since I stood up and saw my face shining from my wisdom . . . I began to explain each and every angel in each and each palace."[38]

Rabbi Nehunia ben Ha-Kanah's trance journey in *Hekhalot Rabbati* occurs in similar circumstances. He sits and contemplates among his students in the terrestrial realm and beholds the throne of glory in a vision. When his students wish to call him back from his state of trance to ask him questions, they request Rabbi Ishmael, as their delegate: "see if you can bring him back from the visions which he has glimpsed."[39] Rabbi Ishmael then touches his teacher's body on Earth with an impure piece of fine wool. Consequently, Rabbi Nehunia ben Ha-Kanah is "dismissed from before the throne of glory where he had been sitting and beholding."[40]

Attention to the introspective spiritual nature of the journey does not contradict its description as a concrete and physical expedition into cosmic regions. A variety of Hekhalot and Merkavah accounts repropose the spiritual-inner voyage as a corporeal quest into super natural worlds through several mythological themes and modes of expressions. The seekers' conceptual experience of attaining God, its progressive stages, and the inner transformation at its end, are all conveyed in terms of external actions and manifested deeds, accomplished in imaginary sites outside of the phenomenological realm.

In his discussion of Near Eastern mythology R. J. Clifford notes:

> In the religions of the ancient near east, to characterize rather broadly, divine presence was sought not so much in mystical inward searching of the soul but in symbolism where a relationship was established between the natural and supernatural worlds.[41]

Such a pattern of reaching the divine is clearly evident in the Hekhalot and Merkavah mysticism, which exhibits aspects of the voyage through a variety of corresponding mythological themes and images. The descenders to the chariot ascend to heaven by foot or on the wings of a divine being. They cross cosmic geographical regions or climb up on a cosmic pole. They reestablish intimate, direct communication with God, as in the first days of creation in the Garden of Eden. The Merkavah devotees enter closed entrances guarded by terrifying guards and encounter dangers, tests, and trials, all in order to prove their virtues and to advance towards the upper divine sphere. A physical transformation at the end of their journey completes the adventure. In such a manner, the mystical spiritual voyage and its various phases are actualized and becomes concrete. Following are examples of such representations.

A Journey Through Cosmic Realms

> Between one bridge and another are twelve myriads of parasangs,
> in its ascent are twelve myriads of parasangs,
> and in its descent are twelve myriads of parasangs . . .[42]

Mythological Patterns

A common feature of the mythopoeic thought is its concrete conception of space, scholars have long recognized.[43] It does not imagine space to be infinite, continuous, and homogeneous but rather as discernible, demarcated, and visible. Examples are evident in mythological accounts of Mesopotamia as well as in biblical references, which depict the conceptual division between the divine and human realms through commonplace images of Heaven, Earth, and the Underworld.[44]

Tangible depictions of divine reality are evident in various mythological accounts of Mesopotamia. The realm of the high gods is illustrated as a tangible world situated up in the sky. As W. G. Lambert, W. Horowitz, and other scholars have shown, this celestial realm is one of cosmic levels.[45] Imagined as several superimposed heavenly layers of equal size and shape, the transcendent realm emerged as concrete. A detailed description of the cosmic physical structure occurs, for example, in two ancient texts reflecting similar traditions. They present a six-tiered universe, composed of three heavens and three earths.[46] In the upper realm, each one of the heavens is made of precious stones and is considered the domain of one distinctive god:

> The upper heavens are of luludanitu-stones, of Anu,
> He settled the Igigi therein.
> The middle heavens are of saggilmu-stone, of the Igigi.
> Bel sat therein on the lofty dais in the chamber of lapis lazuli.
> He lit a lamp of elmesu-stone.
> The lower heavens are of jasper, of the stars,
> He drew the constellations of the gods thereon.

Elsewhere we find a model of heaven with seven levels. A Sumerian incantation from the late second millennium B.C.E. reads: "Seven gods of the broad heavens. Seven gods of the broad land . . . Heaven seven, Earth seven . . ."[47]

Based to such tactile illustration of the divine sphere, various sources also determine concrete manners of reaching it. Thus, attempts to overcome the polarity between gods and humans are often depicted as physical excursions from the human terrestrial to the divine supernatural domains. Several models are commonly employed: crossing the heavens by foot or soaring on the back of a winged guide, traveling in divine unfamiliar territories and roads, and entering blocked gates of celestial palaces.[48]

The legend of Etana, for instance, describes this mythological figure crossing the gap between Heaven and Earth on the wings of an eagle with the hope of attaining the plant of life from the gods. He ascends to Heaven, passes through the seven divine regions of the gods Anu, Enlil, Ea, Sin, Shmash, Adad, and Ishtar, and enters their seven heavenly gates:[49]

> After they had [flown up to the heaven of Anu],
> [They passed] through the gates of A[nu, Enlil, and Ea].
> The eagle and [bowed down together]
> [They passed through the gates of Si[n Shamash, Adad and Ishtar].
> The eagle and [bowed down together].[50]

Portrayed as a guide-figure, the eagle carries Etana on his wings and directs his cosmic tour while indicating the significant sights revealed during the journey:

> He put his arms over its sides,
> put his hands over the quills of its wings.
> [the eagle] took him upward for a mile.
> "My friend, look at the country!
> How does it seem?"[51]

A similar mythical structure of the upper realm is found in a temple's inscription dedicated to the god Anu and his consort Antum, S. Dalley has observed. According to the temple's inscription, attributed to Anu-uballit Nikarchos in 222 B.C.E., the temple's structure included significant symbolic features. It had three gates which open outwards, and seven courts around a courtyard in which the shrine of destinies is found.[52] According to Dalley, this temple's plan reflects at once the arrangement of the universe, as it was conceived at the time of building, and the way of approaching the high god. Thus, seven heavens or palace-courts had to be crossed before the worshiper comes face-to-face with the enthroned deity of cosmic destinies.

A corporeal ascent to the celestial realm is pictured as well in the myth of Adapa. In order to reach the high god Anu Adapa, human, leaves the boundaries of the earthly world, walks through divine trails, and mounts his way to the highest heaven. Before his departure the god Ea instructs Adapa, outlining the procedures.

> He made him take the [Pa]th of Heaven,
> and he went up to heaven.
> When he went up to heaven
> drew near the Gate of Anu,
> Tammuz and Gizzida were standing at the Gate of Anu.[53]

Gilgamesh's quest for immortality is also conceived as a corporeal expedition in super-natural domains. Departing from the boundaries of the human world, he goes on a tangible journey to the mythical realm of the gods, where the only human survivor of the flood, Utnapishtim, dwells. In the course of his route, Gilgamesh visits various legendary locations such as the mountain Mashu, the mythical mountain of the sun, or the jewel garden in which "trees are blossoming with gemstones."[54] Distrustful, he roams divine territories while trying to find directions to regions where no man has tread before:

> Give me directions, [whatever they are];
> give me directions.
> If it is possible, I shall cross the sea;
> If it is possible, I shall roam open country again.[55]

Biblical sources offer a multifaced image of the divine reality depicted as heaven or sky by the Hebrew term *shamayim* (**שמים**).[56] This term, which appears with the standard dual ending, is in fact plural in its grammatical form. Thus, several scholars have derived a biblical notion of plural heavens from this form. Furthermore, the Hebrew phrase "heaven and the heaven of heaven(s) has been thought by some to state a cosmic image which includes multiple heavens. A concrete concept of the upper realm is expressed in several biblical sources. For example, Genesis 1:6–8 depicts a material lower heaven, namely the firmament or dome (**רקיע**), which serves to barricade the water of the upper heaven.[57] Allusion to God's creation in Isaiah 45:12 offers a visual and tangible view of heaven as the world's canopy or cosmic tent: "I made the earth, and created humankind upon it; it was my hand that stretched out (**נטה**) the heavens." Exodus 24: 9–10 describes the concrete heaven revealed to Moses, Aaron, Nadab, Abihu, and seventy of the elders of Israel on Mt. Sinai, when they "saw the God of Israel. Under his feet there was something like a pavement of sapphire stone, like the very heaven for clearness."

Hekhalot Mysticism

Several Hekhalot and Merkavah accounts conceptualize God's reality neither as a transcendent, boundless sphere, nor a conceptual realm.

Instead the reality of the divine is pronounced through a widespread imagery as the tangible, highest district of heavens. Clusters of mythical features give shade and color to this picture, echoing, it seems, biblical and Near Eastern themes. Seven parallel superimposed levels make up the upper cosmic sphere. Each is viewed as a demarcated geographical region, defined by a name and containing its own particular conditions. In several accounts the names of the seven heavens are given: Aravot, Makon, Maon, Zebul, Shehaqim, Raqia, Wilon.[58] Other descriptions give additional detail to substantiate the mythical image of the divine sphere. According to *3 Enoch*, for example, God's palaces are located in distinct upper realms, each is governed by a divine prince:

> There are seven lofty, fearful, marvelous, and noble princes who are in charge of the seven havens. . . . They are all princes over a heavenly host, and every one of them is attended by 496,000 myriads of ministering angels.
> Michael, the Great Prince, is in charge of the seventh heaven, the highest which is in Aravot;
> Gabriel, Prince of the Host, is in charge of the sixth heaven, which is in Makon;
> Shatqiel, Prince of the Host, is in charge of the fifth heaven, which is in Maon;
> Shahaqiel, Prince of the Host, is in charge of the fourth heaven, which is in Zebul;
> Baradiel, Prince of the Host, is in charge of the third heaven, which is in Shehaqim;
> Baraqiel, Prince of the Host, is in charge of the second heaven, which is in Raqia;
> Sidriel Prince of the Hosts, is in charge of the first heaven, which is in Wilon.[59]

Clearly the upper realm of Hekhalot and Merkavah mysticism is not discerned as an abstract, infinite continuum, but rather as a series of separate, finite celestial realms identified by names, and guarded by celestial governor-princes.[60] Majestic palaces are situated in each of the heavenly realms, adding more detail to this mythical landscape. A description in *3 Enoch* pictures this hierarchical, structural sphere comprised of seven heavens, seven palaces, and seven angelic guards:

> The guardian of the entrance of the first palace, when they see the guardians of the entrance of the second palace, they remove their splendid crown and fall prostrate. The guardian of the entrance of the third palace, when they see the guardians of the entrance of the fourth palace, they remove

> their glorious crown and fall prostrate. The guardian of the entrance of the fourth palace, when they see the guardians of the entrance of the fifth palace, they remove their splendid crown and fall prostrate. The guardian of the entrance of the fifth palace, when they see the guardians of the entrance of the sixth palace, they remove their glorious crown and fall prostrate. The guardian of the entrance of the sixth palace, when they see the guardians of the entrance of the seventh palace, they remove their glorious crown and fall prostrate.[61]

It is important to note that this picture is not employed in a symbolic manner to be deciphered thereafter. It is introduced rather as an alternative mythical reality which the descenders to the chariot experience and explore in a direct and personal fashion. The spiritual pursuit of divine presence is depicted in many passages as an active, corporeal ascent through these heavenly realms. Rabbi Ishmael in *3 Enoch*, for example, states his experience:

> When I ascended to the height to behold the vision of the chariot, I entered six palaces, one inside the other, and when I reached the entrance of the seventh palace, I paused in prayer before the Holy One . . . [62]

We find here, as in other Hekhalot and Merkavah accounts, a common presentation of mystical notions conveyed in mythological modes. The presence of God is found within his actual and concrete abode in heaven. The mystic-hero ascends to heaven, crosses the different realms, walks in God's halls, steps into the seventh palace and then utters his prayers. In this passage active verb forms exhibit the spiritual process. The focus shifts from an internal, personal perspective to an external, cosmic scene.

An additional mythological metaphor represents the notion of seeking the divine. The Merkavah devotees are portrayed as travelers trying to find their way in foreign regions. They ask for directions, look for geographical locations, estimate distances and inspect the celestial topography. In a passage in *Ma'aseh Merkavah* we read the following:

> How many bridges (are there)? How many rivers of fire? How many rivers of hail? How many treasures of snow? How many wheels of fire? How many angels of service? (There are) twelve thousand myriads of bridges, six above and six below. Twelve thousand myriads of rivers of hail, six above and six below. Twelve thousands myriad of storehouses of snow, six above and six below. (There are) twenty-four myraids of wheels of firs, twelve above and twelve below.

> And surrounding the bridges, the rivers of fire, the rivers of hail, the treasures of snow, the angels of service—how many angels of service (are there) at each passage and passage? And each creature and creature stands in the midst, facing all paths of heaven.[63]

Often the Merkavah seeker verifies specific details with another experienced traveler, who is able to offer directions and to point the right track in the upper unfamiliar domains. Thus, we read Rabbi Ishmael's testimony:

> I asked Rabbi Akiva how many measures are between one bridge or another? He said to me: Between the one bridge and the other are twelve myriads of parasangs, in its ascent are twelve myriads of parasangs, and in its descent are twelve myriads of parasangs. Between the rivers of awe and the rivers of fear are twenty-two myriads of parasangs. Between the rivers of hail and the rivers of darkness are thirty-six myriads of parasangs. Between the chambers of lightening and the clouds of consolation are forty-two myriads of parasangs. Between the consoling clouds and the Merkavah are eighty-four myriads of parasangs.[64]

The interior components of these upper zones are also distinguished in a tangible manner. Chariots, cherubim, ophanim, sacred camps, and palace's chambers serve as the mythical landmarks of the private divine space. Their location needs to be registered and marked by the traveler who searches the route to his final destination, namely, God's throne of glory:

> Between the Merkavah and the cherubim are one hundred sixty-eight myriads of parasangs. Between the cherubim and the ophanim are twenty-four myriads of parasangs. Between the ophanim and the chambers of the chambers are twenty-four myriads of parasangs. Between the chambers of chambers and the holy beasts are forty thousand myriads of parasangs. Between one wing and another are twelve myriads of parasangs. And their width is similar. From the holy camps to the throne of glory are thirty myriads of parasangs. And from the foot of the throne of glory to the place on which sits the holy King, high and exalted ANPKA YHWH God of Israel, are forty thousand myriads of parasangs. And his great name is declared exhalted there.[65]

In many of these descriptions the corporeal aspects of the journey are emphasized. Yet, the inner dimensions of the process are likewise acknowledged. The transition from Earth to Heaven through superimposed and stratified celestial regions corresponds to the seeker's spiritual development and his inner moral-ethical progress. A passage in *Ma'aseh Merkavah,* discussed earlier, articulates this concept:

> I asked Rabbi Akiva how many measures are thus between one bridge and the other. Rabbi Akiba said to me: "Were straightness and righteousness in your heart then you would know how many measures are in heaven." He said to me: "When I was in the first palace, I was righteous, in the second palace, I was pure, in the third palace, I was upright, in the fourth palace, I was perfect, in the fifth palace I arrived holy before the king of king of kings, blessed is his name."[66]

An additional mythological theme which expresses the contemplative journey is that of flight. A winged heavenly being helps and guides the human adept to come closer to God's seventh heaven. In *3 Enoch,* for instance, Enoch is carried to the height of heavens on "the stormy wings of the *Shekinah.*"[67] The same account pictures Rabbi Ishmael's mythical flight. After ascending to the seventh palace, he is rescued from the fierce gatekeepers by Metatron, prince of the divine presence. Metatron places him on his wings and leads him through the heavenly realm, explaining its unfamiliar sites:

> Come and I will show you where water is suspended in the height, where fire burns in the midst of hailstones, where lightning flashes in the midst of mountains of snow, and where thunders rumble in the height of heights, and where flame blazes in the midst of burning fire . . . and I went with him. Taking me by his hand he bore me up on his wings and showed me all these things."[68]

Echoing the mythic depiction of Elijah's chariot of 2 Kings 2:11, a "wagon of radiance" or a "fiery" chariot are additional parallel images by which the spiritual-contemplative journey becomes concrete.[69] As a passage in *3 Enoch* attests, the angel Anafi'el carries Enoch to heaven "in great glory on a fiery chariot with fiery horses and glorious attendants."[70] In *Hekhalot Rabbati,* in a similar manner, the accomplished adept is a heavenly rider, whose merits are verified, written down by the angel Gabriel, and posted on a celestial carriage. In this carriage the visionary crosses heavenly spheres, accompanied by angels and the blowing of myriads of horns, so the fierce gatekeepers realize his distinction, sheathe their weapons, and allow him into the seventh palace:

> When the guards of the gate of the seventh palace see him, with Dumiel and Gabriel and Katspiel proceeding before the carriage of the man who is deserving and descends to the Merkavah. They cover their faces, which were wrathful

> and sit. And they stand and loosen their taut bows and return their sharp swords to their sheaths.[71]

An Ascent on a Cosmic Pole

> It is like having a ladder in one's house
> on which he ascends and descends . . .
> and being able to go up and down at will.[72]

Mythological Patterns

A common mythological concept is that of an *axis mundi,* or a cosmic pole which links together the regions of the universe. Images, such as mountains, ladders, ropes, trees, temples, or staircases, give concrete representation to this idea. Each of these, in its way, establishes a tangible link between the Heavens, the Earth, and the Underworld. They enable the passage from one level to another, or from one mode of existence to a higher or a lower one.[73]

Various Near Eastern examples exemplify this notion. Cosmic poles are often depicted as cables, ropes, mountains, ladders, or temples.[74] According to Mesopotamian and biblical views, they allow movement and communication between cosmic regions.[75]

In the *Enuma Elish* known as the Babylonian creation story, for example, the god Marduk builds his temple in Babylon, which unites the three cosmic realms, Heaven, Earth and the Underground Apsu, and thus establishes communication between the upper and the lower gods:

> Whenever you come up from the Apsu for an assembly,
> Your night's resting place shall be in it, receiving you all
> Whenever you come dawn from the sky for an assembly,
> Your night's resting place shall be in it, receiving you all.[76]

This description marks out Marduk's temple tower, or ziggurat, as a cosmic pole. Its name, *Esagila,* literally "the House that lift its head (high)," affirms this designation. Titles of other Babylonian sanctuaries reflect a similar intent, implying that temples, and specifically temple towers link the Heaven and Earth: the temple of the God Anu at Uruk is titled the "Palace of Heaven and Underworld." The ziggurat at Borsippa is known as the "House which Gathers the Seven of Heaven and Underworld." The ziggurat of the God Adad in Assur is the "House where Heaven and Underworld Mingle." Ishtar's temple at Nippur and the ziggurat at Larsa are "The Bond of Heaven and Earth."[77] Temple hymns are associated with similar images. The hymn for the ziggurat Eunir states: "Eunir, which has grown high (uniting) heaven and earth, Foundation of heaven and earth." The hymn for the Kesh temple declares: "Temple, whose platform is suspended from heaven's midst, whose foundation fills the Abzu."[78]

A relief dated 850 B.C.E. from the reign of the neo-Babylonian king Nabu-Apla-Iddina establishes a pictorial and highly symbolic manifestation of this mythical idea.[79] The relief depicts a scene from the temple of the sun God in Sippar, in which the temple, represented in the relief as a pillar, rests on the lower parts of the cosmos and reaches the celestial level where the God Shamash sits. As T. N. D. Mettinger has noted, in the right half of the relief, the god Shamash sits on his throne above. The left half depicts a procession in Shamash's temple below. Events in the temple, it appears, occur simultaneously on the terrestrial and the celestial spheres, exhibiting the temple's role as the link between the two realms.[80] Seals from Anatolia, Syria, and Assyria contain similar pictorial representations of this concept. They display a winged disk, representing the sky above, supported by one or two pillars which are rooted in the Earth below.[81]

References to mythic imagery of cosmic pillars are present in various biblical sources as well.[82] The book of Job, for example, states: "The pillars of heaven tremble and are bewildered at his rebuke" (26:11).[83] In Psalm 11:4 the temple is depicted as a pole between heaven and earth: "Yahweh is in his holy temple, his throne in heaven."[84] A similar mythical image appears in Jacob's dream when he sees "a stairway set up on the earth with its top reaching the heavens" (Gen. 28:12).

Hekhalot and Merkavah Mysticism

Hekhalot and Merkavah accounts employ compatible concrete representation of cosmic poles in order to convey the manner in which communication with the divine can be achieved. A passage in *Hekhalot Rabbati* describes an *axis mundi* on which the universe is constructed. This image consists of a pole which links Heaven and Earth, or a ladder which stands on Earth and leads to Heaven and to the throne of God. When Rabbi Nehunia ben Ha-Kanah reveals to the members of his circle, the "heroes of the assembly" all the secrets of ascent he recounts:

> I will reveal before them (members of the assembly) the mysteries, the hidden, the suppressed, wonders, and the weaving of the web on which the completion of the world and its exultation stand. And the axle of heaven and earth on which all the wings of the earth, and all the wings of the universe, and the wings of the high firmament, bound, sewed, attached, are suspended. And the path of the heavenly ladder, with its one end on earth, and one end on the right foot of the throne of glory.[85]

The ambiguous term *bandaba* in *Hekhalot Zutarti* exhibits a similar conceptual image. A cosmic pole established at the beginning of time, prior to the creation of Heaven and Earth, connects the upper and lower realms:

> Before YHWH worked the heavens and the earth,
> [he] fixed a *bandaba* to heaven to ascend [by] it
> and to descend [by] it.[86]

A description in the *Genizah* depicts a cosmic pole around which the world exists. It is imagined as an axle "on which the perfection of the world is fastened and tied to its top."[87] In *Hekhalot Rabbati,* an image of a peg, founded in the dawn of time, denotes a similar concept:

> . . . when you insert the peg of the weaving of the web,
> on which the completion of the world and its exaltation stand,
> many years, generations without end.[88]

The cosmic poles assume a practical function in several Hekhalot and Merkavah accounts, enabling mortal and divine beings to move from one cosmic sphere to another. A passage in *Hekhalot Rabbati* mentions a ladder on which the angels ascend from Earth to Heaven.[89] Additional accounts, as well, describe a rope, which joins the terrestrial and celestial realms and allows worthy mystics to ascend and descend safely.[90] A ladder is also considered a means of ascension in this literature, as Rabbi Ishmael states: "It is like having a ladder in one's house on which he ascends and descends and there is no creature who can prevent him."[91]

A Return to Paradise

> When the Holy One, removed me
> from the generation of the Flood,
> he . . . brought me into the great palaces
> in the height of the heaven Aravot
> where the glorious throne of the *Shekinah*
> is found . . . [92]

Mythological Patterns

Several studies have explored the mythical concept entitles by M. Eliade as a "nostalgia for paradise," and its presence in the Hebrew bible.[93] This mythical concept conveys, through narratives and images, the desire to transcend the human condition, return to a mythical perfect past, recover a direct means of communication with God and even attain a divine state of existence.

One of its expressions appears in various traditions of Eden, which reflect longing for an ideal form of existence preceding the rift between the divine and human. M. Fishbane discusses the implications of this mythical concept in ancient Israel: "The garden of Eden thus symbolizes primordial harmony and order in space, a channel of divine blessing and beneficence which has ruptured with the primordial human transgression of the divine interdiction."[94] Fishbane relates the topological replication of the archaic imagery of Eden to other institutions and texts. He notes: "It is the basis for a profound inner biblical nostalgia for spatial harmony that attached itself—repeatedly in history—to certain spatial institutions or loci which were left to embody this longing."[95] For instance, in several biblical accounts, echoes from Eden are associated with Canaan, Zion, and the temple of Jerusalem. In this way, these places and institutions became the focus for future hope and yearning.[96]

Hekhalot and Merkavah Mysticism

The theme of "nostalgia for paradise," evoked in Hekhalot and Merkavah mysticism, offers an additional pattern of a tangible attainment of God. The opening passages of *3 Enoch* illustrate this notion. The account of Enoch's ascension to heaven opens with a description of the ideal harmonious state of the past. As the account asserts, at the beginning human and divine realms were connected, even after the expulsion from Eden. God's presence, the *Shekhinah,* remained accessible on Earth, allowing humans to experience the divine and even to gaze at his image. Rabbi Ishmael quotes Enoch's nontraditional version of the Eden narrative, and outlines the nature of this harmonious and blissful time:

> From the day that the Holy One, blessed be he, banished the first man from the garden of Eden, the *Shekinah* resided on a cherub beneath the tree of life. The ministering angels used to jump and come down, sections from heaven, to roam the whole world. And the first man and his generation sit at the entrance to gaze at the image of the brilliance of the *Shekinah,* for the brilliance of the *Shekinah* was travelling from one end of the world to the other end . . .[97]

The passage speaks then about human wrongdoing and idolatry, which caused the total separation of the divine and human realms:

> . . . until the coming of the generation of Enosh, who was the chief of all the idolatrous in the world. What did this generation do? They treaded the world from end to end, each of them brought silver, gold, precious stones, and pearls, in mountains and heaps. And they fashioned them into idols in the four quarters of the world . . .[98]

As a consequence of these sins, God removed his *Shekhinah* from Earth, away from the presence of wicked people:

> Immediately, the Holy One, blessed be removed the *Shekinah* from the earth from their midst. At that time the ministering angels came, and the cohorts of the hosts . . . They took trumpets and seized the horns in their hands, and surrounded the *Shekinah* with hymns and songs, and it ascended to the heavenly heights.[99]

This narration in *3 Enoch* articulates clearly the primordial separation between human beings and the divine. The account proceeds to suggest a possible method of reestablishing the perfect situation of the beginning. Even after this divorce between divine and human, several distinguished and exceptional human beings, such as Enoch, can still ascend to heaven and regain the presence of God. In his personal and direct encounter with the divine, Enoch experiences, once again, undivided existence just as before the rupture:

> . . . when the Holy One removed me from the generation of the Flood, he lifted me up on stormy wings of the *Shekinah* to the highest heaven and entered me into the great palaces in the height of the heaven Aravot, where there are the glorious throne of *Shekinah* and Merkavah . . .[100]

Enoch transcends human terrestrial reality and attains an existence shared with the divine. In Hekhalot and Merkavah mysticism he becomes, in effect, a prototype for all Merkavah seekers. He is one who has accomplished this goal, leading the way for others. This pattern of "returning to paradise" is not exclusive to Enoch, however. The journey suggested in several Hekhalot and Merkavah accounts is one that can be repeated by all qualified members of the Merkavah circle who follow Enoch's model.[101]

This account in *3 Enoch* evokes echoes from two other biblical mythological narratives, namely Genesis 2–3 and Ezekiel 28:11–19. Themes from these sources seem to be reapplied in *3 Enoch* in a mystical context. They give background to the goal of transcending the human condition and of recovering direct and personal communication with God.[102] The two biblical accounts present a transition from the harmonious primordial existence to a separated and thus imperfect reality. Each story attributes this shift to wrongdoing, sin, and disobedience.[103] The Genesis narrative describes first the harmony in Eden and then the expulsion of the first couple from this ideal divine habitation, after transgressing God's command. In Ezekiel 28, the prophet Ezekiel announces God's judgment against the prince of Tyre. He compares the proud prince of Tyre to an anointed cherub, full of wisdom and perfect in beauty, who dwelled in Eden. Reminiscent of Genesis 2–3, this Eden also represents the divine abode, identified as both the garden and the mountain of God. Because of his sin, the cherub is cast out of the garden and thus primeval harmony is broken:

> You were the signet of perfection, full of wisdom and perfect in beauty. You were in Eden, the garden of God; every precious stone was your covering, carnelian, chrysolite, and moonstone, beryl, onyx, and jasper, sapphire, turquoise, and emerald; and worked in gold were your settings and your engravings. On the day that you were created they were prepared. With an anointed cherub as guardian I placed you; you were on the holy mountain of God; you walked among the stones of fire. You were blameless in your ways from the day that you were created, until iniquity was found in you In the abundance of your trade you were filled with violence, and you sinned; so I cast you as a profane thing from the mountain of God, and the guardian cherub drove you out from among the stones of fire. Your heart was proud because of your beauty; you corrupted your wisdom for the sake of your splendor. I cast you to the ground (Ezekiel 28:13–17).

Ancient Mesopotamian mythological echoes of both Genesis and Ezekiel 28 have long been noted.[104] In the context of this discussion, however, we leave aside questions of origin, source, textual connections, and interpretation of these tradition. Instead, we examine several selected themes and terms, which seem to re-emerge in *3 Enoch.*

The notion of ideal human-divine harmony is associated in Genesis and in Ezekiel with images of both the Garden of Eden and the Garden of God. A cherub figure appears in the two biblical accounts. In Genesis, the cherubim guard the way to the tree of life, after the expulsion from Eden (Gen. 3:24); In Ezekiel, a cherub exists in the garden, covered with precious stones (Ezekiel 28:14). Both biblical stories identify disobedience and the overstepping of boundaries as the main reason for the ending of ideal primeval harmony between god and humanity. The Genesis account describes the transgression of divine order and commands by human beings; Ezekiel condemns the cherub's sins of arrogantly transgressing the legitimate limits of his powers.

Several of these mythological themes seem to be reintroduced in *3 Enoch.* These include the Garden of Eden, the cherub, the precious stones, and the notion of sinning and violating ideal harmony. The absolute perfection of the beginning is depicted in *3 Enoch* by referring to the Garden of Eden, in which divine and human beings communicated freely. Thus, we read: "The first man and his generation dwelt at the gate of the garden of Eden so that they might gaze at the bright image of the *Shekinah*." A cherub is mentioned also in this context: "the *Shekinah* resided on a cherub beneath the tree of life." Acts of sinning and transgressing limits are the main reasons for breaking the divine-human mutual existence in *3 Enoch*. The narrative presents the transgressive acts of Enosh and his generation as the reason for removing God's presence, the *Shekhinah*, from Earth to Heaven. Precious stones, a typical motif in Ezekiel 28, reappears in *3 Enoch* as part of Enosh's generation's idolatry: "each of them amassed silver, gold, precious stones, and pearls in mountainous heaps and piles."

These mythological references are not used in their original form but are rather reshaped and readjusted in order to convey new mystical notions. Unlike the biblical accounts, *3 Enoch* provides a redemptive option by introducing a mystical alternative of attaining the Merkavah and the presence of God. Several deserving human beings such as Enoch, Rabḇi Nehunia ben Ha-Kanah, Rabbi Akiva, Rabbi Ishmael, and the worthy descenders to the chariot, can cross the gap between the terrestrial and the celestial realms and reconstruct the Edenic harmony of the beginning. They behold God and his *Shekhinah*, and are thus able to overcome the rift between the two realities during the extent of their mystical experience. Such is Rabbi Akiva's experience reported by Rabbi Ishmael to the members of the Merkavah circle:

> Rabbi Ishmael said:
> Thus Rabbi Akiva said to me:
> I recited a prayer and beheld the *Shekhinah*
> and saw everything that one does
> before the throne of glory.[105]

Heaven's Gates

> At the entrance to the seventh palace stand and rage all heroes,
> ruthless, powerful and hard, terrible and frightening,
> higher than mountains and more polished than hills.[106]

Mythological Patterns

Images of guarded doors, blocked gates, bolts, bars, and locks are characteristic to various mythological traditions including that of the ancient Near East. Many accounts situate the gates between the human world and the realm of the gods.[107] The gates define boundaries between the celestial and terrestrial worlds, and emphasize the fundamental distinction between gods and humans in a concrete fashion. Examples are many. Etana goes up to Heaven and passes the seven gates of the gods, namely, Anu, Enlil, Ea, Sin, Shamash, Adad, and Ishtar.[108] In other sources, the same imagery is repeated in relation to the same gods, as the hymn to the sun god Shamash demonstrates:

> O Shamash, you have opened the bolts of heaven's doors.
> You have ascended the staircase of pure lapis lazuli.
> You open up the closed bolts of heaven.[109]

Babylonian texts such as the hymns to the Gods of the night likewise employ images of gates: "the great gates of the b[road] heavens are open."[110]

Despite a clear distinction between gods and human beings, according to Near Eastern sources, mortals often try to overstep the divinely imposed boundaries, and move from the natural to the super-natural world.[111] Thus, doors, gates, or entrances to the divine spheres are often safeguarded by gatekeepers, whose main duty is to protect this realm and prevent human intruders from trespassing. For example, Gilgamesh and Enkidu enter the sacred cedar forest of the god Enlil, which is located outside the phenomenological realm. This forest, as the texts attests, is protected by the guardian Huwawa, whose main duty is to keep the divine realm out of human reach. He is often described as a gigantic being, protected by layers of terrifying radiance, whose appearance is frightful:

> Huwawa whose shout is flood-weapon,
> whose utterance is Fire, and whose breath is Death . . .
> Enlil destines to keep the Pine Forest Safe,
> to be the terror of people.[112]

The divine forest is prohibited to human beings and its nature is not intended to be uncovered. People who dare to enter this out of boundary realm endanger themselves and risk their life. Huwawa's reaction to Gilgamesh and Enkidu's invasion affirms this notion. He describes their offensive act, which should have led to their suffering by physical harm at the entrance to the forest:

> You have found out the nature of my forest,
> the nature [of my dwelling]. . .
> I should have taken you (and) slain you at the
> entrance to my forest's growth.
> I should have given your flesh to be eaten
> by the fire of the forest, roaring lions,
> birds of prey and scavengers.[113]

The attempt of human beings to overcome the disparity between divine and mortal and to exceed their reality is often depicted through mythical themes such as confrontation with divine guards, appeasement of protective watchmen, and public presentation of merits. Gilgamesh, in his quest for immortality, for example, encounters the dreadful guards of the mountain Mashu "whose aura is frightful, and whose glance is death. Their terrifying mantles of radiance drape the mountain."[114] Amazed at his presence in the realm of the gods, they inquire: "Someone has come to us . . ."[115] They then find out his human status, which immediately disqualified him.[116] They refuse to admit him through the "great-gate" of the mountain, declaring:

> It is impossible, Gilgamesh,
> nobody has passed through the mountain's
> inaccessible tract.[117]

Etana, as well, must justify his entry at the gates of the seventh heaven. He relies on the God Ea's plan. This enables him to answer the two divine guards, appease them, and proceed in his quest:

> Ea, aware of heaven's ways, touched him
> And [ ] made him wear his hair unkempt,
> [Clothed him in] mourning garb,
> Gave him instructions.
>
> ---
>
> When you go up to heaven,
> When you approach the gate of Anu,
> Dumuzi and Gizzida will be standing in the Gate of Anu,
> Will see you, will keep asking you questions . . . [118]

A similar mythological concept is present in the story of Inanna's *Descent to the Nether World*.[119] Though this is a narrative of descent rather then ascent, the familiar element of guarded gates establish the underworld as inaccessible using a similar structural pattern. The goddess Inanna must appease the gatekeeper and comply to his demands in order to accomplish her journey and reach her sister Ereshkigal.[120]

Heavenly gates emerge as well in various biblical texts. Jacob's dream is an dominant example. After seeing a staircase reaching up to heaven, Jacob comes to the conclusion: "This is none other than the house of God and this is the gate of heaven (Gen. 28:17).[121] Blocked entrances maintain the separation between the divine and human, as the image of the cherubim, guarding the east of the Garden of Eden "with a sword flaming and turning," demonstrates (Gen. 3:23–24).

Hekhalot and Merkavah Mysticism

The inward progress of moving beyond human restrictions towards an awareness of transcendent reality is often depicted in Hekhalot and Merkavah mysticism as an outward, corporeal process. Heaven's entrances or gates protected by fierce watchmen and terrifying divine gatekeepers, commonly manifest the inaccessible nature of divine reality. Such are the gates of the seventh heaven, secured by the mighty guards at the seventh palace:

> At the entrance to the seventh palace stand and rage all mighty ones, ruthless, powerful, and hard, terrible, and frightening, higher than mountains and sharper than hills. Their bows are strung before the countenance; their swords polished in their hands. Bolts of lightning from their eyeballs, channels of fire from their noses, and torches of coal from their mouths. They are adorned (with) helmets and armors, lances and spears adorn them hanging on their arms. Their horses are horses of darkness, horses of the shadow of death, horses of gloom, horses of fire, horses of blood, horses of hail, horses of iron, horses of fog . . . And a cloud is there over their heads, dripping blood over their heads and the heads of their horses. And this is the mark and measurement of the guardians at the entrance to the seventh palace, and such is the entrance of each palace.[122]

As I. Gruenwald notes, these guards do not represent evil powers. Their main function is to prevent unqualified adepts from entering the most sacred seventh palace.[123] The hero mystic who attempts to penetrate this realm is stopped by fearsome gatekeepers. They "fix their gaze on him," pose questions, and verify whether he deserves to set foot in heaven.[124] The visionary's human essence is clearly considered an obstacle, as Enoch-Metatron reports in *3 Enoch:* "As soon as I reached the heavenly heights, the holy creatures . . . smelled my odor . . . they said, 'What is this smell of one born of a woman?' "[125]

In order to establish his claims and merits, the Merkavah adepts are directed to exhibit specific seals to the gatekeepers at the entrance of each heaven or palace. Following this verification, the gatekeepers allow the adept to move forward and proceed into the next sphere:

> When you come and stand at the gate of the first palace, take two seals in your two hands. One of TWTRWSY YHWH, Lord of Israel, and one of Surya, the prince of the Presence. Show the one of TWTRWSY YHWH to those who stand on the right, and show the one of Surya to those on the left.[126]

The nature of the seals is not thoroughly clear, but they seem to function as amulets which transcribe powerful names, letters, or magical formulas, and are used for theurgic practices and rituals of power.[127] Several accounts describe an enigmatic process in which the adept seals himself during the process of ascent.[128] This use of seals can be associated with recurring concepts found in the ancient Near Eastern mythological lore. An attempt to link amulets and stones with divine influence is well-known in texts dating from late Assyrian times.[129] Different powers were ascribed to amulets which were used in certain combinations in order to cure illness or avert impeding disaster. For example, the Sumerian-Akkadian myth *Lugal-e,* still read in the late Assyrian court, recounts how the god Ninurta defeated the stones and then blessed or cursed them according to their nature. Zachalias of Babylon, during the second century C.E., wrote works which ascribe to stones the ability to influence fate and the affairs of those who wore them.[130] Pictorial images demonstrate as well inscriptions of formulas and names on worshipper's bodies.[131]

The significance of seals displayed by the descenders to the Merkavah to the guards of each heaven may be also understood in light of the original function of the seal in the ancient Near East, and its depiction in narratives. Emerged as a legal mark of ownership or contractual obligation by an individual, it has been suggested that the seal represents and comprises the "essence" of a person.[132] A similar concrete depiction seems to be suggested the Hekhalot and Merkavah descriptions. Qualified adepts who can demonstrate their merits and "essence" by showing the seals can pass unhindered and enter God' s palaces.[133]

Tests and Trial

> When you reach the pure marble stones,
> do not say: Water! Water![134]

Misleading trials and deceptive tests are common themes in mythological presentations of the hero quest. Often the hero figure is required to prove his worth and aptitude by passing them successfully. In this way, he exhibits his qualification and ability to partake in divine worlds despite his human nature.[135]

In the context of Mesopotamian myth, for example, Gilgamesh is challenged to justify his adequacy for immortality by overcoming sleep, associated with the human life cycle. Not being able to resist prolonged drowsiness, Gilgamesh fails the test by falling asleep. Thus, he displays his human limitations in a tangible fashion, and misses the opportunity to gain eternal life and to be aligned with the gods.[136] A similar test is offered to the hero Adapa. When he enters the seventh heaven, the god Anu invites him to drink the water of life and to eat the bread of life. Being falsely informed that they entail death, Adapa refuses to accept such gifts. Thus, he fails the divine test, demonstrating human, limited perception which prevents him from realizing the true meanings of the offer. Consequently, Adapa loses the opportunity to achieve immortality, which could have been gained by accepting the water and bread of life.[137]

Hekhalot and Merkavah Mysticism

As demonstrated in chapter 2, the Hekhalot and Merkavah adepts, at the end of their journey, transcend their human limitations and attain new modes of perception. They are then able to see heavenly visions from a mystical perspective and recognize their hidden meanings. Before they reach this stage, however, the mystics must prevail in the crucial "water test."[138] Every worthy adept is required to recognize the marble stones with which the palace is furnished, despite their watery appearance.

This test seems to demonstrate the spiritual stance of the mystics not in abstraction but in a concrete and tangible fashion. It examines their abilities to give up their mortal perspective in favor of a higher, divine-like perception. Only qualified individuals, who are capable of decoding the meaning of this manifested vision, pass the test and enter the seventh heaven.

An additional entrance test, designed perhaps to determine the inner sense perception and spiritual skills of the Merkavah adepts is depicted in a tangible manner as a corporeal process which takes place at the entrance of the seventh heaven. A passage in *Hekhalot Rabbati* attests:

> If the was qualified to descend to the Merkavah: When they [the angels] would say to him: "Enter!" he would not enter; they once again would say to him: "Enter!" and he immediately would enter, [then] they would praise him and say: "Surely this one is from the descenders of the Merkavah." But if he is not qualified to descend to the Merkavah: When they [the angels] would say to him: "Enter!" and he would immediately enter, they would immediately throw iron cutters at him.[139]

Although not all features of this test are clear, it appears that adepts are required to resist the immediate human instincts and not to enter at once into the seventh palace. Such a response, perhaps, demonstrates a state of mind in which human senses and logic are not of primary importance and may be misleading. Adepts are not expected to react in the predictable fashion, advised by their human reason, senses, and instincts. Instead they are encouraged to avoid them, to develop an alternative response, and to demonstrate this spiritual adequacy in a concrete test.

MYSTICAL-MYTHICAL TRANSFORMATION

> After all this the Holy One, blessed be he, made for me a throne like the throne of glory, and he spread over it a coverlet of splendor . . . like the coverlet of the throne of glory . . . He placed it at the door of the heaven and sat me down upon it.[140]

Mythological Patterns

A pattern of transformation, found in a variety of mythical versions, introduces a change of human standing and position which often occurs at the end of journeys. Several Mesopotamian mythological sources visualize such a process through tangible examples and corporeal images such as passing through gates, ascending to heaven, physical changes of rank.

In the *Poem of the Righteous Sufferer,* for example, a certain nobleman relates how he met with every conceivable calamity and was eventually restored to health and prosperity by the God Marduk, introduced as the Lord of Wisdom.[141] The transformation of his position, according to the poem, materializes when he passes through several gates and in each receives a blessing corresponding with the names of the gates:

> [In the] "Gate of Prosperity" prosperity was [given me,]
> [In the] "Gate of the . . . Guardian Spirit"
> guardian spirit drew [nigh to me,]
> [In the] "Gate of Well-being" I found well-being,
> In the "Gate of the Sun Rise" I was reckoned among the living,
> In the "Gate of Splendid Wonderment"
> my omens were very plain,
> In the "Gate of Release of Guilt"
> I was released from my bond,
> In the "Gate of Worship" my mouth inquired,
> In the "Gate of Resolving of Sights" my sights were resolved,
> In the "Gate of Pure Water"
> I was sprinkles with water of purification.[142]

Another example, portraying the transformation in the context of heavenly ascent, is the Sumero-Akkadian tradition of Enmeduranki, King of Sippar, the legendary founder of the diviner cult. This mythical figure is introduced in various sources as the seventh Antediluvian king, who is brought into heaven to join the divine realm during his lifetime and is given the secrets of the Gods. One particular fragmented cuneiform text, reconstructed and translated by W. G. Lambert, relates a full version of his mythical story.[143] Among other notions, the account denotes a process of transformation from one mode of standing to another.

It opens with a description of the state of primeval existence. King Enmeduranki, mortal, is taken by the gods Shamash and Adad from the terrestrial realm and is brought into the celestial region. There, he is accepted to the divine assembly. His selection is justified in the text by his great love of the high gods Anu, Enlil, and Ea:[144]

Shamash in Ebabbarra [appointed]
Enmeduranki [king of Sippar],
the beloved of Anu, Enlil [and Ea].
Shamash and Adad [brought him in] to
their assembly.[145]

In heaven Enmeduranki undergoes an elaborate process of external transformation. The gods honor him, grant him a golden throne, and put in his hand the cedar rod, an emblem of power and authority. The gods give Enmeduranki, the "tablet of the gods" which, according to Mesopotamian mythological tradition, contains the decrees, destinies, and norms which constitute all aspects and functions of life, past, present, and future.[146] The "tablet of the gods" or the "tablet of Destinies" is considered to be a central emblem of authority and the means by which supreme power is granted to its keeper. Enmeduranki also receives the divine mysteries, which the gods reveal to him. These include divinatory techniques essentially related to the act of observation:

Shamash and Adad [honoured him],
Shamash and Adad [set him] on a large
throne of gold. They showed him
how to observe oil on water,
a mystery of Anu [Enlil and Ea].
They gave him the tablet of the gods, the
liver, a secret of heaven and [underworld].
They put in his hand the cedar- (rod), beloved of the great gods.[147]

This transformation involves changes which serve to mark Enmedranki's new identity, position, power, and responsibility. Enmeduranki is taken to heaven and is assigned a role and place in the celestial realm. Equipped with divine knowledge, Enmeduranki gains access to the mysteries of the gods. He is able to observe manifested signs, see hidden meanings ordinarily concealed from mortal eyes, and behold veiled occurrences beyond time and place.

It is important to note, at this point, that Enmeduranki is considered to be the founder of the bārû cult. The term is derived from the Akkadian verb "bārû," which literally means "to see," "to observe," or "to watch."[148] The tradition asserts that under specific circumstances, the gods reveal the future to human beings through manifested signs. The qualified bārû (literally "the one who sees," or "the one who observes"), versed in the mysteries of the gods, is able to see the divine signs, decipher their concealed significance, and subsequently disclose them to humankind.[149]

After this transformation, the account presents Enmeduranki as an official power in Heaven and the guardian of divine mysteries. He sits above on a golden throne alongside the gods, welcomes people who ascend to heaven, directs them, and reveals the celestial secrets to them. It is important to notice that Enmeduranki is not an independent divine power. Even after his radical transformation, Enmeduranki acts on behalf of the gods and in accordance with their will. His main responsibility, it seems, is to decode veiled secrets by divinatory techniques and to mediate between the divine and human worlds. His descendants, the barus, "observers," share this mediatory role. These specialists, as scholars have noted, rigorously trained and then initiated into the secrets of their art. Their main role is to observe the signs of the gods, understand them, decipher their hidden meaning, and then reveal it to humankind:

> Then he, in accordance with their [wor(?)] brought
> the men of Nippur, Sippar and
> Babylon into his presence,
> and he honored them. He set them on thrones before [him].
> He showed them how to observe oil
> on water, a mystery of Anu,
> Enlil and Ea;
> he gave them the tablet of the
> gods, the liver, a secret of
> heaven and underworld;
> he put in their hands the cedar
> (rod), beloved of the great gods.[150]

The Mesopotamian mythological model presents King Enmeduranki's transformation from an earthly man to a heavenly being who can interpret divine secrets encoded in signs. Several key themes structure the metamorphosis in a concrete manner: (1.) The beloved king is chosen by the gods to be taken to heaven; (2.) in heaven, he receives from the gods divine emblems of status and power, which demonstrate his new position as a member of the celestial assembly; (3.) King Enmeduranki is granted divine knowledge and learns the secrets of the gods. These include the art of divination through techniques of seeing signs, observing them correctly, and understanding their hidden meaning. It is important to note that Enmeduranki's knowledge of divination and his ability to discern the meaning of divine secrets are granted, directed, and dependent on the gods; and (4.) as a receiver of divine mysteries, King Enmeduranki becomes a mediator between Heaven and Earth and a model for members of the bārû cult.

The influence of this Mesopotamian tradition on the Enochic traditions, from Genesis through to the Jewish Apocalyptic writings, has long been demonstrated in significant studies.[151] Already during the time of the authorship of the Genesis Priestly source, the figure of

Enoch existed as a Jewish counterpart to heroic figures of Mesopotamian myth such as the flood hero Utnapishtim, Gilgamesh, Utuabzu, and king Enmeduranki. In the context of this discussion, we will not concentrate on the correspondence between these figures and the manner in which traditions have been transmitted and evolved, but rather on the Mesopotamian model of transformation and its later mystical utilization in the Hekhalot and Merkavah literature.

Hekhalot and Merkavah Mysticism

As noted earlier, several Hekhalot and Merkavah accounts denote a shift from conventional to mystical awareness in terms of inner spiritual and conceptual process, which leads to a perception of transcendent reality. Stages of such inner transformation are discerned in concrete metaphors, pictorial images, and mythological patterns of expressions which correspond to both sources mentioned above, the *Poem of the Righteous Sufferer* and the Enmeduranki narrative.

3 Enoch, which follows the transformation of the human Enoch to Metatron, the Prince of the Countenance, will be our focus. The account first describes how Enoch is chosen by God to ascend to heaven. God selects him, separates him from his human generation, and takes him up to heaven to the higher celestial divine palace. God's love for Enoch is one reason for his elevation:

> Out of the abundant love and great compassion where with the Holy One, blessed be he, loved and cherished me more than all the denizens of the heights.[152]

In Heaven, Enoch's metamorphosis becomes apparent first as an external physical transformation. Enoch is enlarged, sheds his human form and becomes an enormous winged glowing figure. He is also granted a place in the celestial hierarchy. Several concrete emblems mark his elevated position and status: a majestic robe, a kingly crown, an aurora of brilliance and a heavenly throne, similar to the throne of glory. God places this throne at the door of the seventh palace and sits Enoch down upon it:

> After all this the Holy One, blessed be he, made for me a throne like the throne of glory, and he spread over it a coverlet of splendor . . . like the coverlet of the throne of glory. . . . He placed it at the door of the seventh heaven and sat me down upon it. And his herald went out into every heaven and announced concerning me: "I have appointed Metatron my servant as a prince and a ruler over all the denizens of the heights. . . . Whatever he says to you in my name you must observe and do."[153]

Enoch is also granted a profound wisdom, knowledge, divine understanding, and other attributes, which enable him to extend his perception beyond human limitations. This transformation materializes when heavenly gates are opened for him, each containing a certain blessing :

> Before the Holy One, blessed be he, set me to serve the throne of glory, he opened for me 300,000 gates of understanding, 300,000 gates of prudence, 300,000 gates of life, 300,000 gates of grace and favor, 300,000 gates of love, 300,000 gates of Torah, 300,000 gates of humility, 300,000 gates of substance, 300,000 gates of mercy, 300,000 gates of reverence. . . . [154]

Moreover, Enoch-Metatron receives the *pargod,* (**פרגוד**) or heavenly curtain. In this context it seems that the *pargod* of Enoch and the heavenly tablet of Enmeduranki function in a similar manner. The course of human history, its norms, its past, present, and future are all engraved upon the surface.[155]

> . . . the curtain of the Omnipresent, which is spread before the Holy One, blessed be he, and on which are printed all the generations of the world, and all their deeds whether done or to be done, till the last generation. [176]

Enoch learns the secrets of God and understands their hidden meaning. Here we can note a significant development in the Mesopotamia mythological pattern. Enoch-Metatron does not receive methods of divination. Instead, God grants him divine wisdom which enables him to understand and interpret all mysteries. Subsequently, he is qualified to comprehend hidden levels of reality from a divine perspective. Enoch looks beyond time and space, beholds profound visions which no human has ever seen, and unravels the meaning of enigmatic mysteries above and below:

> The Holy One, blessed be he, revealed to me from that time onward all the mysteries of wisdom, all the depths of the perfect Torah and all the thoughts of men's hearts. All mysteries of the world and all the orders of nature stand revealed before me as they stand revealed before the creator. From that time onward I looked and beheld deep secrets and wonderful mysteries, Before a man thinks in secret, I see his thought; before he acts, I see his act. There is nothing in heaven above or deep within the earth concealed from me.[157]

Following the metamorphosis, Enoch becomes a mighty, awesome celestial being, Metatron, the Prince of the Countenance. His form, position, and inner perception are semidivine. Enoch-Metatron becomes the bearer of divine wisdom and thus comprehends both revealed and concealed levels of reality. In this status, he sits on a heavenly throne, and judges the heavenly dwellers:

> At first I sat upon a great throne at the door of the seventh palace, and I judged all the denizens of the heights on the authority of the Holy One, blessed be he.[158]

Enoch-Metatron welcomes the Merkavah seekers who ascend to heaven, such as Rabbi Ishmael, and the "Other" Aher, "who came to behold the vision of the chariot." Misled by the dramatic transformation of Enoch, Aher wrongly concludes: "There are indeed two powers in heaven."[159] In this way, he fails to understand that Enoch-Metatron is not an independent divine power, but rather an agent directed by God. In his new position, Enoch-Metatron acts not only as a guide and a mediator to the ascenders to the chariot, but also reveals celestial mysteries and future events to them, in a process perhaps analogous to King Enmeduranki's patronage of the bārû cult. For example, after he shows Rabbi Ishmael all the heavenly sites, archives, and secrets, he discloses to him the heavenly tablets and explains in detail how to read, understand, and behold their secrets:

> Metatron said to me: "Come and I will show you the curtain of the Omnipresent which is spread before the Holy One, blessed be he." . . . I went and he showed them to me with his finger, like a father teaching his sons the letters of the Torah.[160]

In this way, Enoch-Metatron's role as a link between humanity and God becomes clear. He mediates between the two realms, explains God's secrets, deciphers their hidden meanings, and reveals them to other accomplished members of the Merkavah circle.

We can conclude, it seems, that Enoch's transformation from a human being to the divine power Metatron, is depicted in *3 Enoch* by evoking and appropriating a mythological model drawn from the Mesopotamian tradition. Many themes related to Enmeduranki's transformation in a mythological context, present Enoch's essentially mystical metamorphosis. His human status is elevated by the divine, and he is able to join the celestial sphere as an angelic being seated on a heavenly throne. He receives heavenly emblems of power and authority which manifest his elevated status. He undergoes an external physical transformation, which coincides with an ability to discern the hidden meaning of visions. Enoch-Metatron's ability to decode divine mysteries corresponds to the ancient mythological pattern. Unlike the

Mesopotamian mythological king, however, he does not relay on divinatory methods but is inspired by divine wisdom.

As we have seen, the ancient mythological pattern of transformation which leads to attainment of divine mysteries resurfaces and acquires new implications in *3 Enoch*. Other Hekhalot and Merkavah accounts do not display such an explicit affinity with the ancient mythical model, but can be said to be structured in a similar pattern. In its original mythological setting the mythological model of transformation enables a human being, King Enmeduranki, to attain mysteries of the gods through methods of divination.

In *3 Enoch*, Enoch-Metatron experiences a transformation which entails the attainment of divine wisdom. In other passages of Hekhalot mysticism, a process of transformation results in the ability to behold and interpret divine mysteries and revelations, as we have seen in chapter 2. The mythological pattern of transformation is part of the mystical context. Cultivated and achieved through inner experiences and spiritual development, a transformation in awareness and consciousness enables the adepts of the Merkavah to behold meanings of divine secrets as their human perception matches that of the divine. Accomplished visionaries are depicted as sitting in heaven. They are placed in front of the throne of God, a position which demonstrates their new spiritual status and abilities, gaze at the Merkavah, and behold the King's beauty:

> . . . the Ophannim of might embrace him, the Cherubim of majesty kiss him, the living creatures raise him up, the morning star dances before him, and the Hashmal sings before him, and the wind of living splendor raises him up, until they lift him up and set him down before the throne of glory; And he beholds and sees the king at his beauty. . .[161]

Following this stage the mystics descend to the human realm to give testimony of revelations and visions before all members of their mystical circle. In this way, they bridge Heaven and Earth in a very similar way to both Enmeduranki and Enoch.

CONCLUSION

This chapter examined how the spiritual journey is articulated in several Hekhalot and Merkavah literary traditions. Three main aspects were treated: the image of the Hekhalot "ideal mystic," the voyage, and the transformation at its end. As the discussion demonstrated, these aspects of the spiritual-conceptual path are often stated using a mythological language involving pictorial images, concrete metaphors, and figurative expressions, as well as themes and patterns rooted in Mesopotamian and biblical mythology.

An indirect exegetical dimension is also of great significance in this presentation. Mythological images in Hekhalot and Merkavah mysticism are not elucidated by midrashic or philosophical methods, nor are they deciphered in the symbolic manner, frequently used in later kabbalistic texts. Instead, the new context seem to infuse ancient mythological themes with new meanings and with alternative connotations so that, effectively, they come to express mystical content. Embedded in the Hekhalot and Merkavah mystical imagination are mythological images and specific themes rooted in historical-textual traditions and sources. These elements resurface in a different setting to present new spiritual notions in the Judaism of late antiquity. They offer eloquent expressions of a spiritual-contemplative process of crossing conceptual boundaries. They convey a mystical, inner reality as they describe the visionaries' stages of mental-spiritual progress and awareness. It appears, thus, that collective, ancient mythological themes and patterns of expression are remodeled and reapplied in Hekhalot and Merkavah mysticism to give expression to subjective, mystical notions which by their nature, perhaps, stand beyond clear verbal expression and familiar vocabulary.

5

The Concept of God: Mystical and Mythological Dimensions

INTRODUCTION

Abstract images of spirit and soul are employed to express the essence of God in Hekhalot and Merkavah mysticism. Many statements, likewise, convey God's inconceivable and sublime nature, beyond human or angelic perception. Other descriptions, in sharp contrast, denote the divine in figurative, tangible, and corporeal images. God is portrayed as an anthropomorphic mighty king. Draped in regal garments, wearing a royal crown, God sits on a lofty throne in the celestial realm, holding the signet ring of Heaven and Earth in his hand. His magnificent palaces, majestic thrones, and royal chariots substantiate his greatness and affirm his supremacy. Huge in body and size, beaming with radiance, glory, and beauty, God reigns from above while other divine beings praise him, exalt his name and, in unison, accept his absolute authority. These two conflicting images of God, the abstract and the concrete, are already evident in the biblical and midrashic traditions.[1] In Hekhalot and Merkavah mysticism we find them integrated in a mystical context and reconciled by spiritual exegesis.

This complex presentation of God, both abstract and concrete, is the focus of this chapter. It suggests that the tangible depiction of a figurative God is not in conflict with an abstract conception of a transcendent, spiritual deity. Rather, the concrete portrayal expresses the concept of God in a mythological fashion through pictorial images and visual language. In addition, specific Near Eastern mythological patterns and imagery, rooted in biblical and Mesopotamian traditions, are reintegrated in various descriptions in order to convey God's absolute mastery and his infinite nature. These include, for example, enormous physical size, exclusive kingship, majestic appearance, and tangible supremacy.

This concrete depiction of God is incorporated into the mystical context of the Hekhalot and Merkavah literature and seems to be interpreted through a mystical-exegetical lens. Those Merkavah adepts who come to possess an ability to behold divine visions with an "understanding of the heart" can look at manifestations of God's tangible kingdom and his anthropomorphic image and recognize God's spiritual powers and true essence of soul and spirit. Thus, I will suggest that the two seemingly conflicting descriptions of God, the abstract and concrete, appear to be complementary from the exegetical perspective of the Hekhalot and Merkavah mystics.

This chapter will examine these topics in further detail. It will demonstrate the manner in which the concept of God is asserted by evoking both mythological forms of expression as well as specific themes rooted in biblical and Mesopotamian traditions. The discussion will be divided into three sections. The first will examine descriptive illustrations of God's kingship. The second will analyze manifested figurative images of God. The third will demonstrate how such representations are decoded by mystical exegesis.

MYSTICAL-MYTHICAL KINGDOM

> Who is like you in heaven and on earth?
> Holy in heaven and holy on earth.
> He is a holy King, he is a blessed King,
> He is a mighty King over the entire Merkavah.[2]

Distinct views, present particularly in Deuteronomistic and priestly sources of the Hebrew bible, negate a figurative conception of YHWH, emphasizing instead the divine's transcendence and his verbal, auditory manifestation. These sources reflect a tendency to shun any kind of personal or anthopomorphic language when referring to God. They also disassociate him from specific cultic locations, and refrain from mentioning any relationship of possession between God and his dwelling place.[3] An avoidance of such mythic imagery is not, however, a sole characteristic of the biblical corpus. Concrete, corporeal conceptions of God are introduced in a variety of biblical traditions. Non and pre-Deuteronomistic sources, as well as later works including prophetic and post exilic, priestly traditions, evidently utilize figurative, tangible language and imagery in their depictions of God.[4]

It is such mythic depictions which are often selected and applied in Hekhalot and Merkavah mysticism, and are evident in many of its narrations. Mythological forms of expression were accepted, it seems, as valid ways of articulating its concept of the divine. Thus we see that in Hekhalot and Merkavah mysticism a dominant concept of God is that of a mighty, anthropomorphic king.[5] Moreover, the notions of his kingship is not conceived as an abstract metaphor or as a symbolic concept. Instead, it is presented as a concrete reality manifested in several primary ways. God truly resides in heaven, many accounts affirm. His illustrious palaces, awesome thrones, royal chariots, extensive royal court, and absolute authority over other divine powers, make evident his greatness and affirm his supremacy in a visible, tangible fashion. Following are examples of such representations.

Palaces and Royal Court

> In seven places TWTRWSYY YHWH, God of Israel, dwells
> chamber within chamber, and at the gate of each palace
> are eight doorkeepers, four at the right of the lintel,
> and four at the left of the lintel.[6]

Mythological Patterns

A common mythological convention of the Mesopotamian and related traditions is the use of metaphors of human kingship to denote notions of authority and superiority.[7] Divine qualities of transcendence and supremacy are often expressed by images of the gods as lofty, cosmic kings. These images emphasize their exalted position and might in the super terrestrial regions of the cosmos. The gods reign from on high. They reside in heaven in celestial palaces, characterized in several ways.

The heavenly palaces confirm the supremacy of the high God.[8] They are not conceived as earthly temples, built by human beings as places of worship, but rather as structures designed to function as dwellings for the gods. Textual details in various sources often emphasize these aspects. For example, in the fifth tablet of *Enumah Elish*, the god Marduk refers to the private quarters of his abode as he plans to build his temple. He also speaks of this temple as a tangible verification of his powers:

> I shall make a house to be a luxurious dwelling for myself,
> And I shall found my cult centre within it,
> And I shall establish my private quarters and confirm my kingship.[9]

Similarly, the goddess Ishtar's palace is asserted as her private abode, as Etana and the eagle discover when they reach her heavenly house:

> I saw a house with a window that [had no] seal.
> I . . . went inside.
> Sitting therein was a [young woman];
> She had the dignity of a crown, and was fair of countenance.
> A throne had been set for her and the ground around it

> had been trodden down.
> For at the base of the throne [fierce] lions were ly[ing]. [10]

A parallel mythic conception of palaces is prominent in Ugaritic mythology. The palace of Baal, for instance manifests his hierarchical position. The god El's palace is depicted as a seven-room house in which he hides from the furious goddess Anat.[11]

Palaces of the gods are often situated at the heavenly end of the cosmic pole.[12] They are frequently considered as archetypal models for earthly temples. For example, Gudea, the king of the city of Lagash, builds his earthly temple in accordance with "the holy stars" or "the heavenly plan" revealed to him by the god Ningirsu.[13] Celestial palaces are also perceived as situated parallel to temples on Earth. Descriptions in *Enumah Elish* illustrate this connection, depicting the earthly temple in Babylon as parallel to the heavenly palace, *Esharra*.[14]

An elaborate administrative system serves the high god in his palace and manages his affairs. A divine staff is responsible for various chores, duties, and rituals.[15] In addition, various cosmic and natural aspects as well as abstract moral concepts are personified. They are represented by minor divine beings cast as God's helpers in the celestial realm. For example, in Mesopotamian mythology the god Ishkur (Adad) embodies the power of storms. The god Gibil (Girra) represents fire in all its aspects. The god Nannna is the moon god. The god Utu personifies the power of Righteousness and Justice.[16] In Canaanite myths, in a similar way, abstract notions such as Holiness (*qds*), Justice (*msr*), and Righteousness (*sdq*), are represented by specific deities.[17]

In biblical sources Yahweh is often viewed as a mighty king, ruling over the cosmos from his palace.[18] These sources also reveal various details concerning God's palace, delineated as both his heavenly dwelling and a manifestation of his powers. The principal Hebrew term for Yahweh's residence is palace (*hekhal*, היכל).[19] The term is used to denote both a human-king's royal residence (e.g., 1 Kings 21:1; 2 Kings 20:18, 39:7), and Yahweh's residence (e.g., Mic. 1:2; Hab. 2:20; Ps. 11:4, 18:7; 36:9). In his examination of temple and community in ancient Israel, M. Haran thus affirms:

> Just as every temporal king, and indeed any man, has his own domicile, so the divine king, in whose shadow the community finds protection, has a residence of his own. And in this dwelling place, just as in every luxurious house, the master of the residence is provided with all his "needs." . . . In this dwelling place, moreover, the master of the residence

> has his own servants, the priests, who care for his necessities and keep the house in order—just as any reigning monarch has his palace servants and retinue surrounding him constantly and performing his order.[20]

Connection between the temple as Yahweh's earthly dwelling and the heaven as his celestial abode are evident in postexilic sources, such as psalm 48, which discerns Mount Zion as an *axis mundi* and God's temple as situated on its top.[21] Aspects of God's royalty are often associated with a divine court, administrative royal bureaucracy, divine attendants, and officials: "divine assembly," "assembly of holy beings," "council," "assembly," "hosts," "servants," "attendants" are several applications of such designations.[22]

Hekhalot and Merkavah Mysticism

God's heavenly palaces (Hekhalot, **היכלות**) are associated with the mystical conception of God and the divine sphere.[23] In many accounts, however, these palaces are also envisioned as concrete structures situated in a mythological realm in which God, the king, resides. Following mythological patterns of expression, God's royal palaces attest to his high position, kingship, and supremacy. They are depicted as heavenly abodes, or as "princely households," which contain rooms, doorways, thresholds, archives, and courts:[24]

> In seven palaces TWTRWSYY YHWY, God of Israel, dwells chamber within chamber, and at the gate of each palace are eight doorkeepers, four at the right of the lintel, and four at the left of the lintel.[25]

Various accounts of God's realm reintroduce themes from Ezekiel's throne vision. Yet, in contrast to descriptions in Ezekiel, in which the divine is perceived in an open cosmic setting, God in Hekhalot and Merkavah mysticism is often enclosed in a celestial residential palace which contains rooms, closed doors, and courts as Rabbi Ishmael attests:

> When I ascended to the height to behold the vision of the chariot, I entered six palaces, one inside the other, and when I reached the door of the seventh palace, I paused in prayer before the Holy One, blessed be he.[26]

Other references to doorways and entrances of God's various quarters are mentioned. In *Hekhalot Rabbati*, for example, the angel Anafi'el "keeps the keys of the palaces of the heaven of Aravot." His responsibility as a doorkeeper is described as well:

> . . . when a man wishes to descend to the Merkavah, the angel Anafi'el opens the doors of the entrance to the seventh heaven and that man enters and stands at the threshold of the entrance to the seventh heaven. . . .[27]

The angel Dumi'el, similarly, is depicted as posted at the right side of the entrance to the sixth palace. A passage in the *Genizah,* likewise, speaks of God's palace in which he hides in inner rooms.[28]

Other features demonstrate further correspondence between descriptions in Hekhalot and Merkavah mysticism and conventional patterns rooted in Near Eastern mythology. The seventh palace of God is situated at the heavenly end of the cosmic pole. Thus, we hear of "the heavenly ladder with its one end on earth and one end on the right foot of the throne of glory."[29] God's heavenly palace in the seventh heaven, *raqia* seems to be a model for the earthly temple which is placed parallel to it:

> Raise your eyes to heaven opposite your house of prayer in the hour when you say before me: "holy." Teach them: I have no joy in all my world that I created but when your eyes are raised to my eyes and my eyes are raised to your eyes.[30]

An administrative system is also part of the royal celestial court. Official, divine powers organize the palace's daily functions and activities. These include, for example, gatekeepers, "serving angels," "angels of revelations," the Ophanim, Cherubim, Seraphim, Galgalim, and other groups.[31] The palace routine is detailed. Every day God sits on the throne of judgment in the celestial law court.[32] Three times a day God descends from the eighth heaven to the seventh heaven where his throne is located.[33] Every day, when dawn approaches, God blesses the living creatures.[34] We find detailed reports of other activities inside the palace, conducted by divine workers. Angels are in charge of heavenly archives and their scrolls. One such angel is Radweri'el, who "takes out the scroll box, in which the book of records is kept . . . breaks the seals of the scroll box, opens it, takes out the scrolls and puts them in the hand of the Holy One."[35] Serving angels make crowns of life, setting precious stones and pearls into them, while others mix all kinds of perfumes and prepare wine, spices, and fragrances for righteous people in future days.[36]

Aspects of nature are personified and associated with the domination of angelic masters:

> These are the names of the princes who guide the world: Gabri'el, the angel of fire; Baradi'el, the angel of hail; Ruhi'el,

> who is in charge of wind; Baraqi'el, who is in charge for lightning; Zaami'el, who is in charge of whirlwind; Ziqi'el, who is in charge of comets; Zi'iel, who is in charge of tremors; Zaapi'el, who is in charge of hurricane; Raami'el, who is in charge of thunder; Raasi'el, who is in charge of earthquakes, Salgi'el, who is in charge of snow; Matari'el, who is in charge of rain; Simsi'el, who is in charge of day; Laili'el, who is in charge of night; Galgalli'el, who is in charge of the orb of the sun; Opanni'el, who is in charge of the disk of the moon; Kokabi'el who is in charge of the stars; Rahati'el, who is in charge of the constellations.[37]

God's courtroom is represented as concrete. Likewise, abstract concepts, such as Justice, Mercy, and Truth are personified as autonomous divine figures, who act as God's assistants. His servants Justice, Mercy, and Truth, thus, stand beside him as attendants in the celestial court:

> When the Holy One, blessed be He,
> sits on the throne of judgment,
> Justice stands on his right hand, Mercy on his left,
> and Truth stands directly facing him.[38]

These concrete heavenly palaces and the active royal household do not appear to be presented as symbolic images. Instead, they are introduced as part of the Hekhalot and Merkavah mystical reality, which can be witnessed and explored by human observers. The descenders to the chariot enter doors of the palaces, step into divine quarters, and behold YHWH, God of Israel who dwells inside. Rabbi Akiva and Rabbi Ishmael are prime examples. Rabbi Ishmael's attests: "I saw the King of the Kings sitting on a high and exalted throne, and his servants were attending Him on His right and on His left."[39] Rabbi Akiva attests: ". . . when I went and asked this question before the throne of glory, I saw Him, YHWH, God of Israel. "[40]

In various religious-mystical writings mystical experiences are often characterized as experiences of a "different reality," in R. Otto's words, which is distinct in essence from the mundane, phenomenological reality of everyday life.[41] In Hekhalot and Merkavah mysticism, such a conceptual "different reality" assumes tangible form and visible substance. Wondrous divine beings with numerous eyes, fantastic winged creatures, and radiant sacred beasts with human, lion, bull, and eagle faces, populate the heavenly domain roaming around the celestial upper court.[42] Some of these images are inspired by Ezekiel's throne vision, which derived several of its images from Mesopotamian tradition, as scholars have long demonstrated.[43] Hekhalot and

Merkavah accounts, in turn, both revive and reintegrate such images into their mystical context. The mythical beasts appear to be animated in the mind of the visionaries as visible aspects of the mystical "different reality." Adepts who reach God's heavenly household, encounter these creatures as part of their experience:

> Rabbi Akiva said: "when I ascended and gazed upon God,
> I saw all the creatures that are in the roadways of heaven,
> their length above and their width below,
> their width below and their length above."[44]

THRONES

> . . . because upon a high and exhaulted, frightful and terrible
> throne do you reside in the chambers of the lofty palace.[45]

MYTHOLOGICAL PATTERNS

The throne itself is another concrete, visible manifestation of divine status and authority in Mesopotamian mythological traditions. A Sumerian hymn to the god Enlil elucidates this notion, making evident the link between the god's throne and his sovereign power:

> Enlil, whose command is far reaching,
> Lofty his word (and) holy. . . .
> When father Enlil seats himself broadly on the holy dais,
> on the lofty dais,
> When Nunammir carries out to supreme perfection
> lordship and kingship.
> The earth-gods bow down willingly before him.
> The annuna humble themselves before him.[46]

Thrones are often conceived as charged with the power of divine kingship.[47] An Ugaritic text, thus, describes how both "Divine Thrones" and "Divine Seats" receive various forms of cultic devotion.[48] As principal personifications of divine essence, thrones are often depicted as surrounded with a glorious aura of light and brightness.[49] References to empty thrones representing divinity appear also in several accounts. These thrones are set up for the gods, as visible symbols of authority, so that they may sit on them when circumstances allow.

The iconography of the ancient Near East parallels these literary references, as scholars have noted. Empty thrones appear in Mesopotamian iconography from the period before the Iron Age. T. N. D. Mettinger has denoted a pictorial image of such a throne on an Assyrian cylinder seal from the eleventh and twelfth centuries B.C.E.[50] Similar images are also found in later periods. A series of representations of winged empty thrones, known as the "sphinx thrones," are another example of this image. An ivory model of a winged throne from the Late Bronze Age was found in Megiddo. Its outer wings can be clearly seen; the inner wings seem to be located under the throne.[51]

Sphinx thrones were found as well around Sidon, Tyre, Syria Larissa, and Beth-Shean. As scholars have observed, in several cases thrones themselves were objects of adoration and worship.[52] Several sources mention the position of "throne-bearer" assigned to a divine being whose duty was to serve the throne. For example, Sumerian sources speak of the god Igalima, the throne-bearer of the god Ningirsu.[53] The importance of occupying a throne, as a symbol of kingship and order, is apparent in several sources such as the standard Babylonian version of the *Anzu* myth. In this account the rebel-figure Anzu is able to take control of the god Enlil's power and sovereign position because Enlil, temporarily, left his throne empty and unprotected.[54]

An additional attribute occasionally associated with divine thrones in Mesopotamian mythology is their mobile quality. In a hymn to the god Enlil, his throne is imagined as a dynamic object hovering in heaven:

> Enlil . . .
> Made permanent his great princeship;
> Places the crown upon his holy locks.
> He sets up his dais in the mountain mist.
> He rotates it in heaven like a rainbow,
> He makes it roam about like a floating cloud.[55]

Biblical accounts often proclaim the throne of God as representing his kingship, as many examples attest.[56] The prophet Micaiah ben-Imlah testifies: "I saw the Lord sitting on his throne with all the host of heaven standing beside him" (I Kings 22:19). Daniel sees thrones that were set in place and the Ancient One on his fiery throne (Daniel 7: 9–10). The prophet Ezekiel describes: ". . . something like a throne in appearance like sapphire" (Ezekiel 1: 26; 10: 1). Various psalms express a similar conception of thrones, the manifestation of God's kingship, as psalm 104:19, for example, suggests: "The Lord has established his throne in the heavens." In a similar manner, the throne functions as a concrete symbol of kingship and divine order after God's victory over the forces of chaos, as, for example, in Psalm 93: "The Lord is King . . . he has established the world; it shall never be moved; your throne is established from the old; you are from everlasting" (1–2).

Of importance, too, is the empty cherubim-throne in the cult of the First Temple in Jerusalem (1 Kings 6: 23–28).[57] Mettinger has clearly demonstrated the role of the cherubim-throne in the cult of Yahweh Sabaoth in Solomon's temple. As he has shown, the cherubim-throne embodied the conception of kingship, in a fashion parallel to the Near Eastern model. On it God was invisibly enthroned as a king, as his divine epithet, "he who is enthroned upon the cherubim" (יושב הכרובים), affirms. This empty throne, above the Ark, has been characterized by Mettinger as an example of "sacred emptiness" since it generates in the onlooker the mental image of a deity as a king on his throne.[58]

Hekhalot and Merkavah Mysticism

A mythological treatment of the throne is notable in Hekhalot and Merkavah mysticism. The "throne" (כסא הכבוד), is often conceived as a concrete image of absolute power and authority. It proves and demonstrates God's sovereignty, as the following wording from *Hekhalot Rabbati* indicates:

> . . . because upon a high and exhaulted, frightful and terrible throne do you reside in the chambers of the lofty palace.[59]

God's throne, a visible sign of divine power, is in many cases personified and functions almost as an independent being. At times it also receives some form of cultic devotion, which is set apart from that of God. Praise and hymns are presented directly to the throne. Thus, we read in *Hekhalot Rabbati*:

> Sing, sing exalted seat! Shout, shout for joy, precious vessel which was made with wonderful wonder. Gladden, the king who is on you . . .[60]

Similar to images of the dynamic or winged thrones from ancient Near Eastern sources, the throne in Hekhalot and Merkavah mysticism is also a mobile object, hovering in heaven:

> Your throne hovers since the hour when you inserted the peg of the weaving of the web, on which the completion of the world and its exhaltation stand, many years, generations without end. And he still does not rest his feet upon the ground of the Aravot heaven but like a hovering bird, he stands underneath you.[61]

The throne is set up for God, and, as a personified object, it invites him to sit down upon it. Thus, God's supremacy is again substantiated in a concrete fashion by an icon of his throne, available at all time:

> And three times daily, the throne of glory prostrates itself and say to you: "ZHRRY'L, YHWH, God of Israel, be honored

> and sit down upon me, glorious King,
> as your burden is pleasant for me and not heavy."[62]

An important task of some angels is the bearing of the throne, P. Schäfer has noted.[63] These angels are often addressed as the "bearers," or the servants of the throne and "[all of them] stand crowned under the throne of glory." They lift it high, "with powerful, strength and might."[64] The animated throne, as well, joins the angels in their praises and exaltations and its hymn is the climax of the heavenly songs of glorification:

> . . . like the singing voice of the throne of glory,
> which mentions and exalts the glorious King,
> abandance of voices and much great uproar,
> and many voices were helping him, the throne of glory,
> to assist him, to strengthen him, when he sings and praises
> Him, the Mighty One of Jacob,
> as is written: "Holy, holy, holy" (Isaiah 6:3)[65]

God in several descriptions recognizes the magnitude of occupying his throne. He pledges not to leave it and vows by "the throne of my splendor, which consists of my honor, which I have not left since it was created, and [I] will not leave in eternity."[66]

Chariots

> When He rides upon a swift cherub,
> between placing one foot on its back and
> placing the other foot on it,
> He perceives 18,000 worlds at a glance;
> He discerns and sees into all of them.[67]

Mythical Patterns

In written texts as well as in iconographical sources from the ancient Near East, gods and goddesses are often visualized as riding chariots as they travel. They ride over land and sea in their chariots, which often have meteorological associations, such as clouds, storms, and winds.[68] According to a seventh-century B.C.E. document, the god Utu is thought to ride his chariot across the sky by day, and through the "interior of heaven" by night.[69] In a hymn to the god Iskur, he is illustrated as the "lord who rides the storm." The god Adad is known by the title "rider of clouds." In one of the later texts of *Atrahasis*, the Babylonian flood story, the god Adad rides on the four winds as the flood approachs.[70] In Ugarit sources, the god Baal is often entitled "the rider of the clouds." He is described as riding on a winged chariot.[71]

Biblical traditions often refer to corresponding images such as winds, cherubs, clouds, and chariots in their depiction of the riding God.[72] Psalm 68: 5, for example, introduces Yahweh, the "rider over the steppes" (רכב ערבות). Psalm 18: 11 portrays Yahweh riding on the wind, an image which appears again in depictions of divine chariots in Ezekiel 1: 10 as well as in Psalm 65:12. Similarly, Psalm 18:10 affirms: "He rode upon a cherub (כרוב) and flew. He sped upon the wings of the wind" (כנפי רוח). The notion of God riding a chariot is clearly depicted in Habakkuk 3: 8 and 15 (רכב במרכבה).

Hekhalot and Merkavah Mysticism

Hekhalot and Merkavah mysticism associates the term "chariot" (מרכבה) with a mystical concept of the divine sphere.[83] Several descriptions, nonetheless, embrace mythological images of chariots, presented as vehicles in which God rides as he travels the cosmos. In various texts, God's concrete chariots are mentioned and identified. One example is found in *3 Enoch*:

> How many chariots has the Holy One, blessed be he?
> He has the chariot of the cherubim. . . .
> He has the chariot of the wind . . .
> He has the chariot of the clouds. . . .[74]

Another account in *3 Enoch* reports in detail the act of riding the chariot: God mounts the chariot, places his two feet on it, one after the other, and rides in heaven while glancing at his kingdom:

> When He rides upon a swift cherub, between placing one foot on its back, and placing the other foot on it, he perceives 18,000 worlds at a glance; he discerns and sees into all of them.[75]

References to Rikbi'el (רכביאל), the angel in charge of God's chariot, attest the tangible perception of God's chariots as instrument of transportation. These references give an explanation based on the angel's Hebrew name, Rikbi'el, "God's vehicle," or "God's chariot":

> Why is his name called Rikbi'el?
> Because he is in charge of the wheels of the chariot
> and they are committed to his keeping."[76]

The Yoke of God's Kingdom

> . . . thousands of thousands of thousands
> and myriads of myriads of myriads
> give praise and exaltation to your
> great, mighty and awesome name.

> Before you stand all the mighty ones.
> Who are powerful in praise and in chant.[77]

MYTHOLOGICAL PATTERNS

The divine realm is shared by many monarchical deities, according to Mesopotamian mythology. They are responsible for various aspects of nature and portions of the cosmos. They also embody abstract moral concepts. In addition they control particular city states and nations.[78] Each one of the gods is considered divine, yet they are not equal in power and hierarchical position. Instead, they are subordinate to one high, supreme god, the head of the pantheon. The royal title, "King of the Kings," used often in prayers and hymns addressed to various deities, expresses this notion of one god, superior in status and authority.[79] In an Akkadian hymn, for instance, the god Enlil, chief god of the Sumerian-Assyrio-Babylonian tradition, is entitled: "Lord of lords, king of kings."[80] An Akkadian hymn, dedicated to the god Marduk, likewise proclaims his superiority above all other gods:

> There is [none] among all the Igigi-gods
> who can boast before you.
> You have no rival above or below.
> Whatever the gods of all the inhabited world
> may have done, they cannot be like you, Lord![81]

Several sources associate divine kingship with a cosmic struggle. According to such traditions, the head of the pantheon gains his position after winning a battle in which he proves his powers, leadership, and superiority. Other deities consequently express their recognition of his kingship and proclaim their loyalty in a formal ritual. In his discussion of divine kingship, M. Weinfeld has asserted several distinct integrated actions, which form the ritual of accepting the supreme god's kingship: prostration, repetition of his names, and praise of him in unison.[82] By performing these ritualistic actions, the gods of the pantheon affirm the lofty position of their leader and accept his ultimate authority. *Enumah Elish,* as noted by Weinfeld, presents an example of such a ritual. It recounts how the god Marduk defeats the goddess Tiamat; her army fashions the cosmos and establishes order. Consequently all gods accept him as their king. They bow down, prostrate themselves before him, and address him in a speech:

> They did obeisance to him and the gods spoke to him.
> They addressed their lord Lugal-dimmer-ankin,
> "Previously the Lord was [our beloved] son.
> But now he is our king. We shall take heed of his command."[83]

To express their acceptance of his kingship, all the gods together pronounce Marduk's various names, using a threefold formula of sanctification as they bow down:

> Anshar, Lahmu, and Lahamu called his three names.
> They pronounced them to the gods, their sons.
> "We have given him each of these three names.
> Now you, pronounce his name as we did!"[84]

> The great gods assembled
> And made Marduk's destiny highest.
> They themselves did obeisance . . . .
> Thus they granted that he should exercise
> the kingship of the gods
> And confirmed for him mastery of
> the gods of heaven and earth.
> Anshar gave him another name: ASARLUHI.
> "At the mention of his name we shall bow down!
> The gods are to pay heed to what he says.
> His command is to have priority above and below."[85]

In several biblical sources, mythical imagery is utilized to depict God's kingship.[86] In addition, various of texts express God's supreme kingship in heaven by portraying divine beings who acknowledge his unequaled rule by acts of prostration, repetition of names, and praising in unison. Originally such divine groups, like "the sons of god" (בני אל בני אלים), "the council of the holy ones" "Morning Stars" (כוכבי בוקר) and the host of heaven (צבא השמים), were thought to represent independent beings, other than the one God, as scholars have demonstrated.[87] Psalm 89: 5–6, for example, illustrates this notion in its presentation of divine beings accepting YHWH as a king over the gods by praising and exulting him:

> Let the heavens praise your wonders, O Lord,
> and your faithfulness in the assembly of the holy ones.
> For who in the skies can be compared to the Lord?
> Who is like the Lord among the heavenly beings?

Psalm 29:1–2 envisions the gods giving praise and prostrating themselves before Yahweh:[88]

> Ascribe to the Lord, O heavenly beings.
> Ascribe to the Lord glory and strength.
> Ascribe to the Lord the glory of his name.
> Prostrate yourselves to the Lord when he appears in holiness.

Several other sources include similar representation of divine beings praising God, repeating his names, prostrating themselves, singing in one voice, and repeating the threefold sanctification. The prophet Isaiah sees divine beings speak to one another and praise Yahweh: "Holy holy holy is the Lord of (the heavenly) hosts" (Isa. 6: 3).[89] In Job 38: 7, members of Yahweh's council sing to him jointly: "While the morning stars sang together and all the heavenly beings shouted together." In accordance with Israel's monotheistic perspective, these independent divine beings have been transformed into ministers of the Lord or serving angels. Accordingly, the meaning of the pattern of praise has been altered as it has come to express the greatness of the one God. Nonetheless mythological themes are present. They allude to independent divine beings, who accept the kingship of the supreme god by prostration, repetition of his names, and the praise of him in unison.

Hekhalot and Merkavah Mysticism

As we examine various Hekhalot and Merkavah accounts, the ancient Near Eastern model of recognizing God's ultimate authority seems to reappear. It is possible that this mythological, ritualistic pattern gains a special significance in this literature because of the composite and mixed concept of the divine realm it depicts.[90] R. Elior has examined the nature and development of the angelic realm in the Hekhalot and Merkavah literature, noting that its extensive presentation of the angelic world is unparalleled in any other Jewish source. This literature recognizes very openly the existence of many independent divine beings other than the one God. Their traditional biblical role as God's messengers or servants is far surpassed. The Hekhalot and Merkavah angels are almost autonomous operating by God's side.[91] These divine beings, moreover, share many of God's sacred characteristics: names, attributes, features, responsibilities, and even some creative powers.

Various examples illustrate this perception. There are the "eight revered and awesome princes, who are called YHWH by the name of their King."[92] God's ineffable name is given to the angel Metatron who is called "lesser YHWH." He sits on a throne "like the throne of glory," adorned with God's crown and draped with a royal cloak. He also knows "the wisdom of this world and the wisdom of the world to come," like the Creator himself.[93] Prince Anafi'el is another example. He is crowned with "the bough of his majesty, glory, crown and brilliance and his splendor overshadows all the chambers of the highest heaven, like the creator of the world."[94] As a divine being, almost equal to God, he also keeps the divine emblems: "the signet ring of heaven and earth is in his hand."[95] In addition, there are various angels with specific divine roles and privileges, such as the Prince Hayli'el YHWH, "a prince who is able to swallow the whole world at one gulp. . . . he is in charge of the creatures." These include also "Soperi'el

YHWH who puts to death" and "Soperi'el YHWH who makes alive."[96] The angel Keruvi'el is another example of the Hekhalot tendency to offer a mythical depiction of an independent divine being, powerful in nature, who operates next to God. This angel resembles God in appearance and shares many of his powers, attributes, and qualities of holiness:

> Keruvi'el YHWH is his name, a valiant prince, full of boundless power; a majestic prince with whom is majesty; a righteous prince with whom is righteousness; a holy prince with whom is holiness; a prince glorified by thousands of hosts, a prince extolled by countless legions. At his wrath the earth quakes; at his rage camps tremble; the foundations shudder from fear of him and Arabot quakes at his rebuke. His body is full of burning coals; it is as high as the seven heavens, as broad as the seven heavens, as wide as the seven heavens. The opening of his mouth blazes like a fiery torch, and his tongue is consuming fire. His eyelashes are as the splendor of lightning. His eyes are like brilliant sparks, and his face looks like a blazing fire. A crown of holiness is on his head with the sacred name engraved upon it, from which lightning flickers. The bow of the *Shekinah* is across his shoulders.[97]

In his discussion of the angelic world in the Hekhalot literature, J. Dan observes: "the term 'angels' in its biblical meaning certainly does not apply to them, for they are powers in their own right, at least to a certain extent, and they carry the supreme holy name in their own right."[98] Although it is clear that these powerful divine beings do not share God's sovereign power, the differences between them and the supreme God in some cases are not clear. What seems apparent in the Hekhalot literature is a fear of "two authorities in heaven."[99] In this context, the nature of the angelic praises appears to be of great importance.

Hekhalot and Merkavah mysticism admits a certain correlation between God and other principal divine beings. This correlation echoes a mythological notion of a multitude of divine powers, which could obviously have been regarded as a potential threat to traditional monotheistic views, especially in light of Gnostic and other Christian and pagan influences. Therefore, Hekhalot and Merkavah mysticism, while allowing the existence of such divine beings and according them a significant role, nonetheless emphasizes their subordinate position to the one God. These divine powers are portrayed as subservient to God's control and authority in a traditional mythological pattern, similar to the one presented above. They all accept God's kingship by praising him, prostrating themselves before him, and repeating his names in unison. A passage in *Ma'ashe Merkavah* describes a heavenly ritual of exalting God and praising his name:

> ... thousands of thousands of thousands
> and myriads of myriads of myriads
> give praise and exaltation
> to your great, mighty and awesome name.
> Before you stand all the mighty ones;
> Who are powerful in praise and in chant.[100]

All creatures, including angels and other divine beings, must prostrate themselves, praise God, and affirm his eternal kingship:

> Before you, YHWH God of Israel, kneel and prostrate
> those on high and on low. Before you, YHWH God of Israel,
> Seraphim glorify and sing. Before you, YHWH God of Israel,
> Seraphim sing and rejoice. The throne of your glory praises you
> and gives you pride, and much strength and splendor.
> Before you, YHWH God of Israel,
> your servants crown you with crowns,
> and sing to you a new song. They enthrone you eternally,
> and you shall be called One forever and ever.[101]

It seems that in order to display a complete acceptance of God's kingship, all divine powers must sing together the hymns of praise. Any departure from this practice is severely punished, perhaps to avoid any potential threat to the supremacy of the one God:

> Therefore, they have intent, and hurry, and shine, and gather in fear, purity, and holiness, and they say commendation and chant, adoration and praise with one voice, with one speech, with one knowledge, with one sound. And not only this, but from them fall thousands and thousands, myriads and myraids into rivers of fire and are burned. Since when they sing songs and sanctification before the King of the Kings of Kings, there is no early and late, no one who lowers or no one who elevates. Therefore, he who sings earlier or later than his friends will be burned.[102]

These heavenly rituals are not presented simply as poetic, literary descriptions. It is the absolute duty of all creatures in heaven to engage in them, including the human visionaries who reach the upper level. All descenders to the chariot, who enter the celestial realm, are obliged to participate in the heavenly praise, accept the yoke of God's kingdom, and express their absolute obedience to him, using the threefold sanctification:

> And every knee kneels before you and every tongue testifies
> and every dignified one bows and falls down
> before you, YHWH our God.

To the glory of your name they will give honor.
And all of them will accept the yoke of your kingdom.
And you will reign over them soon, forever and ever.
Because yours is the kingdom
and you will reign in glory forever.
And I will sanctify your name great, and mighty and awesome,
holy, holy, holy. . . .[103]

This requirement for Hekhalot devotees to join in the praise of God is highlighted, perhaps, because of a new and daring option which the Hekhalot and Merkavah mysticism allows. Human beings can initiate and make an ascent to heaven to join the divine realm. They can even acquire several divine-like qualities.[104] Hekhalot and Merkavah authors, however, insist upon the adepts' obligation to praise God and accept his kingship. Thus, their presence in the celestial divine realm can in no way be interpreted as a threat to God's superior authority. For this reason, perhaps, the accounts emphasize again and again the need to declare clearly an unconditional recognition of God's supreme kingship, an obligation which is required of all creatures when they reach the divine.

A prayer in *Ma'ashe Merkavah* offers a short conclusion to this section. It expresses the magnitude of God through specific concrete elements — heavenly palaces, thrones, and chariots — which manifest his majesty and supremacy in conventional mythological patterns:

Great is your name on the entire earth.
In heavens you founded your throne.
And your dwelling place in the highest heights.
Your chariot you placed in the height of heaven,
in the pure mist.
Hosts of fire praise your glory.
Seraphim of fire stand before you.[105]

GOD'S SPIRITUAL-FIGURATIVE IMAGE

The great, mighty and fearsome, grand and powerful God,
who is hidden from the eyes of all creatures
and concealed from the serving angels,
but is revealed to Rabbi Akiva
through the work of the Merkavah.[106]

Descriptions of God's figurative image are prominent in Hekhalot and Merkavah mysticism. What we find in several accounts are two principal ways of speaking of God. One introduces the divine by referring to his body and organs and detailing their names and measurements. The second is concerned with God's other physical attributes such as his majestic radiance, personified names, regal garments, crowns, other emblems of authority and his specific physical features. This figurative pattern of representation seems to express God's transcendent and sublime attributes in mythological language and images, as the discussion below will demonstrate.

The Measure of the Divine's Body (*Shiur Komah*)

> Anyone who knows this measure
> and the praise of his Creator,
> who is covered from all people,
> is promised to be among those of the world to come.[107]

Mythological Patterns

In a variety of Near Eastern myths and iconographical presentations, deities are often depicted in an anthropomorphic or zoomorphic fashion. Through these depictions, the powers and characteristics of the deities are communicated in a direct, explicit manner. In addition to these depictions, several literary accounts reveals an alternate pattern of representation, according to which the figurative description of the form and body of the gods, paradoxically, serves to express their inaccessible, transcendent, and abstract nature. In his discussion of aniconism and anthropomorphism in the ancient Near East, R. S. Hendel has entitled this model of portrayal as "transcendent anthropomorphism," a title which clearly exemplifies a dialectical tendency to denote the deities' inaccessibility and ultimate transcendence through descriptions of their figurative or anthropomorphic manifested form.[108] Several figurative and concrete images are often used: anthropomorphic or zoomorphic form, fiery essence, huge cosmic size, lists of bodily parts and their names. At times names of different deities are equated with these bodily parts.

An effective example is the depiction of the god Marduk in *Enuma Elish*. An account of Marduk's birth, in tablet I: 79–100, presents speculations on his nature. The passage describes his anthropomorphic form and stature, relates the enormous size of his figure, and asserts his unique bodily features and fiery essence. These corporeal characteristics of the god Marduk, the text attests, are far beyond human perception. They are distinguished as "impossible to understand, too difficult to perceive" and express, it seems, his inconceivable nature. Thus, the elaborate portrayal of the god's manifested anthropomorphic form and stature proclaims his nonhuman features and his imperceptibility:

> Proud was his form, piercing his stature,
> Mature his emergence, he was powerful from the start

> Elevated far above them. He was superior in every way.
> His limbs were ingeniously made beyond comprehension,
> Impossible to understand, too difficult to perceive.
> Four were his eyes, four were his ears;
> When his lips moved, fire blazed forth.
> The four ears perceived everything.
> Highest among the gods, his form was outstanding.
> His limbs were very long, his height outstanding.[109]

The details presented clearly refer to Marduk's visible stature and to specific corporeal characteristics such as limbs, organs, and appearance. Yet a quality of inscrutability is applied to the god through the descriptions of his huge body, specific organs, and luminous fiery essence. These seemingly recognizable features exceed both human form and normal human perception. They, thus, emphasize Marduk's inaccessible, unknowable mysterious essence, "made beyond comprehension." In addition, the god Marduk is exalted above the other gods to the degree that his body transcends their anthropomorphism. He is 'other' from the ordinary gods insofar as he is 'other' from human form.[110]

An earlier example, found in the Sumerian Gudea cylinders, presents a similar dialectical pattern of "transcendent anthropomorphism."[111] In the context of complex cultic and ritual issues, the Gudea cylinders introduce a simple narrative plot. According to Cylinder A, the man Gudea, in his dream, receives a vision of the god Ningirsu who commands the construction of a new temple for himself. Gudea recounts his dream for interpretation, describing the appearance of the god Ningirsu, whom, at this point, he does not recognize. In this description specific figurative images are applied. Gudea describes the god's cosmic, gigantic form. He also portrays the god in an anthropomorphic and a zoomorphic manner, as a man, encompassing a god's face, an eagle's arms and a body of storm:

> In the dream there was a man as gigantic as heaven, as gigantic as the earth. According to his head he was a god; according to his arms he was the eagle; according to his lower body he was a storm; on his right and left lions were standing; he commanded me to build his house; his (precise) intent I did not understand.[112]

Explicit corporeal, visible images undoubtedly predominate in this portrayal. Yet, paradoxically, these express the god's imperceptible nature, which Gudea, a human being, cannot fathom. As A. Livingstone has observed, in Mesopotamian mystical and mythological descriptions such as this, the figurative delineation of the god's form presents "the ineffable nature of the divine by offering descriptions which are only barely conceivable."[113] Figurative details regarding Ningirsu's gigantic anthropomorphic and zoomprphic form, his god's face, eagle's arms and his body of storm, do not intend to reduce the god to a familiar form. Rather, they give expression to his unknowable, inaccessible nature. The imagery used also highlights the full dialectic of the "transcendent anthropomorphism" pattern by equating the god's tangible, corporeal body with the image of the storm, which denotes his abstract, limitless, nature.

A Mesopotamian hymn to the god Ninurta, from the first millennium B.C.E., reflects an additional example. This hymn exalts the god Ninurta by portraying his body, to which several parallel dimensions are ascribed: an anthropomorphic form, cosmic size, a list of organs, and the specific names of these organs, associated with various divine beings and with aspects of the cosmos. The hymn includes a series of sentences, each containing a reference to an organ of Ninurta's body and its name which is aligned to the various gods of the pantheon:

> O Lord, your face is like the sun god.
> Your eyes, O Lord are Enlil and Ninlil.
> The pupils of your eyes are Gula and Belit-ili.
> The irises of your eyes are the twins Sin and Shamash.
> The lashes of your eyes are the rays of the sun god. . . .
> The appearance of your mouth, O Lord, is Ishtar of the stars.
> Anu and Antum are your lips, your command.
> Your tongue (?) is Pabilsag of the above.
> The roof of your mouth, O Lord, is the vault
> of heaven and earth, your divine abode.[114]

This portrayal is illustrative of the "transcendent anthropomorphism" model. Ninurta is depicted in what seems to be human form. Specific features such as the god's eyes, pupils, irises, lashes, mouth, lips, and tongue are mentioned. This presentation, however, has no coherent meaning or sense. Instead, it transcends human comprehension and conveys Ninurta's uniqueness and transcendence.

The god's corporeal features are of infinite cosmic dimension, compared in size to Heaven and Earth. It is also important to note that Ninurta's seemingly anthropomorphic body is totally different from a human form. The hymn equates Ninutra's bodily features with various deities and thus seems to ascribe to him a metaphysical, all-encompassing stature. The pattern of correlating parts of one god's body with other gods is probably a theological attempt to synthesize diverse gods into the image of a supreme single god, who embraces the sum total of their qualities. This aspect, however, is denoted through the figurative depiction of Ninirta's revealed body, which conveys his omnipotent, ultimate nature, imperceptible to human's comprehension. "Nintuta's body is transcendent," attests Hendel, "his body is inconceivable as his authority is all encompassing."[115]

Central views present in biblical traditions, particularly in Deuteronomistic sources, clearly negate the visible, figurative features of God, emphasizing instead the divine's transcendence and his verbal, auditory manifestation.[116] Yet, an avoidance of figurative imagery is not a common characteristic of the biblical corpus.[117] Sufficient evidence demonstrates that a corporeal conception of God was acceptable in a variety of biblical traditions.[118] Non- and pre-Deuteronomistic sources, as well as later works including prophetic and postexilic, priestly traditions, evidently utilize figurative, iconic, anthropomorphic imagery in their conceptions of God. The verbal expressions found in these sources do not endorse an acceptance of worshiping iconic cult statues.[119] Various linguistic expressions, nonetheless, presuppose a "mental anthropomorphic" conception of the divine.[120]

Aligned with the notion of "mental iconography" is the employment of the "transcendent anthropomorphism" model in several biblical presentations of God. According to the observation of Hendel, earlier biblical descriptions, clearly non- and pre-Deuteronomistic, exercise a model of "transcendent anthropomorphism" especially in their "God sighting" episodes. These sources confirm the visible presence of Yahweh, described as having an anthropomorphic form. This vision, nonetheless, entails fatal danger to most human beings, as the following examples demonstrate. In Genesis 32:30, Jacob attests: "For I have seen God face-to-face and yet my life is preserved." In Exodus 33:20, God announces to Moses: " You cannot see my face, for no one shall see my face and live." The prophet Isaiah declares:" I am lost for I am a man of unclean lips . . . yet my eyes have seen the King, the Lord of hosts" (Isa. 6:5). A similar perception is raised by Maanoah in Judges 13: 22: "We surely shall die for we have seen God." "Like the body of Marduk, Ninurta, and Ningirsu" asserts Hendel, "Yahewh's body was believed to be incommensurate with mundane human existence: it has a different degree of being than human bodies."[121]

The deadly effect of seeing the body of God is rooted in the biblical conception of purity and danger, according to which that which is holy is also dangerous. As the most holy, God's form is a source of extreme danger and the vision of it is impossible to most humans. The dialectic of holiness and danger, thus, exemplifies the model of "transcendent anthropomorphism" in these biblical traditions. Paradoxically, the manifested divine body conveys a conception of God, who is inaccessible and inscrutable. In Hendel's words: "it is a transcendent anthropomorphism not in its form but in its effect, approachable only by the most holy, and absent in material form in the cult."[122]

This perspective indicates tension between the manifested God's form and the human's ability to behold it. Examining theophanies in biblical traditions, J. Barr suggests that the main significance of God's theophanic descriptions is not whether God is portrayed in human form but, rather, why such anthropomorphic revelations occur to specific selected individuals: "The central truth is the ability of God to assume a form and to let this form be seen by men."[123] "Nothing is indeed more significant about the anthropomorphic theophanies than that they have occurred to special and isolated persons in the past."[124]

The significance of God's form, therefore, is derived from its function. Only a few selected individuals can behold visions of God and endure his holiness and awesomeness, which destroy most humans. Seeing God and surviving, thus, is a form of blessing, an indication of spiritual merits, and a legitimization of role and position. The ones who see God are elevated into a state of holiness in which they can experience his presence directly, in a personal manner.[125] A very telling example is Moses, described, for example, in Numbers 12:8 as the one who "beholds the form of the Lord," to whom God speaks clearly mouth to mouth (**פה אל פה אדבר בו ומראה ולא בחידות ותמנת יהוה יביט**).[126]

In addition to these presentations, several biblical sources, such as Isaiah 6 and Ezekiel 1, utilize a model of "transcendent anthropomorphism" comparable to the Mesopotamian model. These sources also present Yahweh's theophany in a manner which transcends a corporeal perception of the divine and asserts his otherness, boundlessness and indefinableness.[127] Ezekiel, for example, describes God's *kavod,* which he saw seated above the throne in his heavenly vision, as "something that seemed like a human form" (1:26).[128] This depiction is highly anthropomorphic, primarily since Ezekiel uses terms *demut* and *mar'eh* which imply a concrete representation.[129] Yet the cautious language of Ezekiel, J. M. Miller has asserted, suggests that the appearance of God's glory "defies adequate description."[130]

Hekhalot and Merkavah Mysticism

The *Shi'ur Komah* doctrine, found in various versions in the Hekhalot and Merkavah literature and in other sources, presents a unique conception of the divine.[131] According to this doctrine, God is assumed to possess a corporal, visual form, accessible to initiated Merkavah visionaries. The *Shi'ur Komah* descriptions refer to God's stature. They list the specific features of his body, identifying them by name and measurement. These texts ascribe to God's body and organs immeasurable cosmic dimension, and distinguish these bodily features by illegible names, composed of unknown combination of letters, or of letters identified with the letters of God's ineffable name. This direct, corporeal, figurative portrayal of God clearly stands in contrast to the conventional conception of the transcendent, abstract nature of the divine. Thus, questions regarding the origin of the *Shi'ur Komah* unequaled doctrine, as well as the aim and the meaning of its corporal portrayal of God, have been the subject of much controversy from early to more recent times.[132]

One explanation of the figurative portrayal of the divine in the *Shiur Komah* traditions, modern scholars have suggested, is rooted in the fundamental distinction between God's indefinable essence and his manifested appearance.[133] In contrast, a different understating of the *Shi'ur Komah* tradition perceives no distinction between God's hidden and visible aspects, only a paradox of transcendence and immanence.[134] Study of the origin of the *Shi'ur Komah* tradition has stressed links between this doctrine and several themes found in Gnostic sources.[135] The Talmudic scholar, S. Liberman, and other scholars have contended that the *Shi'ur Komah* tradition grew as an ancient esoteric exegesis on the Song of Songs, especially on chapter 5:10–11.[136]

From a different perspective, I suggest, it is possible to examine the *Shi'ur Komah* traditions in light of the mythological "transcendent anthropomorphism" model of description. It seems that such a model, embedded in ancient Near Eastern traditions and found later, in a more restricted fashion, in various biblical and apocalyptic sources, is evoked in the *Shi'ur Komah* context of Hekhalot and Merkavah mysticism.[137]

The *Shi'ur Komah* descriptions make clear that their main concern is the manifested, visible aspect of the divine body. In order to provide answers to questions such as: "How much is the measure of the stature of the Holy One, blessed be he?" several parallel descriptions are provided.[138] They assert God's corporeal form, list his various bodily features and elucidate their measurements. For example:

> The parasangs of His feet fill the entire world,
> as it is said: "Heaven is My throne
> and the earth is My footstool" (Isaiah 66:1).
> The height of His soles is 30 million parasangs.
> His right sole is called PRMSYYH ATYRKNY
> and the left AGTMTZ.
> The height from His sole to the ankle is 150 million
> parasangs. Similarly the left.
> The right ankle is called TZGMTNYH
> and the left ASTMZ.
> From His ankle to the knees is 190,005,200 parasangs.
> Similarly the left.[139]

This depiction is clearly highly anthropomorphic. The measurements assigned to God's various organs, however, are given in enormous multiplied units of ten million parasangs (Persian miles) which cannot be grasped. The smallest unit of these huge dimensions is compared to God's little finger which stretches from one end of the world to the other, indicating that the size of the *Shi'ur Komah* is, in fact, infinite, immeasurable, and inaccessible to human imagination:

> Every parasang equals three miles, and every mile equals ten thousand ells, and every ell equals two small fingers, like His small finger. And His small finger fills the whole world."[140]

Each cosmic part of God's body is given an illegible name, composed of an unknown combination of letters, or of letters identified with the letters of God's ineffable name:

> The right knee is called Satmagatz Yehamiyi and that of the left is called Maghanuriyah. The right thigh is called Shashtastafarnisiyi and the left is called Tafganichaziza. From [God's] thighs to the neck is 240 million parasangs. [God's] thighs are called Astanah . . . dadiyah.[141]

These names seldom convey any meaning. They mostly amount to indecipherable expressions far beyond human understanding. Mentions of seemingly familiar characteristics, such as specific corporeal parts and their measurements and names are, in fact, beyond human comprehension. They serve to convey, therefore, the incomprehensible nature of the inscrutable God:

> The nose, Kngbziha is its name. . . . His tongue from one end of the universe to the other. . . . The width of His forehead is Mssgyhuyvayyh. The name of the width of His forehead is Istanyahu Stnyhn. . . . The black of His right eye is 10,000,500 parsangs and so is the left. The name of the right [eye] is az dhyh attysvname and its prince is Rahbiel.[142]

Images of light, fire, sparks, lightening, and torches are often used to characterize God's figure in the *Shi'ur Komah* tradition: "You are fire" the text declares. It also alludes to the "form of his beauty and splendor," and describes "the splendor of [God's] glory" as "luminous, awesome in the darkness."[143] The radiant splendor of God, suggests E. R. Wolfson, assumes the shape of a human form. Yet, insofar as it "applied to the enthroned form of the glory, it connotes at once corporeality and luminosity; indeed, the one is expressed through the other.[144]

As scholars have stressed, the figurative descriptions of God serve to convey God's incomprehensible, and transcendent nature, which is far beyond human comprehension. In Scholem's view, "The enormous figures have no intelligible meaning or sense-content . . . they are better calculated, on the contrary, to reduce every attempt at such vision to absurdity."[145] Dan asserts that the descriptions emphasize that "the divine 'body' is beyond all knowledge, transcending comprehension . . ."[146] According to Elior the anthropomorphic descriptions of God intend to "glorify Him, to transcend Him and to create endless distance between man and God."[147] "The point of completely absurd calculation, asserts Schäfer, is to demonstrate that God cannot be conceived of in human categories.[148] Wolfson's analysis suggests that beyond "the 'reductio ad absurdum' of these anthropomorphic speculation on God . . . it is necessary to embrace the paradox in its full dialectic: the divine form in conceivable in its imperceptibility, revealed in its hideness."[149] These observations seem to demonstrate that the new and daring depiction of God in the *Shiur Komah* traditions corresponds, in fact, to the ancient pattern of "transcendent anthropomorphism" and its dialectical conceptual principles.

It is also important to note that *Shi'ur Komah* and ancient Mesopotamian descriptions share a similar literary style and imagery, as various examples illustrate. First, as part of the *Shi'ur Komah* depiction of God's figure, specific divine princes are equated with several of his body parts: "The name of the right [eye] is az dhyh attysvname and its prince is Rahbiel."[150] This aspect is not dominant in the *Shi'ur Komah* doctrine. Surprisingly, however, it parallels the Mesopotamian description of the god Ninurta's bodily parts, which are aligned with various divine figures. Second, the *Shi'ur Komah* lists include certain specific parts of the divine body which are strikingly reminiscent of the Mesopotamian depiction of the god Ningirsu: the soles of God's feet, his heels, hips, hands, neck, head, beard, nose, forehead, and cheeks as well as God's right and left eyes, pupils, iris, mouth, lips, and tongue.[151] A similar literary style, according to which a series of sentences contain references to both an organ of the deity's body and to its name and qualities, is also found in the ancient Mesopotamian hymn and the *Shi'ur Komah* presentation.

Finally, in addition to anthropomorphic characteristics, several descriptions ascribed zoopomorphic features to God, which cannot be reconciled with the human body:

> Sitting in his palace, his feet surrounded by clouds of fire . . . like the sun, like the moon, like the stars, like the face of a man, the face of an eagle, the talons of a lion, the horns of an ox. His countenance is compared to that of a spirit, to the form of a soul that no creature can recognize. His body is like chrysolite, filling the entire world. Neither

> the near nor the far can look upon him. Blessed be his name forever.[152]

As this passage connotes, God embraces figurative features associated with a man, an eagle, a lion, and an ox. The God's appearance expresses his inaccessibility and ultimate transcendence, metaphorically, through use of images of spirit and soul that no creature can recognize. Details of this description recall the Mesopotamian anthropomorphic-zoomorphic-transcendent portrayal of the god Ninurta, in Gudea Cylinder A examined above, as a man embodying a god's face, an eagle's arms, and a body of storm.

GOD'S APPEARANCE

> . . . from His beauty the deeps are burned,
> and from His stature the heavens are burned.
> His stature emits proud ones
> and His crown shatters mighty ones,
> and His garments sweep precious.[153]

MYTHOLOGICAL PATTERNS

Several attributes of the gods are repeatedly presented in ancient Near Eastern iconography and literary sources: majestic radiance, personified names, regal garments, crowns, emblems of authority, and specific physical features. These often express notions of divinity, superiority, and high status manifested in a tangible fashion..

Qualities of radiance and light are thought to be the divines' inherent characteristics. The Sumerian term "NI" and the Akkadian term "*melammû*" (literally, radiance, splendor luminosity) defines the gods' supernatural awe-inspiring quality. It is a brilliant, visible glamor, exuded by gods, heroes, and sometimes by kings, that induce awe and fear in the believers.[154] In his discussion of "why Mesopotamian religion should not be written," A. L. Oppenheim explains the nature of its religious thought: " . . . the deity in Mesopotamia is experienced as an awesome and fear-inspiring phenomenon, endowed with a unique, unearthly and terrifying luminosity. Luminosity is considered to be a divine attribute and is shared in a varying degree of intensity by all things considered divine and holy. We find again the same groping of the expression of the ineffable in terms of a fearful supernatural radiance emanating from the deity."[155]

Mythological patterns of thought often perceive names as integral parts of the phenomenon they represent. This conception is present in ancient Near Eastern sources in which the names of the gods are considered to be manifestations of their being. They embody the essence of the gods and are regarded as identical with their bearers.[156] Furthermore, as S. Olyan observes, divine names are often considered independent and sometimes appear to be corporeal. According to several ancient Near Eastern accounts, such names often receive forms of cultic devotion.[157]

Divine emblems likewise exhibit the high position of the gods. For example, "the rod and ring" indicate divine authority in a concrete fashion. These emblems are depicted as a pair of measuring instruments. They symbolize divine justice and kingship, as we see in textual and artistic representations.[158] Sometime the rod and ring appear to be a staff and a chaplet of beads, likewise representing divine status. The seals of the gods are an additional emblem. These represent their kingship and ensure their royal authority. According to Babylonian tradition, for example, in the New Year ceremony the fates for the coming year were fixed by writing on the tablet of destinies.[159]

In other representations Mesopotamian deities are often crowned. They are distinguished as well by specific garments of notable symbolic value. A. L. Oppenheim has examined texts and monuments relating to such "golden garments of the gods." Of the numerous neo-Babylonian texts of the seventh century B.C.E., which refer to the garments of the gods, several describe garments with golden stars or clouds. These decorations perhaps endowed these garments with an aura of divinity and emphasized the status of the gods.[160] A passage in *Enumah Elish* describes Marduk's rise to power. It speaks of several features which manifest divine kingship and make it perceptible: a princely garment, a royal aura, a crown, and a staff:

> He put on a princely garment,
> A royal aura, a splendid crown.
> He took up a mace and grasped it in his right hand.[161]

The quality of beauty is also often attributed to the gods as well as specific facial features.[162] For example, a beard is a characteristic of several gods. One example is the Babylonian god Enki, represented often as a seated god with long beard, a cap, and a robe.[163] The god El, head of the pantheon in Ugaritic mythology, is also depicted as a bearded god, as texts and iconography attest. El's beard is mentioned by the goddess Ashera as a symbol of his greatness: "You are great, O El, and indeed wise; your hoary beard instructs you."[164] The goddess Anat mentions El's gray beard as well.[165]

Concrete patterns of depiction are present occasionally in biblical sources. God's uniqueness and superiority are expressed at times by references to his physical appearance, in particular his illustrious radiance, names, garments, emblems of authority, and physical features.

Divine aspects, such as God's name and glory, describe his presence in priestly and deuteronomist traditions. As Mettinger has demonstrated, deuteronomic sources present Yahweh enthroned in Heaven but his name dwells on Earth. Thus, the name embodies God and represents his presence. For example, God's sanctuary is "the place where the Lord will choose to cause his name to dwell" (Deut. 16: 2). In Jeremiah as well God's name is thought to dwell in the temple.[166] The divine name is clearly personified in Exodus 23: 20–21, where it is said to lead Israel. Olyan notes that in contrast with ancient Near Eastern sources, however, God's names never receive any form of cultic devotion in biblical descriptions.[167]

Priestly circles present Yahweh's qualities of splendor or radiance as *kavod* (כבוד), or *hod* (הוד). This is the brilliant radiance thought to emanate from his being.[168] Habakkuk 3: 3–4 describes a theophanic vision of God: "His splendor covers the heavens. The earth is filled with his radiance. There is brilliant light with his rays on every side." The seventy elders of Israel saw God: "Under his feet there was the likeness of a pavement of sapphire like the very sky for purity" (Ex. 24: 10). Ezekiel sees "radiance all about him" (Ezek. 1: 27–28). Psalm 104 describes God "clothed with honor and majesty, wrapped in light as with garment" (1–2).

Diverse biblical texts portray God as a king enthroned with a crown.[169] Several passages allude to God's garments (Isa. 6: 1; Ezek. 16: 8; Dan. 7: 9; Isa. 63: 1–3; Ps. 60: 10), and even his sandals (Ps. 108: 10). Daniel describes God's garments as well as his white hair: "And the ancient of days took his seat. His garment was like white snow and the hair on his head like pure wool" (Dan. 7: 9). Isa. 33:17 ascribes beauty to God, parallel to other passages (e.g., Ps. 45:3–4).

Hekhalot and Merkavah Mysticism

Hekhalot and Merkavah mysticism conveys the excellence and superiority of God by applying several images which correspond to ancient Near Eastern mythological convention discussed above. Majestic radiance, personified names, royal garments, crowns, emblems of authority, and specific physical features are linked together to express the supremacy of God in a tangible manner.

God of the Hekhalot and Merkavah is a crowned king. He is also surrounded by an awe-inspiring radiance and light:

> King of kings of kings, God of gods,
> Lord of lords,
> He who is exalted with chains of crowns,
> Encircled by branches of brilliance,
> Who "covers the heavens" with the branch of his glory.[170]

The image of the rays of brilliance in this passage seems to coincide to God's *kavod* or *hod* and to the Mesopotamian NI or *melammû*. In Hekhalot and Merkavah mysticism, it receives a visual dimension and becomes the object of beholding.

God's names, likewise, are described in this literature as embodiments of God's essence. A formula repeated in several Hekhalot descriptions attests to this concept:

> He is His name and His name is Him.
> He is in Him and His name is in His name.[171]

The names also contain God's substance and qualities:

> His name is like His might and His might is like His name.
> He is His power and His power is Him
> and His name is like His name.[172]

God's names are not seen as titles or epithets. Instead, they appear to be autonomous and accessible to human perception as such.[173] Likewise they receive ritual adoration from divine beings who "bring to [God's] name, great, mighty and awesome, adornment and glory," and proclaim: "Let your name be declared holy in the sanctification. Let it be magnified in greatness. Let it be made mighty in might. . . ."[174]

A ring and a seal similarly give a concrete representation of God's supremacy. Various accounts state that God sealed Heaven and Earth with the signet ring in his hand.[175] God's beauty, including his beard, is an additional attribute which manifests his uniqueness in a concrete fashion. God's face, in particular, is the focus of attention:

> Fine countenance, adorned countenance, countenance of beauty,
> countenance of flame is the countenance of YHWH,
> the God of Israel, when He sits upon His throne of glory
> and His praise is high in the seat of His splendor
> His beauty is finer than the beauty of valor.[176]

The beauty of God's face is awesome and overwhelming. Thus, it has an harmful effect upon fearful observers:

> Those who serve Him today will not serve Him tomorrow, and those who serve Him tomorrow will no longer serve Him. For their strength has lessened and their faces have blacken, their hearts are confused, and their eyes become darkened because of the radiance glory of the beauty of their king. . . .[177]

God's majestic appearance adds to his regal status: "his garment is white like snow; his hair on his head is as pure wool."[178] Furthermore,

God's crown and garment acquire a cosmic dimension which expresses his divinity:

> Who is like our King? Who is like our Creator?
> Who is like YHWH our God?
> The diadem of His head emanates and radiates
> the sun and the moon.
> Pleiades and Orion and Mercury and Venus,
> Constellations and stars and signs
> sweep and emanate from His garment.[179]

As in the mythical model presented earlier, the physical and tangible details in the Hekhalot and Merkavah descriptions express God's loftiness and exaltation. These are recognized and acclaimed.

MYSTICAL EXEGESIS

> The sight of His countenance and the sight of His cheeks
> is like the image of a spirit
> and like the form of a soul.[180]

A cluster of figurative features vividly describes God's image, as we have seen. He is portrayed as an anthropomorphic king, sitting on a glorious throne in the royal seventh palace. His brilliant palaces and thrones and his imperial chariots manifest his supremacy as well as his total authority over other heavenly powers who accept his rule in unison. God's divine body is huge; his limbs are enormous. He wears regal garments and a royal crown, and holds the signet ring of Heaven and Earth in his hand.

Side by side with such figurative, anthropomorphic depiction, various accounts clearly announce God as a transcendent, incomprehensible being. They express his qualities through abstract images, which have no substance or tangible, visible aspect. These include images of spirit and soul and also those of gentle breezes and the breath of life. All of these representations convey spiritual aspects, which cannot be conceived, defined, distinguished, or limited. Thus, a *Shi'ur Komah* account, examined before, attests:

> Sitting in His palace, his feet surrounded by clouds of fire . . .
> like the sun, like the moon, like the stars, like the face of a man,
> the face of an eagle, the talons of a lion, the horns of an ox.
> The countenance of His face is like the image of a spirit,
> and like the form of a soul that no creature can recognize.
> His body is like chrysolite, filling the entire world. Neither the
> near nor the far can look at Him . . .[181]

This description, like several Hekhalot and Merkavah accounts, juxtaposes both tangible and abstract images of divinity. It makes no apparent distinction between the two. It is important to note, however, that this description is not a general and theoretical depiction of God. Instead, its portrayal of God is a testament, introduced by Rabbi Akiva, who witnessed God's presence, and who transmits the knowledge of him to others.[182]

The description clearly pertains to the figure of the enthroned God "sitting in His palace, His feet surrounded by clouds of fire." This vision of God, nonetheless, is not allowed to be seen by humans and angels alike since "no creature can recognize, neither the near nor the far can look at Him."[183] In spite of this prohibition, which is dominant in Hekhalot and Merkavah mysticism, as we have seen, Rabbi Akiva is able to behold God's form that no creature can recognize.[184] He perceives figurative corporeal attributes such as body, form, limbs, and the other specific anthropomorphic-zoomorphic features. At the same time, Rabbi Akiva also recognizes God's spiritual qualities and transcendent nature, presented metaphorically as of soul and spirit.

Such visions of a figurative and abstract God are seen from a mystical perspective as part of the adepts' spiritual experience. They are revealed, at the peak of the journey, only to worthy descenders to the chariot, as Rabbi Akiva attests:

> The great, mighty and fearsome, grand and powerful God,
> who is hidden from the eyes of all creatures
> and concealed from the serving angels,
> but revealed to Rabbi Akiva
> through the work of the Merkavah.[185]

When worthy adepts, such as Rabbi Akiva, acquire an exegetical "understanding of the heart" and consequently a divine-like perspective, they are able to behold manifested divine visions and to understand their true essence. Rabbi Akiva's unique awareness and mystical exegesis, thus, seems to reconcile the concrete and the transcendent concept of God as the passage cited above demonstrates. He beholds the figurative appearance of God and perceives his spiritual aspects of soul and spirit.

An additional personal testament, based on Rabbi Ishmael's own experience, demonstrates the significance of the mystical perception, which allows specific individuals to decode the meaning of divine visions, to conceive the nature of God, and thus to equate their human perspective with the divine reality.

> The sight of His countenance and the sight of His cheeks
> is like the image of a spirit and
> like the form of a soul, and the
> radiance shines and is terrible out of darkness.

> Cloud and fog surround him,
> and all the Princes of the Countenance
> are poured out before him through the
> strength of the stature of His beauty and His glory.[186]

Rabbi Ishmael does not rely on his sensual and logical perception. From his perspective, the visible, concrete, anthropomorphic features of God's countenance and cheeks correlate to abstract, intangible images of a gentle breeze and the breath of life, which connote God's transcendent essence. It seems, thus, that a spiritual exegetical ability allows Rabbi Ishmael to make the transition from an ordinary level of awareness to a deeper level of perception, which enables an attainment of divine truth.

As these examples suggest, the tension between the concrete and transcendent conception of God seems to have been reconciled in Hekhalot and Merkavah mysticism in light of the mystical-exegetical context in which it is introduced. The dialectical concept of God and the unique mystical-exegetical ability to perceive this paradox are linked together. Visions of a figurative and abstract God are seen from a mystical perspective as part of the adepts' spiritual experience. At the peak of the journey to the Merkavah, when worthy descenders acquire a spiritual understanding and consequently a divine-like perspective, they are able to decode and to interpret the true concealed essence of God's manifested visions. Rabbi Akiva and Rabbi Ishmael, exemplary mystics, go far in their mystical comprehension of the divine transcendent and concrete vision. They behold God's revealed figurative and concrete manifestation, deciphers its enclosed meaning, and recognizes God's concealed, infinite, transcendent and spiritual essence.

CONCLUSION

This chapter examined the manner in which mythological patterns and themes come to express the concept of God in Hekhalot and Merkavah mysticism. As we have seen, God's sublime and infinite nature is expressed through the application of concrete images and figurative language, as well as through various themes rooted in Mesopotamian and biblical mythological imagery. Powerful images such as enormous physical size, exclusive kingship, majestic appearance, and tangible supremacy are evoked. Yet, they do not convey a limited perception of God. Instead, such representation conveys his supremacy, transcendent, and inaccessibility through the language of mythology evoked by Hekhalot and Merkavah mysticism.

Integrated with this presentation is the unique awareness and exegetical perception, mystical in nature, which qualifies Merkavah adepts. Hekhalot and Merkavah mysticism emphasizes this spiritual capability which enables selected individuals to perceive concealed truths of external manifestations, to behold the invisible God through his figurative forms, and thus to bridge divine and human perspectives in a manner in which no angel and human usually can. In the process of "spiritual exegesis," the transcendent qualities of God are conceived by worthy visionaries at the end of their spiritual voyage. They behold God as both concrete and abstract. In their descriptions, we see a mystical, human response to divine revelation. The concept of God they present, therefore, depends upon this perception. In Hekhalot and Merkavah mysticism, it appears, it is principally a specific human awareness and state of understanding that defines and gives meaning to visions and images, which convey a mystical conception of God in mythological language.

Examining the presence of myth in Judaism, M. Fishbane has distinguished five stages of myth and myth making. His observations of the fifth stage are based on an analysis of modern poetry. They seem, however, to delineate adequately the interplay between myth, mysticism, and exegesis in Hekhalot and Merkavah mysticism:

> Only rarely will a strong poet release images that appear to arise from the very ground of being. In such cases we are on the brink of myth, and cross over to the realm insofar as images cohere in some narrative sense. I would even say that the poet becomes a mythmaker when his images (or mythlike metaphors) bring new dramatic vitality to the sights and sounds of the world, for himself and for his readers. In the process, the poet may utilize and transform images from earlier tradition; and such a process may even give the new myth an unexpected exegetical freshness. Nevertheless, the new moment is not exegesis per se but a return through subjectivity to the sounds and the sights of existence.[187]

6

Literary, Phenomenological, Cultural, and Social Implications

INTRODUCTION

At the beginning of this study we looked at Rabbi Akiva's question as a framework for this analysis of Hekhalot and Merkavah mysticism of late antiquity. Rabbi Akiva asks:

> Who is able to contemplate the seven palaces
> and behold the heaven of heavens
> and see the chambers of chambers
> and say: "I saw the chamber of YH?"[1]

Thus far the discussion has addressed several aspects of this question. It examined the nature of the meditative process which leads the Merkavah adepts to contemplate the seven heavens, ascend to the celestial realm in a spiritual, mental journey, and behold God in his celestial chambers. It also observed the manner in which these mystical notions were formulated and conveyed through the language of mythology.

An important segment of this question still remains untreated: Who were the adepts of the Merkavah circle in late antiquity? Who are those who are "able to contemplate the seven palaces. . . . ascend and behold the heaven of heavens," and describe their endeavors in writings? In attempting to answer this question, this chapter will consider possible cultural and social dimensions of Hekhalot and Merkavah mysticism and the background of its authors. The enigmatic Hekhalot and Merkavah literature does not offer dependable and definite information, as noted previously. Based on the premise that mystical literature is grounded in a specific religious and social structure, however, it seems beneficial to look at possible cultural and social implications of the literary and phenomenological observations presented above.

This chapter, as a conclusion of this study, will first briefly summarize these previous observations. It will then offer several suggestions regarding the possible cultural and ideological affiliation of Hekhalot and Merkavah mysticism and its authors.

LITERARY AND PHENOMENOLOGICAL OBSERVATIONS

Maintaining the view that scholarly analysis of mystical phenomena is primarily textually based, this study examined Hekhalot and Merkavah mysticism as found in several treatises and literary accounts. In light of current observations and methodological premises in the study of mysticism, several mystical characteristics of this tradition were identified. As exhibited above, Hekhalot and Merkavah mysticism delineates both inner-spiritual experiences and the personal, divine revelations which they entail. These two aspects are interrelated. Mystical goals, practical methods, spiritual stages, inner conceptual transformation, divine revelations, and their spiritual exegesis coincide and create an integrated, common mystical outlook which, despite its noncanonical status, endured over a long period of time.

Various literary traditions provide descriptions of a specific path or *via mystica* which leads the Merkavah seekers to a spiritual awareness of God during a personal, unmediated experience. As part of their effort to attain God, those who journey on this path practice various mystical methods, develop an elevated spiritual perception, and expand their consciousness. These inner-spiritual practices lead to self-transformation which results in their achieving a divine-like status and a new "understanding of the heart." From their new and elevated position, the Merkavah visionaries are capable of beholding visions of God and of deciphering their meaning in a process of spiritual exegesis. Their experience is an expanded one. They do not simply behold such visions with a limited, human perspective. Instead, by beholding and deciphering the meaning of such visions in a process of spiritual exegesis, they reach divine truths. This type of elevated exegesis becomes possible for qualified adepts at the end of their spiritual voyage, when human and divine perspectives correspond.

The analysis above has also demonstrated how these mystical notions are formulated and expressed in Hekhalot and Merkavah mysticism through mythological language. Myth and mysticism are two conceptual frameworks which have no inherent connection. Some schools of mysticism present their ideas and beliefs through use of various modes of expression other than mythology. Other schools, however, evoke mythological elements in their teachings in various ways. As chapters 4 and 5 have demonstrated, several Hekhalot and Merkavah accounts express mystical notions by utilizing mythological language, pictorial images, visual metaphors, and concrete illustrations. Echoes from familiar ancient Near Eastern mythological traditions, biblical and Mesopotamian, are likewise prominent. We find the presence of mythology particularly in relation to two topics: the spiritual journey to God, and visions of the divine in the heavenly realm.

The journey is delineated on two levels. It is presented as a mental-contemplative process, or a spiritual-ecstatic voyage, which takes place in the adepts' imagination, spirit, and mind. Such an experience is depicted often in a tangible fashion as an actual, corporeal ascent to heaven taking place in a mythological, celestial cosmos. The act of crossing conceptual boundaries and gaining a divine-like awareness is expressed through several mythological patterns and specific themes rooted in Near Eastern mythological sources. These include an heroic journey to the forbidden divine realms, an ascent to heaven on a cosmic pole, a symbolic return to the primordial, harmonious state of Eden, entrances through heaven's gates, and various tests and trials. The spiritual shift of awareness is presented in several Hekhalot and Merkavah descriptions by applying a common mythical pattern of symbolic death and rebirth and by evoking a model of metamorphosis from a human status to a divine-like state.

The complex concept of God, attained by the descenders to the Merkavah, is likewise portrayed on two levels. Varying descriptions allude to God's spiritual character, his transcendent nature, and his inconceivable qualities, all far beyond human or angelic comprehension. These abstract dimensions of God are expressed through mythological, concrete imagery. God of the Hekhalot and Merkavah is a king, huge in body and size, draped in regal garments and wearing a royal crown. He sits on his glorious throne in his royal seventh palace while other divine beings praise him, glorify his name, and accept his rule in unison. These essentially anthropomorphic, figurative portrayals do not contradict an abstract conception of a transcendent, spiritual God. Rather, they express this abstract concept in a mythological fashion through the application of pictorial images and metaphorical language, as well as by evoking traditional Near Eastern conventional themes such as enormous physical size, exclusive kingship, exceptional beauty and tangible supremacy.

Such revelations of the divine are not presented in isolation. They are dependent upon the adepts' spiritual comprehension and exegesis. The concrete, anthropomorphic figure of God is revealed to qualified adepts only at the end of their spiritual journey. Then, when the Merkavah devotees reach an optimal mystical stage of consciousness, their human perception coincides with that of the divine. They can behold visions of God, gaze at the King in his beauty, and decipher the meaning of these revelations with "an understanding of the heart." Thus, they comprehend God's essence and speak of his spiritual and inconceivable nature, conveying it in abstract images such as spirit and soul.

In this mythological formulation of mystical notions, it is important to note that mythical images and themes are not presented in their original form in Hekhalot and Merkavah mystical writings. They are interiorized, spiritualized, and reintegrated through distinctive mystical lenses in order to convey new mystical notions in the Judaism of late antiquity. The mythological themes, however, are not interpreted or decoded in light of the traditional Jewish midrashic or symbolic methods, frequently used in rabbinical literature or in later Kabbalistic sources. Instead, in many of the Hekhalot and Merkavah accounts mythological themes are presented directly as an integral and vital part of the mystical content. They give expression to mystical notions such as spiritual experiences and transcendent revelations, which by their nature may stand beyond clear verbal expression and familiar vocabulary.

CULTURAL AND SOCIAL IMPLICATIONS

As we have seen in chapter 1, various questions concerning the social climate in which Hekhalot and Merkavah mysticism developed, as well as the identity of its authors and redactors, and their specific ideological affinities, are still questions debated by scholars. The fictional enigmatic and pseudepigraphic nature of the Hekhalot and Merkavah literature does not offer clear information.[1] Well-known Tannaitic figures such as Rabbi Ishmael, Rabbi Akiva, and Rabbi Nehunia ben Ha-Kanah, are presented in the writings as the main protagonists. Yet, as J. Dan observes, the descriptions often refer to an imaginary reality. Likewise, they repeatedly contradict both historical information and the accepted traditional norms of the first few centuries C.E.[2]

As discussed above, several theories have been suggested in the scholarly literature concerning the social and historical origin of the Hekhalot literature as well as its writers' possible affiliations. According to one view, introduced by G. Scholem, Hekhalot and Merkavah mysticism emerged in the central circles of rabbis, in a context committed to knowledge of rabbinic law and lore, namely, the *tannaim* and *amoraim* of the first centuries C.E.[3] This view has been challenged by D. J. Halperin, who demonstrates differences between the Hekhalot and Merkavah tradition and that of rabbinic Judaism. In his opinion, the Hekhalot and Merkavah literature developed in lower-class groups of people known as *Am ha-Arets* (people of the land, עם הארץ), who operated in a context of social conflict with the rabbis, and expressed their protest through the literature.[4] According to R. Elior, the writers of the Hekhalot and Merkavah literature identify themselves with the priestly class of the first centuries C.E. After the destruction of the temple in 70 C.E., these groups continued their priestly tradition within their visionary experiences in the heavenly palaces, in order to preserve and reconstruct lost Temple traditions.[5] P. Schäfer sees Hekhalot and Merkavah literature as a product of a "post-Rabbinic elite" dating from the late Talmudic period to the late Gaonic era.[6] M. Cohen, P. S. Alexander, and M. Swartz have suggested that the different Hekhalot texts took shape over several centuries in Palestine in the early Amoraic period to the post-Talmudic time in Babylonia.[7] The authors, according to Swartz, came from educated, yet popular groups deprived of formal rabbinic training, found in circles of synagogue functionaries, liturgical poets, and professional scribes. J. R. Davila, likewise, associates professional scribes with the composers of the Hekhalot and Merkavah literature. In a recent study he identifies the people behind the Hekhalot and Merkavah literature as practitioners of ritual power, compared to shamans and shamans/healers.[8]

As I conclude this study, I would like to consider these debated questions regarding the cultural-social background of Hekhalot and Merkavah mysticism in light of the literary, phenomenological evidence discussed above. R. Gimello, in his discussion of mysticism, highlights the significance of historical-cultural factors on every mystical tradition, asserting that mystical content and cultural-social factors are bound together:

> Mysticism is inextricably bound up with, dependent upon, and usually subservient to the deeper beliefs and values of the traditions, cultures, and historical milieu which harbor it. As it is thus intricately and intimately related to those beliefs and values, so must it vary according to them.[9]

Mystical literature, S. T. Katz has attested, is rooted in its particular cultural circumstances and grounded in its specific historical context. Thus, it reflects both phenomenological characteristics and historical-cultural aspects:

> . . . as language and judgment also belong to, indeed are inseparable from, social life, the structural matrix works to locate both experience and the experiencer (the mystic) in a given sociohistoric conceptual field, whose problems and problematic he or she adopts and aims to solve.[10]

Hekhalot and Merkavah mysticism, like other mystical traditions, is an historical phenomenon. As such, its literary traditions and imagery point beyond themselves, reflecting not only a spiritual-mental stance and phenomenological dispositions but also, indirectly, cultural and social ideologies, norms, and attitudes. It appears worthwhile, thus, to attempt to reconstruct the ideologies of Hekhalot and Merkavah mysticism based on the literary evidence discussed above. This is by no means to suggest that such sources are to be treated as straightforward and accurate historical documents but rather to propose that they reflect the self-perception of the authors, redactors, and practitioners of Hekhalot and Merkavah mysticism, as well as their value systems and ideological affinities.

Such observations, regarding self-perception, ideology, and value systems, may associate this mystical literature and its writers with an identified group in the Jewish society of late antiquity. In what follows, I will outline specific perspectives found in Hekhalot and Merkavah mysticism. In light of these I will suggest that a specific group in Jewish society, that of "scribe, sages, and the wise" who were associated with classes of priests, may have been the authors of this mystical literature.

Perspectives in Hekhalot and Merkavah Mysticism

Several observations emerge from the Hekhalot and Merkavah mystical sources regarding the outlooks of its authors and members of the Merkavah group.

First, the descenders to the Merkavah are associated with traditional Jewish teachings, culture, ethics and conventional forms of study. The main visionaries, as noted above, are identified as esteemed tannaitic sages whose traditional scholarly knowledge is very apparent. Furthermore, as various examples attest, a capable descender to the Merkavah is portrayed as a highly educated and qualified person, fully trained in Jewish law, ethics, lore, and the study and Jewish exegesis of the Torah. Members of the Merkavah circles, as Elior has demonstrated recently, were closely affiliated with temple angelic-priestly traditions, literature, and rituals, which were refashioned and transformed in the Hekhalot and Merkavah literature.[11]

Second, despite the emphasis on rabbinic education and tradition, several aspects of Merkavah mysticism stand in tension with aspects of rabbinic Judaism. Several scholars have argued that because the authors of the Hekhalot and Merkavah literature did not retain a recognized status and an esteemed position, they probably stood outside official rabbinic groups.[12] In addition, there are indications of conceptual dissimilarity between traditional rabbinic notions and Hekhalot and Merkavah mysticism. Primary illustrations are attitudes towards the concepts of revelation and communication with God. A central notion in traditional Judaism defines the relationship between God and human beings around the divinely initiated revelation at Sinai and its continuous manifestation in the Torah, which embodies everything relevant for understanding the world and God. This traditional view is substituted in Hekhalot and Merkavah mysticism with an alternative religious option which emphasizes personal, mystical encounters with God and the heavenly realm, initiated by humans.[13]

Third, the notion of deciphering divine revelations and comprehending attained visions is emphasized in Hekhalot and Merkavah mysticism, as we have seen. With "light in their heart and a face shining from wisdom," the Merkavah adepts wish to realize the content of God's secrets,[14] as well as to decode all the mysteries of the world and all the orders of nature, as the Creator himself, so that "there is nothing in heaven above or deep within the earth concealed from them."[15]

Fourth, great value is attributed to written documents which contain the teachings of the Hekhalot and Merkavah mystics, as well as to the acts of recording and transmitting distinct knowledge to members of the circle. The significance of additional varying "scribal" features are likewise noticeable. A passage in *Hekhalot Rabbati*, for example, describes how divine visions and celestial revelations are attained by "those who descend to the Merkavah," and their content are recorded by people whose proficient skill and role are to witness these visions and to transcribe them in writing:

> These are the people whom the descenders to the Merkavah take and situate above them; they seat them (these people) before them and say to them: "Observe, see, hear, and write all that we say and all that we hear before the throne of glory."[16]

Similar scribal activity is demonstrated as well by the act of recording the secret names of the guards of the seventh heaven. These names are recorded by individuals who seem to be scribes of mystical knowledge, as Rabbi Nehunia ben Ha-Kanah's instructions attest:

> Since you say to me: detail (the names) come and stand on your feet; And when the name of each one is pronounced from my mouth, every one of you should bow down and fall down on your faces. Immediately all the heroes of the *havurah*, heroes of the Torah, and all the mighty men of the *yeshiva* came and stood on their feet before Rabbi Nehunia ben Ha-Kanah. And he would speak, and they would fall on their faces, and the scribes would write.[17]

Merits of the worthy mystic, who has proven himself in the study of Torah, Rabbinic exegesis, and ethical deeds are recorded in writing by Gabriel, the angelic scribe, and attached to the ascending wagon:

> Dumi'el needs Gabri'el, the scribe and he writes for him on a paper of the wagon of that person, saying: "such is the wisdom of this person and such are his deeds and he requests to enter before the throne of glory.[18]

A reference to a textual document which contains secret knowledge is associated with the Enoch tradition. In *3 Enoch*, Enoch realizes divine secrets through the act of reading "letters by which heaven and earth, seas and rivers, mountains and hills, trees and grasses, stars and constellations, angels, all heavenly creatures, throne of glory, the world wisdom," and all other phenomena were created.[19] A written document facilitates the transmission of knowledge. Thus, Enoch-Metatron mediates hidden knowledge to his disciple, Rabbi Ishmael, by instructing him to read the letters of the heavenly curtain: "he showed them to be with his fingers, like a father teaching his son the letters of the Torah."[20]

The opening passage of *Hekhalot Rabbati* introduces a book which contains knowledge of the seven celestial divine palaces and of the seventy holy names of God: "This is [the] book [of] [the] seven sacred palaces, in which seventy sacred names are explained."[21] An emphasis on learning secret knowledge from a written book is found, as well, in *Hekhalot Zutarti*:

> Everyone who is careful with this book and purifies himself, he is loved by angels, er'elim, troops, Seraphim, Cherubim, Ophanim, and the throne of glory.[22]

Reference is made to a written text that includes the secrets of the perception of God and divine mysteries. This text is attributed to Moses who is presented in this context as both an ideal mystic and scribe who mediates between Heaven and Earth and reveals transcribed hidden knowledge to the selected members of the Merkavah circle:

> This is the book of wisdom, understanding, and perception, the study of above and below, the secrets of the Torah and of heaven and of earth, and the secrets, which He gave to Moses, son of 'Amram, of the perception of YH YH AH'HYH YAW Sabaot God of Israel.[23]

A description in *Hekhalot Rabbati,* discussed previously, demonstrates as well the process of transmitting esoteric teachings to the members of the Merkavah group, identified as the *havurah* or *yeshiva.* When Rabbi Nehunia ben Ha-Kanah decides to reveal "the secret of the world as it appears to one who is worthy to gaze at the king and on the throne in its glory and beauty,"[24] he instructs Rabbi Ishmael, his student, to bring before him the people who belong to this circle, namely, "all the heroes of the *havurah* and all the mighty men of the *yeshiva.*"[25]

Hekhalot Rabbati depicts as well the manner in which traditional and esoteric knowledge is transmitted from a master teacher to his disciples. Rabbi Nehunia ben Ha-Kanah explains the process to Rabbi Akiva:

> I have put in your mouth Torah, Prophets, and Writings; Mishna, and Midrash of laws and legends, the legal decisions of the permissible and the forbidden. Yet were it not for the secrets of Torah which I have hidden from you, would you come and appear before me at all?[26]

Also of importance is the portrayal of both Moses and Enoch as prototypes of the Merkavah mystics, as demonstrated above. Both heroic figures from the past are traditionally known as "scribal" ancestors. Enoch was known by the third century B.C.E. to have been a "scribe of righteousness" (1 Enoch 12:4 4QEnGiants 8:1–4, ii.14–15), who ascended to heaven in order to transcribe the angelic appeal (1 Enoch 13:4–7). Moses is known as the one who has written God's words at Sinai and other occasions, and thus transcribed the Torah of Moses (Ex. 24:4; Num. 33:2; Deut. 31:9, 22). In the second century B.C.E., this tradition was supplemented by the compilers of the book of Jubilees, who emphasized Moses' scribal role: "And the angel of the presence spoke to Moses by the word of the Lord saying, 'Write the whole account of creation . . .' " (2:1) Moses scribal descenders, then, transmitted his knowledge in a transcribed book.[27] At the same time central Hekhalot and Merkavah heroes, such as Enoch and Rabbi Ishmael, are identified as priests and associated with priestly traditions, rituals and duties, and many literary examples of the Hekhalot and Merkavah literature reveal specific priestly traditions and interests from the First and the Second temple periods, as Elior has attested.

Fifth, an additional aspect of Hekhalot and Merkavah literature is the capacity to express mystical notions through the reapplication and appropriation of biblical and ancient Mesopotamian mythological themes. Affinities with the language of the mystery cults is also suggested by specific descriptions. The presence of biblical traditions in Hekhalot mysticism is obvious. Mesopotamian mythological motifs and the language of pagan cults, however, are elements which seem to suggest a certain familiarity with non-Jewish traditions operating within the Greco-Roman world of late antiquity, as well as the capacity to draw on the symbolic power of such far removed traditions.

In light of the evidence presented above, we can discern several distinctions among the Hekhalot and Merkavah mystical group, as found in their mystical records. The descenders to the chariots are depicted as members of a specific circle of learning, who regard written records not only as primary sources for knowledge, but also as channels through which teachings are transcribed and transmitted. They are portrayed as highly educated and trained in Jewish traditional disciplines, scriptures, rabbinical texts, and interpretations. This group is associated, as well, with priestly temple traditions, ritual and literature which they both transform and continue. Members of this cultured circle, however, not only show interest in the normative teachings and principles of Judaism, but they also see themselves as initiators and recipients of direct divine visions. Much of their practice, moreover, revolves around interpreting and deciphering these mystical revelations as they aim to comprehend their encoded concealed meanings. They also attribute their knowledge to esteemed teachers and models, such as Moses and Enoch, regarded as scribes, priests, sages, and mediators between Heaven and Earth. Like them, the Merkavah adepts aspire to access divine secrets and then to record and transmit these mysteries to other members of their circle. The manner in which several of these notions are expressed in the Hekhalot and Merkavah literature, through utilizing themes from foreign sources, suggests a certain awareness of non-Jewish traditions and proficiency in evoking such traditions in a new mystical context.

What kind of a social-cultural group emerges from these descriptions and what is its ideological affiliation? I would like to suggest that many of the characteristics attributed to members of the Hekhalot and Merkavah mystical circle are shared by other specific groups recognized by titles such as scribes, sages, and wise men associated with classes of priests and with temple traditions. Many of the Hekhalot and Merkavah mystical accounts, likewise, appear to be laced with several features, ideologies, and traditions, associated with distinct concerns of several disciplines of such groups, namely, visionary sages, scribes, or scribes-priests who embrace the pursuit of transcendent divine mysteries and revelations. The following discussion aims to support this hypothesis.

Perspectives of Scribes, Scholars and the Wise

Studying the changes brought about in Judaism as a result of Hellenistic influence, E. J. Bickerman has observed a complex view of late antiquity Jewish society which reflects the existence of different groups of intellectual experts. Bickerman has discerned a stratified system of intellectual circles, placed between the highest rank of the rabbinical elite and the lowest, that of the common class. "Between and beside the nobles and the common people there had always existed groups of technological experts whose power was based on knowledge."[28]

As several scholars have submitted, the designated titles of such Jewish intellectual groups of late antiquity are not rigidly used. Scribes, sages, scholars, wise men are synonymous and fluid titles, distinguishing members of such circles. The evidence for their activities is sparse, scattered, and open to various interpretations.[29] Scribes-sages were neither organized in groups nor did they serve in distinctive identifiable classes of specialists, A. J. Saldarini has asserted.[30] Their status and social classes varied. Likewise, the range of functions and roles they performed was considerably broad. Records describe scribes-sages, scholars, wise men as associated with priests, Levities, prominent families, as well as with lower class officials.[31] In addition to their role as part of the administration, independent scribes-sages in different locations functioned in a wide range of disciplines and expertise. They were known as teachers and textual specialists, and were involved in writing, reading, and producing documents. Scribes-sages were thus known also as experts of the scriptures and the laws, skills which they acquired through reading, coping, and interpreting.

Several classes of scribes were also associated with classes of priests as their roles and traditions overlapped at various times, as several of sources attests. In Mesopotamia from the ar millennium BCE on, scribes were situated in royal courts and temples and were associated with priestly classes, among other positions. Scribal literary culture and traditions were also a phenomenon associated with schools of priests and those who trained in priestly circles in Israel, according to sources included in the Hebrew Bible. Fishbane has demonstrated the difficulty of distinguishing priests, scribes, prophets and other leaders who produced and transmitted the biblical books. Studies of Deuteronomy, edited probably before and during the exile, emphasize its priestly scholastic character and connection with wisdom and Scribal traditions. In the post exilic Jewish community the roles of priests, Levities and scribes clearly overlapped. The most well-known scribe, Ezra is of a high priestly stock. Representing undoubtedly the blending of priestly and Scribal traditions he is depicted as a "scribe skilled in the law of Moses" (Ezra 7:6, 11, 12, 21). Great Scribal activity is attributed to priests and Levities according the Chroniclers depiction (1 Chro. 24:6, 2 Chro. 34:13). The *Testament of Levi,* an apocalyptic work of the second century BCE, is ascribed to the predecessor of a priestly lineage, emphasizing the priestly and Levitecal descent of the scribes (8:17 possibly 13:1–2). Enoch, depicted as a scribe in *1 Enoch* and *4QEn Giants,* is the central hero of the Enochic priestly tradition. Priestly origin is attributed as well to scribes who composed and copied texts found among the Dead Sea Scrolls that speak of a community of the "Sons of Zadok". In addition to specialization in the copying of books and sacred scrolls several groups also drew on secular written documents. Various sources attribute to sages, scribes and "the wise" an attitude of openness to foreign, non-Jewish traditions. Some scribe-sages were also associated with knowledge and wisdom; they were depicted as seers, wise men and seem both to continue and to transform familiar Near Eastern traditions of mantic wisdom.[32]

Only several concerns of the sages and scribes, as described above, are relevant to our present discussion of Hekhalot and Merkavah mysticism and its background. These include an appreciation of scholarship and of transmitting acquired knowledge through written documents and books; extensive education in traditional Jewish scriptures, wisdom, lore, and interpretation; affiliation and devotion to priestly temple traditions; familiarity with foreign, non-Jewish traditions, and specific interest in decoding, and interpreting concealed divine secrets. As a variety of sources attest, specific circles of Jewish intellectuals of late antiquity, associated with Near Eastern traditions of scribal wisdom, demonstrate such interests and approaches. The Hekhalot and Merkavah accounts, likewise, associate its mystics with these concerns, as we have seen, and thus may point to some ideological affinity with the former group of intellectuals, scribes, and sages.

The first three interests of these sages-scribes, namely appreciation of scholarship, knowledge and written documents, the dedication to extensive Jewish education as well as the connection to priestly traditions and literature, have been intensively discussed in various studies.[33] Thus the discussion below will examine the latter concepts, namely, the familiarity with foreign, non-Jewish traditions and, more extensively, the specific interest in decoding and interpreting concealed divine secrets.

Various sources attribute to the sages and scribes an attitude of openness to their neighboring non-Jewish traditions, in accord with a long tradition associated with the learned activity of "the wise." This attitude, which can be identified in early stages of the history of ancient Israel,[34] is documented in several sources from the Greco-Roman period, which demonstrate that knowledge of the Torah and as well of non-Jewish types of wisdom was important for Jewish scribal groups. For example, Ben Sira's portrayal of the ideal sage emphasizes study of the Torah and abiding by the commandments as a primary goal (Sir 6:37, 23:27, 29:11–13). Nonetheless, Ben Sira also accentuates the need not to separate from foreign cultures and to be open to other traditions. Ben Sira's ideal scribe-sage, for example, must be ready to travel to foreign places: ". . . he will travel in the lands of foreign peoples for he has tested the good things and bad among human beings" (Sir 39:4 Greek).[35] Tolerance of other cultures, customs, and traditions is likewise encouraged: "Eat like a man the things set before you" (Sir 31:16a Greek); "Should they choose you to preside over a feast, become among them as one of them (32:1 Greek). Observing Ben-Sira's view, J. Gammie suggests: "It is most probably due to his secular tasks as scholar, sage, and jurist that the necessity of a more cosmopolitan and assimilationist stance was thrust upon him."[36]

Ben-Sira's profile of the ideal scribe is not unique. Daniel, in the book of Daniel, is a Babylonian scribe, familiar with foreign tradition and with the pagan literature of the Chaldeans (1:4). The *Letter of Aristeas* to Philocrates, a pseudonymous Greek-Jewish composition, shows a similar attitude when presenting characteristics of the seventy-two translators, commissioned by the Egyptian king to produce a Greek translation of the Hebrew Bible: ". . . they had not only mastered Jewish literature, but had made a serious study of that of the Greeks as well" (L. Arist, 121).[37] These educated sages are clearly acquainted with both Jewish and non-Jewish traditions and with other traditional views: "They rose above conceit and contempt for other people and instead engaged in discourse and listening to and answering each and every one . . ." (L. Arist, 121). In her discussion of the Jewish scribes in Greco-Roman times, C. Schams clarifies this phenomenon: "Scribes who during their training would have copied different texts, wisdom books, and sacred writings as the classical texts, would have gained some knowledge of the content of these books. Since the sacred books were considered a source of wisdom, they were studied by educated and wise scholars."[38]

An additional specific concern of the scribes, sages, and intellectuals of late antiquity is their distinct interest in the notion of decoding and interpreting veiled divine mysteries. This interest follows well-known traditions associated with scribes and sages dating from ancient times until late antiquity, which are expressed in striking terminological and conceptual similarities.[39] According to Mesopotamian sources, for example, a special kind of knowledge associated with the wisdom of the scribes, enables one to acquire divine understanding and to know the secrets of Heaven and Earth. Such knowledge is attributed to exceptional humans and especially to successful kings.[40] Ashurbanipal (668–627 B.C.E.), for instance, left an account of how he obtained such wisdom through the art of the scribes. "I learned the wisdom of Nabu, I studied all the scribal craft . . ." he claims, and gives specific details:

> Marduk, the wisest of the Gods, gave me wide understanding and extensive intelligence and Nabu, the scribe [who knows] everything granted me his wise teachings. . . . I learned the art of the Sage, Adapa, [so that now] I am familiar with the secret storehouse of all scribe learning [including] the celestial and terrestrial portents.[41]

Nabonidus (555–539 B.C.E.) describes himself as a learned man who possesses knowledge and wisdom and thus is able to understand secret lore:

> I am wise, I am learned, I have seen what is hidden; I do not understand the impressions made by a stylus [but] I have seen secret things; the god Ilte'i has shown me everything. I have found out [secret lore].[42]

As we have seen in chapter 4 above, the fragmentary cuneiform text from Mesopotamia associates King Enmeduranki of Sippar with the tradition of deciphering divine secrets. Endowed with knowledge associated with methods of divination, the ancient king is able to interpret omens, to comprehend the mysteries of the gods, and the secrets of Heaven and the underworld. Letters by scholar-scribes to the neo-Assyrian Kings Esaehaddon and Ashurbanipal demonstrate a similar claim to understanding celestial and terrestrial signs, including a wide range of cosmological observations.[43]

The sages and scribes of Mesopotamia produced and copied cuneiform literature over a long period of time, from the middle of the first millennium B.C.E. well into the Greco-Roman period. As noted above, their tradition continued beyond Mesopotamia throughout the changing political and social scenery of the Near East and into the Hellenistic period.[44] Hellenistic Jewish cultures absorbed much of the culture of Mesopotamia, including various scribal traditions, as seen in several apocalyptic sources.[45] One example of this phenomenon is the Enochic tradition. As studies have shown, the figure of Enoch is modeled after that of the Mesopotamian King Enmeduranki.[46] The Enoch tradition does not continue the tradition of divination, yet it maintains a deep interest in the notion of encoding divine mysteries, as J. J. Collins makes clear. Emphasizing the link of Enochic tradition to the scribes and sages, Collins asserts: "The books of Enoch often speak of a class of the "righteous and chosen," and Enoch, the righteous scribe, must be considered as their prototype. We know regrettably little about this Enochic group . . . they were, or at least included in their number, scribes who were familiar with the name of Enoch."[47] It is important, however, to note the different perspective of the Jewish scribes-sages. As Collins affirms: "They also claimed to know divine mysteries and boasted of an ancient prototype who had ascended to heaven. They were influenced by their Babylonian counterparts in some respects. . . . In accordance with Jewish tradition, they rejected most methods of divination and omen seeking. . . . For the decoding of these mysteries, however, the Jewish sages relied not primarily on divinatory techniques but on what they believed to be divine revelation."[48]

The principal characteristics of Enoch in the Enochic tradition are the marks of a scribe-sage figure, who is familiar with both traditional wisdom and the wisdom of decoding divine secrets.[49] The primary narrative describing Enoch, the *Book of the Watchers* (1–36) introduces him as "Enoch the scribe," or "Enoch the scribe of righteousness" (12: 3-4). His role is to mediate between the angels in Heaven and the fallen angels, or watchers, on Earth, and to "write out for them the record of a petition" (13:4). The opening of the last part of 1 Enoch, the *Epistle of Enoch,* introduces Enoch as the wise scribe of this book, "[Book] five, which is written by Enoch, the writer of all the signs of wisdom among all the people" (92:1). In the *Book of Giants,* included as part of the Enochic writings at Qumran, Enoch 's scribal skills are associated with his ability of interpreting dreams.[50]

Concern with encoded divine wisdom and its interpretation is central to the apocalyptic Enoch tradition. In the *Book of the Watchers,* Enoch travels beyond the boundaries of the Earth, enters inaccessible places, and understands mysteries and cosmological secrets. In the *Astronomical Book* (72–82), the angel Uriel interprets the meaning of divine mysteries, and becomes the source of knowledge. Enoch's statement in the *Apocalypse of Weeks* makes this clear: "That which appeared to me in the heavenly vision, and I know from the words of the holy angels and understand from heavenly revelation" (93:2). Mysteries written on the celestial tablet of heaven are also revealed to him: "For I know this mystery. I have read the tablets of heaven and have seen the holy writings and I have understood the writings in them" (103:2).[51]

The Book of Daniel demonstrates a similar interest in the wisdom of decoding divine secrets, associated with scribes, sages, and intellectual circles.[52] Daniel is a *maskil*.[53] He and his companions are educated as Babylonian scribes who study the letters and language of the Chaldeans (1:4) and are known as "the wise men of Babylon (2:13). Daniel, who "studied the books (9:2) is distinguished not only by his skills in all wisdom but also by his knowledge and loyalty to Jewish tradition and law. There is an emphasis on writing books and on the significance of the intellectuals *(maskilim),* who constitute the religious leadership of Judaism (chap. 12).

Daniel is introduced into the meaning of mysteries. The idea of wisdom encoded in mysterious signs is prominent in chapters 1–6. Chapters 7–12 display the notion of divine revelations, which require comprehension and interpretation. Daniel becomes a recipient of dreams and visions. He receives a vision near the bank of waters in Babylon (10:4), sees a fiery heavenly figure, and falls down to the ground with terror (10:9). He is then raised by this figure, who grants him understanding of the prophet Jeremiah's oracle, treated as a mysterious revelation (10: 11–14). Daniel falls dumb and trembles until the divine being calms him down and an entity "like a a man" touches him and promises to reveal to him the meanings of prophecies that "were inscribed in the true writing" (10:21). Daniel is now able to understand and interpret the hidden messages of the revelations (9, 11, 12:10, 11:33, 35).[54] As a divinely inspired sage, Daniel becomes a seer of mysteries who mediates between the divine and his contemporary generation.[55]

Ben Sira restricts his ideal sage to the Torah, advising him not to search for hidden knowledge: "Search not for what is too wondrous for you and investigate not what is hidden from you. Mediate upon what is permitted to you and deal not with secret things" (Sir 3:20–22). Despite this prohibition, it is evident that Ben Sira is aware of such intellectual pursuits of wonders and hidden knowledge, as scholars have argued.[56] A similar well-known Mishnahic prohibition expresses reservations regarding esoteric wisdom, yet allows one who is learned and intelligent to study the secret knowledge of *Ma'aseh Merkavah*:[57]

> It is forbidden for three persons to discuss the laws of sexual offenses, for two people to discuss *Ma'aseh Bereshit*, and for a single person to discus *Ma'aseh Merkavah*, unless [that person] is learned and intelligent (m. *Hagigah* 2:1).

4 Ezra is an additional source which displays an interest in decoding divine secrets associated with scribes and sages.[58] The text depicts

Ezra as a priest and a scribe who is the author of the twenty-four books of the Hebrew Bible and seventy others, reserved only for the wise. Although Ezra "has never gone down into the deep, and neither ascended into the heavens" (4 Ezra 4:7–9), his interest in esoteric knowledge is clear, and is understood to be the source for his deep understanding of revelations and visions. Invited by God to reproduce the Law, Ezra receives divine revelations as well as a special understanding and wisdom:

> Then I opened my mouth and behold, a full cup was offered to me; it was full of something like water, but its color was like fire. And I took and drank; and when I has drunk it, my heart poured forth understanding, and wisdom increased in my breast, and my spirit retained its memory, and my mouth was open and was no longer closed (39–40).

In *2 Baruch,* the tradition of decoding secrets and revelations is also linked to the wisdom of the scribes and sages.[59] Baruch, the scribe from the book of Jeremiah, is portrayed as a leader of the community who is involved with tradition and law. As a wise man (46:4) he instructs the people to observe the Torah and its laws (44:2–3, 45:1–2, 85:3), and writes to the exiles in Babylon (77:11–87). In addition, Baruch is concerned with visions and revelations which he receives through dreams (36:1, 53:1), and with interpretations which reveal eschatological information: "And while I was pondering these and similar things, behold, Ramael, the angel who is set over true visions, was sent to me and he said to me" (55:3).

It is interesting to find in Josephus' *Jewish War* a reference to scribes and their interest in interpreting mysteries. Recounting events which took place towards the end of the first revolt in 70 C.E., Josephus introduces a list of omens and signs which had supposedly occurred before the outbreak of the war. These omens are linked with predictions of the downfall of Jerusalem. In Josephus' view, correct interpretation of the omens was crucial: "By the inexperienced, this was regarded as a good omen, but by the sacred scribes it was at once interpreted in accordance with other events" (*War* 6.291). Josephus does not elaborate on the identity, background, and status of the group he names as sacred scribes. It is clear, however, that they are seen as learned and experienced interpreters of signs who are therefore able to predict the future.[60]

Several documents of the Qumran community connect intellectual figures such as the wise man, the sage, or the *maskil* to the notion of deciphering the meaning of hidden mysteries. "There is no evidence that the sages of Qumran depended on dream visions or angelophanies as the media of such revelation," C. A. Newsom asserts. There are "repeated references, however, to revelations, the gift of a spirit of knowledge, and inspired revelation, by which secrets and mysteries are decoded."[61] Collins points out that the author of the *Hodayot* claims to be the recipient of direct revelation. This is evident in the following lines, attributed to the Teacher of Righteousness: "These things I know by the wisdom which comes from Thee for Thou hast unstopped my ears to marvelous mysteries"(1QH 1:21).[62] Qumran *Pesharim* as well demonstrates an interest in revelation and interpretation.[63] Words of the scriptures are treated as mysteries which reveal information about supernatural realms, divine mysteries, and God's plan for human salvation at the end of time. These need special interpretation, divinely disclosed to the elect. Lines from the *Rule of the Community* demonstrate clearly the claim for understanding esoteric wisdom: "My eyes have gazed on that which is eternal, on wisdom concealed from men, on knowledge and wise design [hidden] from the sons of men" (1QS 5–6).[64] The source for such concealed wisdom, however, is the will of God made evident through proper understanding of the Torah.[65]

Shared Perspective Indeed?

Several of the principal concerns of the sage and scribe groups described above are significant to our discussion of Hekhalot and Merkavah mysticism and its background. These include: appreciation of scholarship and of transmitting acquired knowledge through written documents; dedication to extensive education in traditional Jewish scriptures, wisdom, lore, and interpretation; affiliation and devotion to priestly temple traditions, rituals and literature; familiarity with foreign, non-Jewish traditions which operated within the Greco-Roman world of late antiquity, and capacity to evoke their symbolic themes; finally, specific interest in decoding and interpreting concealed divine secrets. Though these identifying elements are not the dominant characteristics of all Jewish intellectuals of late antiquity, they do represent interests of specific circles of sages and scribes associated with varying aspects of Jewish education as well as of non-Jewish traditions.

We may note the transformation of such an interest in Hekhalot and Merkavah mysticism. The significance of understanding concealed meanings is clearly maintained. Rather than attributing such wisdom solely to divine inspiration or to an angelic illumination, Hekhalot and Merkavah mysticism seems to narrow the gap between exegesis and experience.[66] It emphasizes the cultivated mystical awareness, consciousness, and "understanding of the heart" as keys to an exegetical understanding of concealed visions, as the opening of *Hekhalot Zutarti* cited above suggests:

> If you want to single yourself out in the world
> so that the secrets of the world
> and the mysteries of wisdom will be revealed to you,
> study this teaching and be careful with it
> until the day of your departure.
> Do not try to understand what lies behind you

and do not investigate the words of your lips.
You will try to understand what is in your heart
and keep silent,
so that you will attain the beauty of the Merkavah.[67]

CONCLUSION

We come now to the end of this study. The last part of our discussion has attempted to identify the social-cultural background of Hekhalot and Merkavah mysticism, its authors, and redactors, in light of views and attitudes present in their mystical writings. As a concluding hypothesis to our analysis, we have examined how several important attitudes and concerns, associated with the Hekhalot and Merkavah mystics, are also present as key interests among Jewish intellectuals in late antiquity in circles of scribes, sages, and "the wise" from ancient to Greco-Roman times. We see several shared perspectives: attention to education, scholarship and transmitting knowledge; proficiency in traditional Jewish scriptures, teachings, and interpretation; allegiance to priestly temple traditions, rituals and literature; certain familiarity with foreign, non-Jewish traditions, and interest in decoding concealed divine secrets. Though these are not precise social, historical, and cultural features which can equate the two groups with absolute confidence, they do seem to reflect a distinct similarity in self-perception and ideological interests. Thus, it seems plausible to consider that the enigmatic Hekhalot and Merkavah mysticism is a product of these Jewish intellectuals of late antiquity associated with classes of temple priests, who, in keeping with the traditions of the wise, reapply several of their principles and concepts to their mystical writings.

These suggestions are presented as possibilities and not as certainties. They neither specifically define the group in which Hekhalot and Merkavah mysticism was compiled, nor do they identify its authors and redactors with absolute confidence. Nonetheless they treat the inclinations of the writers as well as their cultural and social ideologies. Together with the previous discussion of Hekhalot and Merkavah mysticism, both its special mystical notions and the manner in which they are conveyed through mythological forms of expression, as well as through evoking and transforming Mesopotamian and biblical mythological themes, these cultural and social references conclude this study and thus address the last aspect of Rabbi Akiva's question:

Who is able to contemplate the seven palaces
and behold the heaven of heavens
and see the chambers of chambers
and say: "I saw the chamber of YH?"[68]

Notes

CHAPTER 1: THE HEKHALOT AND MERKAVAH LITERATURE AND ITS MYSTICAL TRADITION

1. The term "Merkavah" refers to the "celestial throne" described in several scriptural accounts, such as Daniel 7, Isaiah 6, and Ezekiel 1. Although the term "Merkavah" is not mentioned in the first chapter of Ezekiel, in the rabbinic literature the expression "ma'aseh merkavah" is used in reference to various interpretations of Ezekiel 1. See, for example, *Mishna Hagigah* 2: 1. The earliest surviving use of "Merkavah" referring to Ezekiel's vision is found in Sirach 49: 8. On the relationship of the Hekhalot and Merkavah literature to interpretations of Ezekiel see D. J. Halperin, *The Faces of the Chariot: Early Jewish Responses to Ezekiel's Vision* (Tübingen: Mohr Siebeck, 1988).

2. For recent critical editions of individual Hekhalot and Merkavah texts see R. Elior, *Hekhalot Zutarti; in Jerusalem Studies in Jewish Thought* (Jerusalem: Magnes Press, 1982); P. S. Alexander, "3 (Hebrew Apocalypse of) Enoch," in *The Old Testament Pseudepigrapha,* ed., J. H. Charlesworth (New York: Doubleday, 1983), 1: 223–315; M. Cohen, *The Shiur Qomah: Texts and Recensions* (Tübingen: Mohr Siebeck, 1985). Editions of principal manuscripts composing the Hekhalot and Merkavah literature are P. Schäfer, *Synopse zur Hekhalot Literatur* (Tübingen: Mohr Siebeck, 1981), and *Geniza Fragmente zur Hekhalot Literatur* (Tübingen: Mohr Siebeck, 1984). For the place of previous editions, up to the end of the 1970s, in the synoptic editions, see Schäfer, *Synopse,* x–xvii.

3. See S. Lieberman, "How Much Greek in Jewish Palestine," in *Biblical and Other Studies,* ed., A. Altmann (Cambridge, MA: Harvard University Press, 1963), pp. 123–141.

4. For early date see G. Scholem, *Major Trends in Jewish Mysticism,* 3d ed. (New York: Schoken, 1954), pp. 41–47; *Jewish Gnosticism, Merkabah Mysticism and Talmudic Tradition,* 2d ed. (New York: Jewish Theological Seminary of America, 1965), pp. 7–8. Scholem considered *Hekhalot Zutarti* as the oldest text in the Hekhalot followed in chronological order by *Hekhalot Rabbati, Merkavah Rabbah, Ma'aseh Merkavah* and *3 Enoch.* These views were first challenged by E. E. Urbach, followed by Halperin, who argued for a later date. See E. E. Urbach, "The Traditions about Merkavah Mysticism," in *Studies in Mysticism and Religion Presented to Gershom G. Scholem on his Seventieth Birthday,* eds.,

E. E. Urbach, R. J. Z. Werblowsky, and H. Wirshuvski (Jerusalem: Magnes, 1967), pp. 1–28 [Hebrew]; D. J. Halperin, *The Merkabah in Rabbinic Literature* (New Haven: American Oriental Society, 1980); *Chariot*, esp. pp. 359–363.

5. The medieval manuscripts are included in Schäfer's *Synopse.* For background on the medieval manuscripts see Schäfer's introduction to the *Synopse,* viii–xviii and his collected articles in *Hekhalot-Studien* Texte und Studien zum antiken Judentum 19 (Tübingen: Mohr Siebeck, 1988); D. J. Halperin, "A New Edition of the Hekhalot Literature," *JAOS* 104 (1984): 543–552.

6. On the work of the Karait Salmon ben Yeruhim with references to Hekhalot and Merkavah texts see L. Nemoy, *Karaite Anthology* (New Haven, CN: Yale University Press 1952), pp. 71–82.

7. *Genizah* fragments of the Hekhalot and Merkavah literature are included in Schäfer's edition. The earliest *Genizah* manuscript is T. -S. K 21. 95. S, published in the *Geniza Fragmente,* 9–32. Some of the Genizah fragments were first published by I. Gruenwald, "New Passages from Hekhalot Literature," *Tarbitz* 38 (1968–69): 354–372 [Hebrew]; "'Remarks on the Article 'New Passages from Hekhalot Literature'," *Tarbitz* 39 (1970): 216–217 [Hebrew].

8. See reviews of the *Synopse,* criticizing Schäfer for not including some of the midrashic material and other texts, such as *Alpha Beta de–Rabbi Akiva,* in the Synoptic collection of the Hekhalot and Merkavah texts: P. S. Alexander, "Synopses zur Hekhalot-Literatur," *JJS* 34 (1983): 102–106, 105; R. Elior, "Schäfer's Synopse zur Hekhalot-Literatur," *JQR* 77 (1986/87): 213–217.

9. The complexity of the Hekhalot and Merkavah tradition and problems concerning its texts and redactions have been presented in detail by Schäfer in various studies now included in *Hekhalot-Studien.* See also Scholem, *Major Trends,* 40–79; J. Dan, *The Ancient Jewish Mysticism* (Tel Aviv: MOD Books, 1993), p. 7ff; Gruenwald, "Literary and Redactional Issues," in *From Apocalypticism to Gnosticism* (Leiden and Frankfurt: Peter Lang, 1988), p. 180 ff.; Halperin, *Chariot,* 367; P. S. Alexander, "The Historical Setting of the Hebrew Book of Enoch," *JJS* 28 (1977): 156–180.

10. On the various traditions and their reflections in different texts of Hekhalot and Merkavah literature see summaries in Scholem, *Major Trends,* 43–73; *Merkavah,* 5–7; Dan, *Mysticism,* 7–24; *Three Types of Jewish Mysticism* (Cincinnati: University of Cincinnati Press, 1984), pp. 1–81; Gruenwald, *Apocalyptic and Merkavah,* 127–234; P. Schäfer, *The Hidden and Manifest God: Some Major Themes in Early Jewish Mysticism* (Albany NY: State University of New York Press, 1992), pp. 1–138.

11. For selected recent studies which focus on the Hekhalot and Merkavah literature see: P. S. Alexander, "Comparing Merkavah Mysticism and Gnosticism, An Essay in Methods," *JJS* 35 (1984): 1–18. M. Bar-Ilan, *The Mysteries of Jewish Prayer and Hekhalot* (Ramat Gan: Bar-Ilan University Press, 1987) [Hebrew]; I. Chernus, "Individual and Community in the Reduction of the Hekhalot Literature," *HUCA* 52 (1981): 253–257; "Visions of God in Merkabah Mysticism," *JSJ* 13 (1982): 123–146; "The Pilgrimage to the Merkavah: An Interpre-

tation of Early Jewish Mysticism," *Jerusalem Studies in Jewish Thought* 6: 1–2 (1987): 1–36 [English Section]; J. Dan, "The Religious Experience of the Merkavah," in *Jewish Spirituality: From the Bible Through the Middle Ages,* ed., A. Green (New York: Crossroad, 1986), pp. 289–307; *Three Types; Mysticism;* "The Revelation of the Secret of the World," in *On Sanctity: Religious, Ethics and Mysticism in Judaism and Other Religions* (Jerusalem: Magnes Press, 1997), pp. 179–201 [Hebrew]; J. R. Davila, "The Hekhalot Literature and Shamanism," *Society of Biblical Literature Seminar Papers* 33 (1994): 767–789; *Descenders to the Chariot, The People behind the Hekhalot Literature* (Leiden, Boston, Köln: Brill, 2001); R. Elior, "The Concept of God in Hekhalot Mysticism," in *Binah, Studies in Jewish Thought* ed., J. Dan (New York, Westport, Conneticut, London: Praeger, 1989), 2: 97–120; "Mysticism, Magic, and Angelology: The Perception of Angels in Hekhalot Literature," *JSQ* 1 (1993/94): 3–53; "From Earthly Temple to Heavenly Shrine: Prayer and Sacred Song in the Hekhalot Literature and Its Relation to Temple Traditions" *JSQ* 4 (1997): 217–267; "The Merkavah Tradition and the Emergence of Jewish Mysticism: From Temple to Merkavah from Hekhal to Hekhalot from Priestly Opposition to Gazing upon the Merkavah," in *Sino-Judaica: Jews and Chinese in Historical Dialogue,* ed., A. Oppenheimer (Tel Aviv: Tel Aviv University Press, 1999), pp. 101–158; *Temple and Chariot, Priests and Angels, Sanctuary and Heavenly Sanctuaries in Early Jewish Mysticism* (Jerusalem: Magnes Press, 2002) [Hebrew]; K. E. Grözinger, *Musik und Gesang in der Theologie der fruehen juedischen Literatur* (Tüebingen: Mohr Siebeck, 1982); Gruenwald, *Apocalyptic and Merkavah; Apocalypticism to Gnosticism;* Halperin, *Chariot;* M. Idel, "The Concept of Torah in Hekhalot Literature and Its Metamorphosis in Kabbalah," *Jerusalem Studies in Jewish Thought 1* (1981): 23–84 [Hebrew]; "Enoch is Metatron," *Jerusalem Studies in Jewish Thought* 6: 1–2 (1987): 151–170. [Hebrew Section]; N. Janowitz, *The Poetics of Ascent: Theories of Language in a Rabbinic Ascent Text* (Albany, NY: State University of New York Press, 1989); A. Kuyt, *The "Descent" to the Chariot: Towards a Description of the Terminology, Place, Function and Nature of the Yeridah in Hekhalot Literature* (Tübingen: Mohr Siebeck, 1995); R. M. Lesses, *Ritual Practices to Gain Power: Angels, Incantation, and Revelation in Early Jewish Mysticism* (Harrisburg, PA: Trinity, 1998); C. R. A. Morray-Jones, "Paradise Revisited: The Jewish Mystical Background of Paul's Apostolate, Part 1: The Jewish Sources," *HTR* 86 (1993): 177–217; "Part 2: Paul's Heavenly Accent and Its Significance," *HTR* 86 (1993): 265–92; "Transformational Mysticism in the Apocalyptic-Merkabah Tradition," *JJS* 43 (1992): 1–31; *Transparent Illusion. The Dangerous Vision of Water in Hekhalot Mysticism. A Source-Critical and Tradition-Historical Inquiry* (Leiden, Boston, Köln: Brill, 2002); P. Schäfer, *Hekhalot-Studien; Hidden and Manifest;* Scholem, *Major Trends; Merkabah;* M. Smith, "Some Observations on Hekhalot Rabbati," in *Biblical and Other Studies,* ed., A. Altmann (Cambridge, MA: Harvard University Press, 1963), pp. 149–156; M. D. Swartz, *Mystical Prayer in Early Judaism: An Analysis of Ma'aseh Merkavah* (Tübingen: Mohr Siebeck, 1992); *Scholastic Magic: Ritual and Revelation in Early Jewish Mysticism* (Princeton, NJ: Princeton University Press, 1996); E. R. Wolfson, *Through a Speculum that Shines. Visions and Imagination in Medieval Jewish Mysticism* (Princeton, NJ: Princeton University Press, 1994), pp. 74–124.

12. See H. Graetz, "Die mystische Literatur in der gaonäischen Epoche," *MGWJ* 8 (1859): 67–68, 103–118, 140–153. A similar late dating was suggested by P. Bloch for other reasons. See P. Bloch, "Die Yordei Merkawa, die Mystiker der Gaonenzeit und ihr Einfluss auf die Liturgie," *MGWJ* 37 n. s. 1 (1893): 18–25, 69–74, 257–266, 305–311.

13. See M. Gaster, *Studies and Texts in Folklore, Magic, Medieval Romance, Hebrew Apocrypha and Samaritan Archaeology,* vol. 2. (London: Maggs Bros, 1330); A. Jellinek, Bet ha-Midrasch, 6 vols. 2d ed. (Jerusalem: Wahrman Books, 1967); A. J. Wertheimer, *Batei Midrashot,* 2 vols. (1950–53; reprint, Jerusalem: Katav-yad ve-Sepher, 1989); S. Musajoff, *Merkavah Shelemah* (Jerusalem: Diffus Solomon, 1921).

14. . H. Odeberg, *The Hebrew Book of Enoch or Third Enoch* (1928; reprint, New York: Ktav, 1973).

15. Scholem, *Major Trends,* chap. 2; *Merkavah.* Gruenwald, *Apocalyptic and Merkavah;* Morray-Jones, "Paradise Revisited: The Jewish Mystical Background," "Part 2: Paul's Heavenly Accent "; "Transformational Mysticism"; A. Green, *Keter: The Crown of God in Early Jewish Mysticism* (Princeton, NJ: Princeton University Press, 1997). Other scholars support this view and demonstrate links between this literature and priestly as well as priestly-angelic traditions from the last few centuries of the first millennium B. C. E and the middle of Second Temple period. See, I. Gruenwald, "The Impact of Priestly Traditions on the Creation of Merkavah Mysticism and the Shiur Komah," *Jerusalem Studies in Jewish Thought* 6: 1–2 (1987): 65–120 [Hebrew Section]; R. Elior, "From Earthly Temple to Heavenly Shrine" 217–267; "The Merkavah Tradition," 101–158; *Temple and Chariot.*

16. In Scholem's view, the tradition had emerged in Palestine among the disciples of R. Yohanan ben Zakkai, during the first century C.E., after the destruction of the Second Temple, and from there spread to Babylonia. See Scholem, *Major Trends,* 41–47; *Merkavah,* 7–8. The Talmudic scholar S. Lieberman supported these assertions. Close correspondence has been demonstrated by both Scholem and Lieberman between the mystical accounts of the heavenly ascensions to the Merkavah in the Hekhalot and Merkavah literature and the Talmudic sections dealing with *Ma'aseh Merkavah* (The Work of the Chariot). See Lieberman, "Song of Songs," published as an appendix in G. Scholem, *Merkavah,* 118–126. According to Scholem and Lieberman, the rabbinic homilitical speculations of the "Four Who Entered the *Pardes*" in *Mishnah Hagigah* 2: 1, as well as its various recensions and related traditions in the Palestinian and Babylonian Talmuds, have preserved within them echoes of the same mystical speculations and practices which are part of the Hekhalot and Merkavah literature. Morray-Jones has supported these observations in a recent study which demonstrates the interdependency of the two traditions, see his "Paradise Revisited."

17. See Urbach, "The Traditions about Merkavah Mysticism"; Halperin, *Chariot,* chaps. 1 and 9. For discussions and critiques of these views see R. Elior, "Merkabah Mysticism: A Critical Review," *Numen* 73 (1990): 233–249;

Chernus, "Individual and Community" 253–257. For supporting views see M. Himmelfarb, "The Practice of Ascent in the Ancient Mediterranean World," in *Death, Ecstasy and Other Worldly Journeys,* ed., J. J. Collins and M. Fishbane (Albany, NY: State University of New York Press, 1995), pp. 126–128; *The Ascent to Heaven in Jewish and Christian Apocalypses* (New York and Oxford: Oxford University Press, 1993), p. 108 ff.

18. M. Cohen, *The Shiur Qomah: Liturgy and Theurgy in Pre-Kabbalistic Jewish Mysticism* (Lanham, New York, and London: University Press of America, 1983); *Shiur Qomah, Texts and Recensions;* P. S. Alexander, "3 Enoch and the Talmud," *JSJ* 18 (1987): 40–68; "3 Enoch"; Swartz, *Mystical Prayer; Scholastic Magic.*

19. Attitudes towards history in the Hekhalot and Merkavah literature have been discussed, for example, in Scholem, *Major Trends,* 40–42; J. Dan, "The Revelation of the Secret," 179–201 [Hebrew]; 'The Concept of History," in *Mysticism,* 168–182; Halperin, *Chariot,* 360–363; Elior, "Mysticism, Magic, and Angelology."

20. Dan, "The Concept of History."

21. Scholem, *Major Trends,* 40–41; *Merkavah,* 1–5, 9–13; P. Schäfer, "The Aim and Purpose of Early Jewish Mysticism," in *Hekhalot-Studien,* 277–295; *Hidden and Manifest God;* Halperin, *Merkabah,* 3ff., 183ff.; *Chariot,* 377–387; Davila, "The Hekhalot Literature and Shamanism"; *Descenders to the Chariot;* Swartz, *Mystical Prayer; Scholastic Magic,* 173 ff; Elior, "From Earthly Temple to Heavenly Shrine"; "The Merkavah Tradition"; *Temple and Chariot* [Hebrew].

22. For discussions of common themes see Halperin and Urbach cited above, n. 17. See also Scholem *Merkavah,* 9–13, 24; I. Chernus, *Mysticism in Rabbinic Judaism* (Berlin and New York: de Gruyter, 1982). For textual examples see *Hagigah,* 2: 1, b; *Hagigah,* 11b–16a; *Pesiqta Rabbati,* 20.

23. On links to ancient liturgy see A. Altmann, "'Kedusha' Songs in Ancient Hekhalot Literature," *Melilah* 2 (1946): 1–24 [Hebrew]; Gruenwald, "Angelic Songs," in *Apocalypticism to Gnosticism,* 145–173; Swartz, *Mystical Prayer;* Elior, "From Earthly Temple," 230 ff.; Bar Ilan, *Jewish Prayer and Hekhalot* [Hebrew]. On links to priestly and priestly-angelic traditions see See Gruenwald, "The Impact of Priestly Traditions"; Elior, "From Earthly Temple to Heavenly Shrine"; "The Merkavah Tradition"; *Temple and Chariot.*

24. For a discussion of the connection between Hekhalot and Merkavah and apocalyptic literature see Scholem, *Major Trends,* 51–52; Gruenwald, *Apocalyptic and Merkavah,* 29–72; Alexander, "3 Enoch," 223–254; Halperin, *Chariot,* 63–113; Himmelfarb, *The Ascent to Heaven,* 107–114.

25. On links between Hekhalot and Merkavah literature and Qumran literature see Scholem, *Major Trends,* 43–46, 54, 29, 128; J. Strugnell, "The Angelic Liturgy At Qumran- 4Q Serekh Shirot Olat Hashabbat," VTSup 7 (1960): 318–345; C. Newsom, "Merkabah Exegesis in the Qumran Sabbath Shirot," *JJS* 38 (1987): 11–30; L. Schiffman, "Merkavah Speculation at Qumran: The 4Q Serekh Shirot Olat ha-Shabbat," in *Mystics, Philosophers and Politicians,* eds., J. Reinharz

and D. Swetschinski (Durham: Duke University Press, 1982), pp. 35–45; J. M. Baumgarten "The Qumran Sabbath Shirot and Rabbinic Merkabah Tradition," *Revue de Qumran* 13 (1988): 199–213; Halperin, *Chariot*, 49–55. J. R. Davila, "The Hodayot Hymnist and the Four who Entered Paradise," *Revue de Qumran* 17 (1996): 457–478.

26. For discussion of connections between Hekhalot and Merkavah literature and Gnosticism see early suggestions by H. Graetz, "Die mystische Literatur in der gaonischen Epoche," 104. See later views: Scholem, *Major Trends*, chap. 2; *Merkavah*. See critical review by D. Flusser, "Scholem's Recent Book on Merkabah Literature," *JJS* 11 (1960): 59–68. See also Alexander, "Comparing Merkavah Mysticism and Gnosticism,"1–18; Dan, *Mysticism*, 42 ff.; "Anafiel, Metatron, and the Creator," *Tarbitz* 52 (1982–83): 447–457 [Hebrew]; Gruenwald, *Apocalypticism to Gnosticism*, 123–198; "Knowledge and Vision: Towards a clarification of two 'Gnostic' concepts in the light of their alleged origin," *Israel Oriental Studies* 3 (1973): 63–107; G. G. Stroumsa, "Aher: A Gnostic," in *The Rediscovery of Gnosticism*, ed., B. Layton Bentley (Leiden: Brill, 1981), 2: 808–818; N. Deutsch, *The Gnostic Imagination* (Leiden, New York, Köln: Brill, 1985); *Guardians of the Gate, Angelic Vice Regency in Late Antiquity* (Leiden, Boston, Köln: Brill, 1999), pp. 111–123.

27. On connection between Paul's account in II Corinthians 12: 2–4 and the Hekhalot and Merkavah literature see Scholem, *Merkavah*, chap. 3; P. Schäfer, "New Testament and Hekhalot Literature: The Journey into Heaven in Paul and in Merkavah Mysticism," *JJS* 35 (1984): 19–35; Morray-Jones, "Paradise Revisited"; A. F. Segal, *Paul, the Convert: The Apostolate and Apostsasy of Saul of the Pharisee* (New Haven and London: Yale University Press, 1990), pp. 38–71. On the influence of Hekhalot and Merkavah traditions on early christology including themes of exaltation and divine angelic intermediary see A. Segal, *Two Powers in Heaven: Early Rabbinic Reports about Christianity and Gnosticism* (Leiden: Brill, 1977); C. Rowland, *The Open Heaven: A Study in Apocalypticism in Judaism and Early Christianity* (New York: Crossroad, 1982); J. E. Fossum, *The Image of the Invisible God: Essays on the Influence of Jewish Mysticism on Early Christology* (Göttingen: Vandenhoeck and Ruprecht, 1995); T. Eskola, *Messiah and the Throne: Jewish Merkabah Mysticism and Early Christian Exaltation Discourse* (Tübingen: Mohr Siebeck, 2001).

28. For comparisons with Jewish magical-theurgical traditions see L. H. Schiffman and M. D. Swartz, *Hebrew and Aramaic Incantation Texts from the Cairo Genizah: Selected Texts from Taylor-Schechter-1* (Sheffield: Sheffield Academic Press, 1992); Swartz, *Scholastic Magic*. On links to Jewish incantation literature see P. Schäfer, "Jewish Magic Literature in Late Antiquity and Early Middle Ages," *JJS* 41 (1990): 75–91; "Magic and Religion in Ancient Judaism," in *Envisioning Magic: A Princeton Seminar and Symposium*, eds., P. Schafer and H. G. Kippenberg (Leiden: Brill, 1997), pp. 19–43. Compare traditions in *Sefer ha-Razim*, a book of Hebrew spells and incantations, which have been found in the Cairo *Genizah* or have been preserved in later Jewish sources: M. Margaliot, ed., *Sefer ha-Razim* (Jerusalem: American Academy for Jewish

Research, 1966) [Hebrew]. On links to magical practices in ancient Greco-Egyptian and Jewish cultures see Lesses, Ritual *Practices to Gain Power.*

29. See n. 13 above.

30. See n. 14 above.

31. Alexander, "3 Enoch"; Cohen, *The Shiur Qomah;* Elior, *Hekhalot Zutarti;* Gruenwald, "New Passages"; "Remarks on the Article 'New Passages'"; K. Herrman, *Massekhet Hekhalot: Traktat von den himmlischen Palästen. Edition, Übersetzung, und Kommentar* (Tübingen: Mohr Siebeck, 1994); G. Scholem, "Ma'aseh Merkavah," appendix C in *Jewish Gnosticism, Merkabah Mysticism and Talmudic Tradition* (New York: Jewish Theological Seminary of America, 1965), pp. 103–136.

32. On the *Synopse,* and the *Geniza Fragmente* editions see n. 2 above. The paragraphs in the synoptic edition have been arranged in a synoptic manner, without imposing a final recension, using MS New York 8128 as a fictive basis. Schäfer's explains his principles in several articles included in *Hekhalot-Studien.* The term "macroform" used by Schäfer in this context defines an individual work of the Hekhalot and Merkavah and indicates its "fictive" or "ideal" form as well as its different manifestations in the various manuscripts. The term microform defines smaller units of work. Schäfer has not suggested a global date for the literature, but rather referred to different units. The *Hekhalot Rabbati* is thought by him to be an earlier collection, and following it, in chronological order, are *Hekhalot Zutarti, Ma'aseh Merkavah, Merkavah Rabbah,* and *3 Enoch.*

33. Schäfer has stated his views in several studies collected in *Hekhalot-Studien.* See also "Redactional Identity of 'Hekhalot Rabbati,'" *Jerusalem Studies in Jewish Thought* 6: 1–2 (1987): 1–12 [Hebrew Section]; "Tradition and Redaction in Hekhalot Literature," *JSJ* 14 (1983): 172–181.

34. For discussion of the phenomenological approach to Jewish mysticism see M. Idel, *Kabbalah, New Perspectives* (New Haven: Yale University Press, 1988), p. xix ff., 22 ff. For a discussion of the common ideology of the Hekhalot and Merkavah literature and the phenomenological approach to it see Dan, *Mysticism,* 27 ff.; *Three Types,* 1–8; Gruenwald, "Literary and Redactional Issues," in *Apocalypticism to Gnosticism,* 183–186; Elior, "The Concept of God," 97–100; Wolfson, *Speculum,* 74, 81 ff.

35. Scholem, *Major Trends,* 45 ff; Gruenwald, *Apocalyptic and Merkavah* 98 ff; Dan, *Mysticism,* 25ff; *Three Types* 8–16; Elior, "The Concept of God"; "Mysticism, Magic, and Angelology"; "From Earthly Temple to Heavenly Shrine"; Grözinger, *Musk und Gesang.*

36. Halperin, *Merkabah; Chariot,* 359–363; Schäfer, *Hidden and Manifest,* 150–155; Himmelfarb, *The Ascent to Heaven,* 106–114; "The Practice of Ascent," 126–128.

37. Alexander, "The Historical Setting," *JJS* 28 (1977): 173.

38. Wolfson, *Speculum*, 120. For an analogous view of the context of Jewish mysticism see M. Idel, "The Concept of Torah in Hekhalot Literature," 36 [Hebrew]. For similar views of the mystical phenomena in general see B. Garaside, "Language and Interpretation of Mystical Experience," *International Journal for the Philosophy of Religion* 3 (1972): 93–102; P. Moore, "Mystical Experience, Mystical Doctrine, Mystical Technique," in *Mysticism and Philosophical Analysis*, ed., S. T. Katz (London and New York: Sheldon 1978), pp. 101–131; C. Keller, "Mystical Literature," in *Mysticism and Philosophical Analysis*, ed., S. T. Katz (London and New York: Sheldon 1978), pp. 59–67; B. McGinn, *The Foundations of Mysticism* (New York: Crossroad, 1991), 1: 321.

39. S. T. Katz, "Language, Epistemology and Mysticism," in *Mysticism and Philosophical Analysis*, ed., S. T. Katz (London and New York: Sheldon 1978), p. 26. For a full discussion see pp. 22–24.

40. R. M. Gimello, "Mysticism in Context," in *Mysticism and Religious Traditions*, ed., S. T. Katz (New York: Oxford University Press 1983), pp. 61–88; Keller, "Mystical Literature," 59–67; Moore, "Mystical Experience, Mystical Doctrine," 101–131.

41. McGinn, *Foundations of Mysticism*, xiv.

42. On the relationship between mystical writings, exegesis, experiences and the value of cultures of a specific historical milieu see discussion in Idel, *Kabbalah*, 17 ff., 59 ff.; S. T. Katz "The 'Conservative' Character of Mysticism," in *Mysticism and Religious Traditions*, ed., S. Katz, (New York: Oxford University Press 1983), pp. 3–60; "Language, Epistemology," 22–24; K. Waujman, "Towards a Phenomenological Definition of Spirituality," *Studies in Spirituality* 3 (1993): 5–57; M. Fishbane, The *Exegetical Imagination, On Jewish Thought and Theology* (Cambridge, MA: Harvard University Press, 1998).

43. On considering various different forms of mystical writings as a source for understanding the phenomenological aspects of any mystical tradition, see Keller, "Mystical Literature," 59–67.

44. For a comprehensive presentation of modern theories of mysticism, presented from theological, philosophical, psychological and phenomenological perspectives, see McGinn, *Foundations of Mysticism*, 265–343.

45. McGinn, *Foundations of Mysticism*, xix.

46. McGinn, *Foundations of Mysticism*, xvii. Compare E. Underhill's well known view: "mysticism, in its pure form, is . . . the science of union with the Absolute and nothing else, and . . . the mystic is a person who attains this union." E. Underhill, *Mysticism: A Study in the Nature and Development of Man's Spirituality* (1911; reprint, New York and Ontario: Meridian, 1974), p. 72. For critiques of this and similar limited views that deny validity to experiences other than union see McGinn, *Foundations of Mysticism*, xii–xx, 275 ff., 321 ff. For discussions of various mystical models see D. Merkur, *Mystical Moments and Unitive Thinking* (Albany, NY: State University of New York Press, 1999), pp. 1–25.

47. J. Dan, "In Quest of a Historical Definition of Mysticism," *Studies in Spirituality* 3 (1993): 66.

48. J. E. Collins *Mysticism and New Paradigm Psychology* (Savage, MD: Rowman and Littlefield 1991), pp. xix–xx.

49. D. Merkur, *Gnosis: An Esoteric Tradition of Mystical Visions and Unions* (Albany, NY: State), p. 11.

50. Keller, "Mystical Literature," 77.

51. Merkur, *Gnosis,* 11.

52. These macroforms, published in P. Schäfer's *Synopse* and *Geniza Fragmente,* will be the main sources for our investigation: *Hekhalot Rabbati—Synopse,* 81–121, 152–154, 156–173, 189–196, 196–277; *Hekhalot Zutarti—Synopse,* 335–374, 407–426; *Sefer Hekhalot = 3 Enoch—Synopse,* 1–80; *Ma'aseh Merkavah—* Synopse, 544–596; *Shi'ur Komah—Synopse,* 376–377, 468–484, various fragments relating to Metatron known as *Shivhei Metatron—Synopse,* 384–406, 484–488, and several *Genizah* fragments especially 8 (also known as the *Ozayah* fragment, after the name of the angel Ozayah), 11, and 22.

53. On several recensions of *Hekhalot Rabbati* see Schäfer's discussion in *Hekhalot-Studien,* 63–74; 96–103. The list excludes MS. TS 21. 95S (G1), an important fragment from Cairo *Genizah.* J. R. Davila has argued that the manuscripts of *Hekhalot Rabbati* present little internal variation and a critical text could be produced of it: "Prolegomena to a Critical Edition of the Hekhalot Rabbati," *JJS* 45 (1994): 208–226. On the background of this ascent see discussions of the "story of the ten martyrs": Gruenwald, *Apocalyptic and Merkavah,* 158–159.

54. For diverse views on the term "descent," frequently used in this literature to describe an "ascent" to divine realms, see Scholem, *Major Trends,* 46–47; *Merkavah,* 20 n. 1; Schäfer, *Hidden and Manifest,* 2–3; Halperin, *Chariot,* 226–227; A. Kuyt, "Once Again: 'yarad' in Hekhalot Literature," *Frankfurter Judaistische Beiträge* 18 (1990): 45–69; *The "Descent" to the Chariot;* G. G. Stroumsa, "Mystical Descent," in *Death, Ecstasy and Other Worldly Journeys,* ed., J. J. Collins and M. Fishbane (Albany, NY: State University of New York Press, 1995), pp. 137–153; E. R. Wolfson, "Yerida la -Merkavah: Typology of Ecstasy and Enthronement in Ancient Jewish Mysticism," in *Mystics of the Book—Themes, Topics and Typologies,* ed., R. A. Herrera (New York: Peter Lang, 1993), pp. 13–45. For textual examples see *Synopse,* 94, 163, 234, 236, 335, 407, 565, 672, 685, G8.

55. On the "Pardes" (the Divine "orchard") traditions in Hekhalot and Merkavah literature see *Synopse,* 334–343, 408–410. On the term "Pardes," its origin and place in Rabbinic literature see Halperin, *Merkavah,* 65–105; Morray-Jones, "Paradise Revisited," 177–217; *Transparent Illusion,* 1–53; Scholem, *Major Trends,* 52–53; *Mysticism,* 14–19.

56. See Elior, *Hekhalot Zutarti,* 61; Idel, "The Concept of the Torah," 28 n. 21.

57. On *Hekhalot Zutarti* and its redactions see Schäfer, *Hekhalot-Studien*, 50–62; Elior, *Hekhalot Zutarti*.

58. On *Ma'aseh Merkavah* manuscripts see Swartz, *Mystical Prayer*, esp., 41–62; Janowitz, *The Poetics of Ascent*, 17–28. On *Ma'aseh Merkavah* structure and redactions see Swartz, *Mystical Prayer*, 65–103.

59. On *3 Enoch* see Schäfer, *Hekhalot-Studien*, 84–95; Alexander, "3 Enoch," 223–253; "The Historical Setting of the Hebrew Book of Enoch"; J. R. Davila, "Of Methodology, Monotheism, and Metatron: Introductory reflections on Divine Mediators and the Origins of the Worship of Jesus," in *The Jewish Roots of Christological Monotheism. Papers from the St. Andrews Conference on the Historical Origin of the Worship of Jesus*, eds., C. C. Newman, J. R. Davila, and G. S. Lewis (Leiden: Brill, 1999), pp. 3–18.

60. On *Shi'ur Komah* traditions, provenance, transmission, and dating see G. Scholem, *Major Trends*, 63–67; *Merkabah*, 36–42, J. Dan, "The Concept of Knowledge in the Shi'ur Qomah," in *Studies in Jewish Religious and Intellectual History Presented to Alexander Altmann* eds., S. Stein and R. Loewe (Alabama: University Of Alabama Press, 1979), pp. 67–73; Cohen, The *Shi'ur Qomah;* Gruenwald, *Apocalyptic and Merkavah*, 213–217, "Knowledge and Vision"; Halperin, *Chariot*, 405 ff.

61. See, for example, *Synopse*, 203–204, 225–228, 240, 579–586.

62. See, for example, *Synopse*, 1, 216, 348, 405, 554, 556, 557, 579, 592.

63. See, for example, *Synopse*, 81, 203, 219, 247, 335, 421, 572.

64. For narratives see, for example, *Synopse*, 108–121, 334–345, 408–410. For dialogues see, for example, *Synopse*, 4 ff., 111, 201–206, 484, 558 ff., 570, 579 ff., 595

65. See, for example, *Synopse*, 421, 470, 544–546, 551–553, 585–592, 593–596.

66. See Keller, "Mystical Literature," 77 ff.

CHAPTER 2 : HEKHALOT AND MERKAVAH MYSTICISM

1. Keller, "Mystical Literature," 86.

2. G8; *Geniza Fragmente*, 103.

3. On the homogeneous ideology of Hekhalot and Merkavah literature see Dan, *Mysticism*, 27 ff.; *Three Types*, 1–8; Gruenwald, "Literary and Redactional Issues," in *From Apocalypticism to Gnosticism* 183–186; *Apocalyptic and Merkavah*, 99; Elior, "The Concept of God," 97–100; Wolfson, *Speculum*, 74, 81 ff. On the benefits of consulting a variety of different forms of mystical writings in order to understand clearly the phenomenological aspects of any mystical tradition, see Keller, "Mystical Literature," 59–67.

4. On various "ideal figures" in ancient Judaism see discussion in J. J. Collins and G. W. E. Nickelsburg, eds., *Ideal Figures in Ancient Judaism* (Chico: Scholars Press, 1980). On "models" in mysticism see S. T. Katz, "Models, Modeling, and Mystical Training," *Religion* 12 (1982): 247–275.

5. On the concept of "model" in various mystical traditions see S. Katz, "The 'Conservative' Character of Mysticism," 43–51. On Enoch as a model for "Yordei Merkavah" see Scholem, *Major Trends*, 47; *Merkavah*, 60; Schäfer, *Hidden and Manifest*, 134. On Moses as a model see Schäfer, *Hidden and Manifest*, 63, 67, 73, 88; Elior, *Hekhalot Zutarti*, 61; Idel, "The Concept of Torah," 28, n. 21 [Hebrew]. On Rabbi Ishmael as a model, see Schäfer, *Hidden and Manifest*, 88–89, 108–109. On Rabbi Akiva as a model, see Schäfer, *Hidden and Manifest*, 58–59, 67; Gruenwald, *Apocalyptic and Merkavah*, 146; Elior, *Hekhalot Zutarti*, 61. On Rabbi Nehunia ben Ha-Kanah as a model see Schäfer, *Hidden and Manifest*, 88; Dan, "Secret of the World,"16–21 [Hebrew]. See, for example, descriptions in *Synopse*, 336, 337, 347.

6. G8; *Geniza Fragmente*, 103. This passage is part of the instructions given by the angel Ozayah to the descenders to the Merkavah. Compare Gruenwald, "New Passages," 354–72; Halperin, *Chariot*, 368–369; Kuyt, *The Descent to the Chariot*, 34–52.

7. For a different view that human mind cannot independently conceive the divine see Elior, "The Concept of God," 108 ff., 112 ff.

8. F. J. Streng, "Language and Mystical Awareness," in *Mysticism and Philosophical Analysis* ed., S. T. Katz (London and New York: Sheldon 1978), p. 142.

9. *Hekhalot Rabbati; Synopse*, 218. Compare *Synopse*, 216.

10. Needless to say that both, biblical and rabbinical sources include various parallel conflicting perspectives. On the contrast between the human and divine realms in the Hebrew bible see, for example, Isa. 14: 12–20 (compare Ezk. 28: 11–19); Prov. 30: 2–4 (compare Job 26; 38: 1–42: 6); Deut. 29: 29 and 30: 11–14. On concepts of Heaven and Earth in the Hebrew bible see J. E. Wright, *The Early History of Heaven* (Oxford, New York: Oxford University Press, 2000), p. 52ff. On views concerning visions of the divine in the Hebrew Bible see, for example, Exod. 20: 2–4, Deut. 4: 12, 15–16. On the tendency to abstract God in Deuteronomistic sources see M. Weinfeld, *Deuteronomy and Deuteronomistic School* (Oxford: Clarendon Press, 1972), pp. 191–209; M. Fishbane, *Biblical Interpretation in Ancient Israel* (Oxford and New York: Oxford University Press, 1985), p. 322; R. S. Hendel, "The Social Origin of the Anicoic Tradition in Ancient Israel," *Classical Biblical Quarterly* 50 (1988): 365–382; I. Knohl, *The Sanctuary of Silence: The Priestly Torah and the Holiness School* (Minneapolis: Fortress Press, 1995). On views concerning visions of the divine in rabbinical sources see A. Marmorstein, "The Old Rabbinic Doctrine of God," in *Essays in Anthropomorphism* 2 (London 1937; reprint New York: Ktav, 1968); E. E. Urbach, *The Sages, Their Concepts and Beliefs* translated by I. Abrahams (Jerusalem: Magnes Press, 1975), pp. 66–79; Chernus, "Visions of God in

Merkabah Mysticism"; M. Fishbane, "The Measure and the Glory of God in Ancient Midrash," in *The Exegetical Imagination*, 56–72.

11. This notion, in my view, varies from divinely inspired revelation, discussed by Fishbane, for example, in which visions and revelations are endowed by God and interpreted by a divine voice or inspiration: M. Fishbane, *Biblical Interpretation*, 443–505. See further n. 123 below. For discussion of the new mystical approach found in the Hekhalot and Merkavah literature, in light of former Jewish traditions see Scholem, *Major Trends*, 64; Dan, *Three Types*, 2–7; *Mysticism*, 25–41; Elior, "The Concept of God," 98–100; Gruenwald, "Knowledge and Vision," 88–105; Schäfer, *Hidden and Manifest*, 161–163.

12. For studies of various forms of heavenly ascent in the ancient world, see views in classical works: W. Bousset, "Die Himmelsrise der Seele," *Archiv für Religionswissenschaft* 4 (1901): 136–169, 229–273. For recent studies see I. P. Culianu, *Psychanodia I—A Survey of the Evidence concerning the Ascension of the Soul and its Relevance* (Leiden: Brill, 1983); Himmelfarb, *The Ascent to Heaven;* Rowland, *The Open Heaven*; Schäfer, "New Testament and Hekhalot Literature"; A. F. Segal, "Heavenly Ascent in Hellenistic Judaism, Early Christianity, and their Environment," *Aufstieg und Niedergang der Römischen Welt* II. 23. 2 (1980): 1333–1394; J. D. Tabor, *Things Unutterable: Paul's Ascent to Paradise in its Greco-Roman, Judaic, and Early Christian Contexts* (Lamham, MD: University Press of America, 1986); D. J. Halperin,"Ascension or Invasion: Implication of the Heavenly Journey in Ancient Judaism." *Religion* 18 (1988): 47–67.

13 Compare, for instance, *Synopse*, 1, 81, 93, 159, 169, 198, 248, 259, 335, 403, 407, 408, 409, 421, 545, 554, 557, 570, 579, 592, 595, 688, *Geniza Fragmente*, 103, 105. The source of the phrase "to behold the King in his beauty" is Isa. 33: 17. For an analysis of this and similar expressions see Elior, "The Concept of God," 27–32. For the mystical significance of terms such as "beholding," "seeing," "gazing" and so forth, see Scholem, *Major Trends*, 52–53, 56; *Merkavah*, 14–16, 77; Gruenwald, *Apocalyptic and Merkavah*, 94, 137–138; "Knowledge and Vision," 96.

14. *Synopse*, 545.

15. *Synopse*, 81.

16. *Synopse*, 556. Compare Isa. 6: 1; 1 Kgs 22: 19; 2 Chron. 18: 18.

17. Compare statements in several macroforms: *Synopse*, 159, 198, 248, 259, 407–409, 411, 421, 545, 570, 688.

18. *Hekhalot Rabbati; Synopse*, 218. Compare *Synopse*, 216.

19. *Hekhalot Zutarti; Synopse*, 169. Compare *Synopse*, 163, 164.

20. See *Hekhalot Rabbati; Synopse*, 181. Compare *Synopse*, 198, 220, 224, 229, 791, 811.

21. *Hekhalot Rabbati; Synopse*, 213–214. Compare *Synopse*, 3, 8.

22. *Synopse,* 102. Compare *Synopse,* 276, 966. Following Chernus I read this passage as a description of the fatal dangers involving the vision, contra Scholem who sees it as a description of a mystical transfiguration taking place within the mystic. See Chernus, "Visions of God," 129–130; Scholem, *Merkavah,* 60.

23. Scholem, "Shiur Komah," in *On the Mystical Shape of the Godhead: Basic Concepts in the Kabbalah,* translated by J. Neugroschel (New York: Schoken, 1991), p. 20 ff. *Major Trends,* 66; *Kabbalah,* 17.

24. Gruenwald, *Apocalyptic and Merkavah,* 94. In his more recent studies Gruenwald has altered his opinions and presented the visions of God as the ultimate goal in Merkavah mysticism. See "Literary and Redactional Issues," 184; "Knowledge and Vision," 108–109; "The Impact of Priestly Tradition," 105 n. 7 [Hebrew]. See also Dan's view: "The Concept of Knowledge," 70–71. Morray-Jones identifies a "name-bearing angel who embodies the *kavod*": "Transformational Mysticism," 9. For similar views see G. G. Stroumsa,, "Form(s) of God: Some Notes on Metatron and Christ." *HTR* 76 (1983): 269–288; N. Dethch, *The Gnostic Imagination,* 99–105.

25. Elior, "The Concept of God," 109–110.

26. Elior, "The Concept of God," 113–114.

27. Schäfer, *Hidden and Manifest,* 148–150; 162 ff.

28. Chernus, "Visions of God."

29. Wolfson, *Speculum,* 85. See discussion pp. 82–98.

30. McGinn, *Foundations of Mysticism,* xix.

31. *Hekhalot Zutarti; Synopse,* 335. For a different reading see: Elior, "The Concept of God," 113; Schäfer, *Hidden and Manifest,* 70 ff.

32. Streng "Language and Mystical Awareness," 142 [Italic in the original].

33. Idel, *Kabbalah,* 111.

34. *Hekhalot Rabbati; Synopse,* 203.

35. McGinn, *Foundations of Mysticism,* xvi.

36. Dan, "The Secret of the World" [Hebrew]; "In Quest of a Historical Definition of Mysticism," 58–90.

37. *Hekhalot Rabbati; Synopse,* 202–203.

38. The various methods often overlap. See, for example, mention of both fasting and bodily posture (known as "Elijah posture") in *Hekhalot Zutarti; Synopse,* 424: "Whoever wishes to learn this teaching and to explain the explanation of the Name, will sit in fasting forty days and place his head between his knees until the fasting controls him. He must recite an incantation to earth and not to heaven . . . and if he is a youth, he may recite it so long as he does not have an ejaculation. If he has a wife he must be ready by the third day . . . "

The purpose of these practices is not clear. Nonetheless, according to the previous section, 421–423, they are linked to both, the ability to "behold the work of his creator" (*Synopse,* 421) and to the"ascent and descent of the chariot" (*Synopse,* 422–423). For a different view, that the ritual has anything to do with heavenly journeys, see Halperin, *Chariot,* 374; "A New Edition of the Hekhalot Literature," 550–551. Mention of the fast which "controls" the mystic implies, it appears, a change of attitude. On ascetic practices and mystical techniques see Scholem, *Major Trends,* 44, 49–50; Gruenwald, *Apocalyptic and Merkavah,* 99–102; Idel, *Kabbalah,* 78–79; D. Merkur, "Unitive Experience and the State of Trance," in *Mystical Union In Judaism, Christianity and Islam, An Ecumenical Dialogue,* eds., M. Idel and B. McGinn (New York 1989), pp. 125–153. On "Elijah posture" and its effect see Idel, *Kabbalah,* 89; Scholem, *Major Trends,* 49–50. See Elior's view of this description and its references to ascetic seclusion: *Hekhalot Zutarti,* 59 [Hebrew]. On seclusion as am mystical method see M. Idel, "Hitbodedut as Concentration in Jewish Philosophy," *Da'at* 14 (1985): 35–82; 15 (1986): 117–120. [Hebrew]; Chernus, "Individual and Community," 253–227.

39. See, for example, *Synopse,* 547 in which the vision of God and the celestial realm is associated with prays, praises of God, and a purification ritual: "He said to him to Rabbi Ishmael: How can one behold them and see what does RWZYY YHWH do? Rabbi Akiva said to me: I prayed a prayer of mercy and I was saved . . . and what what do I do and can behold them and see what does RWZYY YHWH do? When Rabbi Akiva heard what, he said to me and revealed that all flesh and blood, who has in his heart the praise of RWZYY YHWH God of Israel this great secret is revealed to him he must complete it on each day a the break of dawn and cleanse himself from falsehood and from wrongdoing and from all evil." For songs, hymns and prayers as mystical techniques compare 81, 94–106; 544, 550, 551–557, 592, 595–596. See discussions: Altmann, "Songs," 1–24; Scholem, *Major Trends,* 56; *Merkavah,* 75–83; Grözinger, "The Names of God and the Celestial Powers: Their Function and Meaning in the Hekhalot Literature," *Jerusalem Studies in Jewish Thought 6: 1–2* (1987): 66–77 [English Section]; Elior, "From Earthly Temple," 230 ff.

40. See for example *Synopse,* 421: "Anyone who wishes to pray this pray and to behold (להתבונן) the work of his creator will recall (יזכור) for himself one of these letters. . ." For mention of names and letters compare *Synopse,* 336, 337, 340, 342, 413–414. See discussion: Scholem, *Major Trends,* 57–63, *Merkavah,* 20–30; Grözinger, "The Names of God," 23–42.

41. For example, see *Synopse,* 554.

42. See, for example, *Synopse,* 204 which associates the descent to the Merkavah with adjuration of the angel Suriah by the repetition of divine names: "When someone wishes to descent into the Merkavah, he calls on Suriah, the prince of the presence, and adjures him one hundred and twelve times by TWTRWSY'Y YWY. . ." See *Hekhalot Rabbati; Synopse,* 204–205.

43. Moore, "Mystical Experience," 120.

44. See views by Scholem, *Major Trends*, 49–60; Gruenwald, "Angelic Songs"; Dan, *Mysticism*, 76–80; Wolfson, *Speculum*, 110 ff.; Idel, *Kabbalah*, 88 ff.; Elior, "The Concept of God"; Merkur, *Gnosis*, 155–180; Davila, "The Hekhalot Literature and Shamanism."

45. *Ma'aseh Merkavah*; *Synopse*, 579–584. See analysis in Swartz, *Mystical Prayer*, 22–23; Janowitz, *The Poetics of Ascent*, 95–97.

46. *Hekhalot Zutarti*; *Synopse*, 337.

47. *Hekhalot Rabbati*; *Synopse*, 107–111.

48. *Hekhalot Rabbati*, *Synopse*, 225–228. For analysis of this passage see Schiffman, *Association for Jewish Studies Review* 1 (1976), 269–281; Lieberman, "The Knowledge of Halakha by the Author (or Authors) of the Heikhaloth," appendix 2 in I. Gruenwald, *Apocalyptic and Merkavah Mysticism*, 241–244; Gruenwald, "Angelic Songs"; Idel, *Kabbalah*, 88–89; Wolfson, *Speculum*, 108; Dan, *Mysticism*, 82.

49. Schäfer, *Hidden and Manifest*, 150–165; Halperin, *JAOS* 104 (1984), 549–551; *Chariot*, 370, 441; Swartz, *Scholastic Magic*. Lesses, *Ritual Practices*. See also Himmelfarb, "The Practice of Ascent," 126–128; *The Ascent to Heaven*, 108 ff.; These scholars rightly observe that the Hekhalot and Merkavah literature also introduces magical-theurgic traditions and ritual practices to gain power, which do not pertain to the ascent to the Merkavah traditions but design to compel angels to descend from heaven to disclose to the mystics esoteric secrets of Torah (*Sar Torah* Traditions). These traditions, which are not part of the Hekhalot and Merkavah literature mystical core, will not examined in this study. Likewise, it is beyond its scope to discuss the many debated theories of magic and theurgy and to examine the Hekhalot and Merkavah literature in light of them. This study subscribes to Werblowsky's views that magic and mysticism are integrated, not exclusive. See R. J. Z. Werblowsky, "Mystical and Magical Contemplation," *History of Religions* 1 (1961): 9–36; "On the Mystical Rejection of Mystical Illuminations," *Religious Studies* 1 (1965/6): 177–184. On magical techniques as part of mystical methods in Hekhalot and Merkavah mysticism, see Scholem, *Major Trends*, 50–51; *Kabbalah*, (New York: Meridian, 1978), p. 15 ff.

50. See Hai Gaon's views in B. M. Lewin, *Otzar Ha-Geonim: Thesaurus of the Gaonic Responsa and Commentaries: Tractae Jom-Tow, Chagiga and Maschkin* (Haifa and Jerusalem: Hebrew University Press Association, 1931) 4: 14–15. Compare Scholem's explanation of the term *"yeridah la-merkavah"* as "those who reach down into themselves in order to perceive the chariot," *Kabbalah*, 6.

51. Halperin, "New Edition of Hekhalot Literature," 543–552.

52. Idel, *Kabbalah*, 90. Idel further comments that this interpretation may bear some affinities to much earlier Jewish views. See *Kabbalah*, 91, 319 nn. 107, 108.

53. These methods effect adepts' perception of God and the Merkavah enabeling "to look," "to gaze," "to look," "to glance," "to peer," "to behold," (**להסתכל לצפות להציץ לראות**). See, for example, *Synopse*, 81, 104, 335 (MS

M22), 414, 421, 424, 544, 547, 550, 595. For discussion of the psychological and mental aspects of mystical experience see Merkur, "Unitive Experiences and the State of Trance,"125–153.

54. *Ma'aseh Merkavah; Synopse,* 591.

55. *Ma'aseh Merkavah; Synopse,* 570.

56. *Ma'aseh Merkavah; Synopse,* 557.

57. *Hekhalot Rabbati; Synopse,* 81.

58. *Ma'aseh Merkavah; Synopse,* 554.

59. Moore, "Mystical Experience," 113.

60. *Ma'aseh Merkavah; Synopse,* 558.

61. For example, see *Synopse,* 93, 199–201, 224, 234. See Scholem, *Major Trends,* 41–42, 52–70; Gruenwald, *Apocalypticism and Merkavah,* 99.

62. For example, see *Synopse,* 181, 204, 247, 335, 421, 572.

63. Moore, "Mystical Experience," 113.

64. *Ma'aseh Merkavah; Synopse,* 544.

65. Scholem, *Major Trends,* 79.

66. *Ma'aseh Merkavah; Synopse,* 558.

67. On the dangers and tests see Dan, *Mysticism,* 93 ff.

68. *Hekhalot Rabbati; Synopse,* 224–228.

69. Idel, *Kabbalah,* 205–206.

70. Dan, "In Quest of a Historical Definition of Mysticism," 66.

71. Scholem, *Merkavah,* 14–19; *Major Trends,* 52–53; Halperin, *Merkabah,* 86–92; *Chariot,* 199 ff.; Dan, *Mysticism,* 93; Schäfer, *Hidden and Manifest,* 38–39; "New Testament and Hekhalot Literature," 28–35.

72. See *Synopse,* 259. Compare *Synopse,* 344–346, 409–410.

73. *Hekhalot Zutarti; Synopse,* 345, cf. 672. On "the Other" (אחר), a prevalent designation for the heretic Eliaha Ben Avuyah, see Y. Liebes, *The Sin of Elisha: The Four Who Entered Paradise and the Nature of Talmudic Mysticism* (Jerusalem: Akademon, 1990) [Hebrew].

74. *Hekhalot Zutarti; Synopse,* 410. Compare *Synopse,* 344–345.

75. *Synopse,* 346. Compare *Synopse,* 673. In this context it is interesting to note a link between the stage of being worthy or being fit to behold divine visions and the ability to behold. The Hebrew term, "to be worthy of," or "to fit" ראוי, is a passive present participle form of the Hebrew root "to behold," ראה.

76. Streng "Language and Mystical Awareness," 142.

77. *Ma'aseh Merkavah; Synopse,* 580–581.

78. This observation disagrees with Scholem who suggests that the Hekhalot and Merkavah mysticism takes no particular interest in human beings, *Major Trends,* 79. On transformation compare Morray-Jones, "Transformational Mysticism," 25 ff.; Idel, "Enoch is Metatron"; V. D. Arbel, "Understanding of the Heart—Mystical Experiences in the Hekhalot Literature," *JSJ* 6/4 (1999): 319–344.

79. On the pattern of "death and rebirth" see A. van Gennep, "Initiation Rites," in *The Rite of Passage,* trans. M. B. Vizedom and G. L. Caffe (Chicago: University of Chicago Press, 1960); C. Bell, *Rituals: Perspectives and Dimensions* (New York: Oxford University Press 1997), pp. 94–102; V. Turner, *The Ritual Process: Structure and Anti-Structure* (London: Routledge and Kegan, 1969), p. 94ff; M. Eliade, *Birth and Rebirth: The Religious Meanings of Initiation in Human Culture.* trans. W. R. Trask (New York: Harper and Row, 1958). On reflection of this pattern in rabbinical literature see Chernus, *Mysticism,* 33–73.

80. See van Gennep, *Rite of Passage,* 6. Compare Turner, *The Ritual Process,* 94.

81. See van Gennep, *The Rite of Passage,* 3.

82. See Bell, *Rituals,* 95.

83. On Metatron see J. C. Greenfield, "Prolegomenon" in *3 Enoch or The Hebrew Book of Enoch.* ed., H. Odeberg. 1982; reprint, New York: Ktav, 1973), pp. 2–165; Scholem, *Major Trends,* 67–70; *Merkavah,* 43–55; S. Lieberman, "Metatron, The Meaning of his Name and his Function," Appendix 1 in I. Gruenwald, *Apocalyptic and Merkavah,* 235–241; Schäfer, *Hidden and Manifest,* 29–32; Dan, *Mysticism,* 108 ff.

84. *3 Enoch; Synopse,* 11; trans. Alexander, "3 Enoch," 256.

85. *3 Enoch; Synopse,* 59. Compare *Synopse,* 60–62, 64–68.

86. *3 Enoch; Synopse,* 66–68.

87. *3 Enoch; Synopse,* 59–68; trans. Alexander, "3 Enoch," 292.

88. *3 Enoch; Synopse,* 60; trans. Alexander, "3 Enoch," 293. Compare *Synopse,* 63, 67.

89. On the term *"pargod,"* its Persian origin and various meanings in Jewish writings see Alexander, "3 Enoch"; Odeberg, *The Hebrew Book of Enoch,* 141; Scholem, *Major Trends,* 72; *Merkavah,* 35.

90. *3 Enoch, Synopse,* 64–65; trans. Alexander, "3 Enoch," 297–298.

91. On the Messiah, the son of Joseph, as a forerunner to the Messiah, the son of David, see Alexander, "3 Enoch," 298.

92. *3 Enoch; Synopse,* 65; trans. Alexander, "3 Enoch," 298.

93. *Hekhalot Rabbati; Synopse,* 124–125.

94. *Hekhalot Rabbati; Synopse,* 125–126.

95. Moore, "Mystical Experience," 121.

96. *Hekhalot Rabbati; Synopse,* 247–251.

97. *Ma'aseh Merkavah; Synopse,* 580–581. Compare a similar but less detailed description, *Synopse,* 595, 596.

98. *Ma'aseh Merkavah; Synopse,* 586.

99. On Enoch's transformation see Elior, "The Concept of God" 20; Idel, "Enoch is Metatron"; Morray-Jones, "Transformational Mysticism," 10 ff.

100. *3 Enoch; Synopse,* 11; trans. Alexander, "3 Enoch," 262.

101. *3 Enoch; Synopse,* 12; trans. Alexander, "3 Enoch," 263.

102. *3 Enoch; Synopse,* 14; trans. Alexander, "3 Enoch," 264.

103. *Hekhalot Rabbati; Synopse,* 83–86.

104. H. Jonas, "Myth and Mysticism: A Study of Objectification and Interiorization in Religious Thought," *The Journal of Religion* 49 (1969): 315.

105. Ibid., 315–329.

106. Ibid., 315.

107. Ibid., 317.

108. The literature on the Mystery cults is extensive. See the bibliographies compiled by B. M. Metzger, "A Classified Bibliography of the Greco-Roman Mystery Religions 1924–1973 with a Supplement 1974–77," in *Aufstieg und Niedergang der römischen Welt,* eds., H. Temporini and W. Haase (Berlin: Walter de Gruyter, 1984), 2: 17. 3, 1259–1423. See also B. M. Metzger, "Considerations of Methodology in the Study of the Mystery Religions and Early Christianity," *HTR* 48 (1955): 1–20. For the term "mystery cults" see comments in K. Rudolph, "Mystery Religions," in *The Encyclopedia of Religion* ed., M. Eliade (New York: Macmillan, 1987), 10: 230–239 and W. Burkert, *Ancient Mystery Cults* (Cambridge, MA: Harvard University Press, 1987). Both scholars emphasize that the term "cults" defines these groups better than the terms "religions" or "churches."

109. See discussion and references in A. J. M. Wedderburn, "The Spread of the Mysteries," in *Baptism and Resurrection* (Tübingen: Mohr Siebeck, 1987), pp. 98–113; J. H. W. Liebeschurtz, *Continuity and Change in Roman Religion* (Oxford: Oxford University Press, 1979), p. 233 ff.

110. See discussion in Wedderburn, "A Common Theology of the Mysteries," *Baptism and Resurrection* 139–148; F. C. Grant, *Roman Hellenism and the*

New Testament (Edinburg and London: Oliver and Boyd, 1962), p. 115ff; Burkert, *Ancient Mystery Cults,* 90, 112–114.

111. See discussion and examples in G. E. Mylonas, *Eleusis and the Eleusinian Mysteries* (Princeton: Princeton University Press, 1961), pp. 224–226; A. J. Festugière, *Personal Religion Among the Greeks* (1954; reprint, Berkeley: University of California Press 1960), p. 77ff.

112. See R. MacMullen, *Paganism in the Roman Empire* (New Haven, CT: Yale University Press, 1981), 23 ff.; Mylonas, *Eleusis and the Eleusinian Mysteries,* 302 ff. Knowledge of the mystery cults become known in the Hellenistic-Roman world as concepts, myths and rites were taken up and reinterpreted, to support the beliefs of other schools, such as Greek philosophers and various Gnostic groups. See discussion in A. D. Nock, *Conversion: The Old and the New in Religion from Alexander the Great to Augustine of Hippo* (Oxford: Oxford University Press, 1933), p. 268 ff.; U. Bianchi, *The Greek Mysteries,* (Leiden: Brill, 1967), p. 6 ff.

113. For discussion, examples, and references see Wedderburn, "A Common Theology of the Mysteries," 139–148.

114. Macmullen, for example, refers to a "generalized initiatory experience," suggesting that a fixed ritual of initiation with similar procedures was found in a number of mystery cults." See MacMullen, *Paganism* 172. See similar views in R. Garland, *The Greek Way of Death* (London: Duckworth, 1985).

115. *Anthology* 4. 52. 49. Cited in M. W. Meyer (ed.), *The Ancient Mysteries, A Source Book* (New York: Harper, 1987), pp. 8–9. As Meyer comments "Plutarch initially notes the similarity of the Greek verbs *teleutan* (to die) and *teleisthai* (to be initiated) and then observe that people who die and people who are initiated go through comparable transformations. The author, most likely was reflecting on the great mysteries of Eleusis in his idealized observations, but the passage may be read in a more general manner as a characterization of the place of death and life in the various mystery religions." Compare Wedderburn, "The Use of Language of the Mysteries," *Baptism and Resurrection* (Tübingen: Mohr Siebeck, 1987), p. 152.

116. Jonas, "Myth and Mysticism," 322–323.

117. Ibid., 323. On initiation and changes in human status see M. Eliade, *Birth and Rebirth,* 78ff; V. Turner, *The Ritual Process: Structure and Anti-Structure* (London: Routledge and Kegan, 1969), 94ff; van Gennep, *Rites of Passage,* 3ff.

118. Jonas, "Myth and Mysticism," 321. Through the initiation process devotees were able to shared some divine-like qualities which a specific God had made available to them. Their status, however, was not equivalent to that of the divine. See See C. H. Talbert, "The Concept of Immortals in Mediterranean Antiquity," *JBL* 94 (1975): 419–439.

119. Jonas, "Myth and Mysticism," 322.

120. McGinn, *Foundations of Mysticism,*, xiv.

121. *Hekhalot Zutarti; Synopse,* 352.

122. *Hekhalot Rabbati; Synopse,* 218.

123. M. Fishbane, *Biblical Interpretation,* 443–524; "From Scribalism to Rabbinism," in *The Sage in Israel and the Ancient Near East,* eds. J. G. Gammie and L. G. Perdue (Winona Lake, IN: Eisenbrauns 1990), pp. 439–456; J. J. Collins, "The Sage in Apocalyptic and Pseudepigraphic Literature," in *The Sage in Israel and the Ancient Near East,* 343–354; *The Apocalyptic Imagination,* 5–6; G. Vermes,"Biblical and Midrash: Early Old Testament Exegesis," in *The Cambridge History of the Bible. From the Beginning to Jerome,* eds. P. R. Ackroyd and C. F. Evans (Cambridge: Cambridge University Press, 1970), pp. 199–231.

124. *Hekhalot Zutarti; Synopse,* 350.

125. *Hekhalot Zutarti; Synopse,* 352.

126. On the doctrine of *Shiur Komah* see Scholem's view that since the enormous measurements describing the anthropomorphic God are entirely beyond human comprehension, they convey, in fact, God's spirituality and transcendent nature, which are beyond the reach of human beings. See *Major Trends;* "On the Mystical Shape"; *Merkavah,* 118–126, 153–186; Cohen, *The Shiur Qomah;* Dan, "The Concept of Knowledge," 67–73; Elior, "The Concept of God," 105–106; Gaster, "The Shiur Komah" in *Studies and Texts,* 1330–1353; Greenfield, "Prolegomena," 34; K. Herrmann, "Text und Fiktion. Zur Textüberlieferung des Shiur Qoma," *Frankfurter Judaistische Beiträge* 16 (1988): 89–142.

127. *Hekhalot Zutarti; Synopse,* 356. Compare *3 Enoch; Synopse,* 51

CHAPTER 3: MYTHICAL LANGUAGE OF HEKHALOT AND MERKAVAH MYSTICISM

1. Moore, "Mystical Experience," 105.

2. S. T. Katz, "Mystical Speech and Mystical Meaning," in S. T. Katz, ed., *Mysticism and Language* (New York: Oxford University Press, 1992), p. 5.

3. S. Ackerman, "Myth," in *The Oxford Companion to the Bible,* eds., B. M. Metzger and M. D. Coogan (New York: Oxford University Press, 1993), pp. 539–541. The literature on former and contemporary theories of myth is vast and cannot be included here. For representative studies and bibliographies see Ackerman "Myth,"; T. S. Sebeok, ed., *Myth: A Symposium* (Bloomington: Indiana University Press, 1986); A. Dundes, *Sacred Narratives, Readings in the Theory of Myth* (Berkeley: University of California Press, 1984).

4. H. Frankfort, and H. A. Frankfort, "Myth and Reality," in *The Intellectual Adventure of Ancient Man: An Essay on Speculative Thought in the Ancient Near East,* eds., H. Frankfort, H. A. Frankfort, J. A. Wilson, T. Jabobsen, and W.

A. Irwin (1946; reprint, Chicago and London: The University of Chicago Press, 1977), p. 5.

5. W. Doniger, *Other Peoples' Myths* (New York and London: Macmillan, 1988), pp. 32–33.

6. W. Burkert, *Greek Religion,* trans. J. Raffan (1977; reprint Cambridge, MA: Harvard University Press, 1985), p. 120. Compare McCurley's suggestion: "On a more general level myth can be used to describe a manner of speaking or writing: a symbolic expression of a real phenomenon which can be expressed in no other way." Cf. B. Batto, *Slaying the Dragon: Mythmaking in the Biblical Tradition* (Louisville, KY: Westminster John Knox press, 1992), p. 1.

7. On the dominant view, even up until the first half of the twentieth century, that mythological traditions are the expression of a polytheistic viewpoint which differs radically from the biblical, monotheistic, historical perspective see, for example, Y. Kaufmann, *History of the Religion of Israel* (New York: KTAV, 1977). For treatment of biblical mythological narratives as faded fragments of pagan polytheistic myths see classic studies: H. Gunkel, *Schöpfung und Chaos in Urzeit und Endzet* (Göttingen: Vandenhoeck and Ruprecht, 1895); G. von Rad, *The Old Testament Theology,* 2 vols. (New York: Harper & Row, 1962, 1965); M. D. Cassuto, *Biblical and Oriental Studies,* 2 vols. (Jerusalem: Magnes Press, 1973).

8. On biblical mythology in contemporary scholarship see representative studies: B. Batto, *Slaying the Dragon,* 4–14; N. Wyatt, "The Problem of Biblical Mythology" in his *Myth of Power: A Study of Royal Myth and Ideology in Ugaritic and Biblical Tradition* (Münster: Ugarit-Verlag, 1996), pp. 373–424.

9. G. H. Davies, "An Approach to the Problem of Old Testament Mythology," *PEQ* 88 (1956): 83–91.

10. M. S. Smith, *The Early History of God. Yahweh and the Other Deities in Ancient Israel* (San Francisco: Harper and Row, 1990), p. 23; N. Wyatt, "The Problem of Biblical Mythology," p. 423.

11. M. Buber, "Myth in Judaism," in *On Judaism,* ed., N. N. Glatzer (New York: Schocken, 1967), pp. 95–107. On the vitality of mythological forms in Judaism from biblical mythological motifs to mythopoetic exegesis of Scripture in the ancient *Midrash,* the Pseudepigrapha, the ancient *piyyutim,* and medieval Jewish mysticism see M. Fishbane, *The Garments of the Torah, Essays in Biblical Hermeneutics* (Bloomington, IN: Indiana University Press 1989), p. 32 ff.; *The Exegetical Imagination,* 1–104.

12. Green, *Keter,* ix.

13. Y. Liebes, "De Natura Dei" in his *Studies in Jewish Myth and Jewish Messianism* (Albany, NY: State University of New York Press 1993), pp. 2–3. On mythical, symbolic imagery in the mystical Kabbalistic literature see Scholem's view of mysticism as the "last stage of religion," which re-integrates myth as a response to the tension between the mythical and historical stages: *Major Trends,* 7 ff., 29 ff., 34–35; See Idel's critique: *Kabbalah,* 157–174.

14. On ancient Near Eastern diverse cultures and literature see T. Jacobsen, *The Treasures of Darkness: A History of Mesopotamian Religion* (New Haven: Yale University Press, 1976); W. G. Lambert, *Babylonian Wisdom Literature* (Oxford: Clarendon Press, 1960), p. 2 ff.; S. N. Kramer and J. Maier, *Myths of Enki, The Crafty God* (New York and Oxford: Oxford University Press, 1989), p. 127ff.; A. L. Oppenheim, *Ancient Mesopotamia: Portrait of a Dead Civilization* (Chicago: University of Chicago Press, 1964), pp. 7–182; S. Dalley, ed., *The Legacy of Mesopotamia* (Oxford: Oxford University Press, 1998).

15. Examples are many. See representative recent studies: S. Dalley, "The Influence of Mesopotamia upon Israel and the Bible," in *Legacy of Mesopotamia*, 57–83; Kramer and Maier *Myth of Enki*, 153 ff.; H. W. F. Saggs, *The Encounter with the Divine in Mesopotamia and Israel* (London: Athlone Press 1978), p. 6ff.; Y. Muffs, *Love & Joy: Law, Language and Religion in Ancient Israel* (New York: Jewish Theological Seminary of America, 1992). On Near Eastern Traditions and the book of Ezekiel see: D. Bodi, *The Book of Ezekiel and the Poem of Erra* (Freiburg and Göttingen: Vandenhoeck Reprecht, 1991); J. F. Kutsko, *Between Heaven and Earth. Divine Presence in the Book of Ezekiel* (Winona Lake, IN: Eisenbrauns, 2000), pp. 101–156.

16. See F. M. Cross, "New Direction in the Study of Apocalyptic," *JTC* 6 (1969): 175–165; W. G. Lambert, *The Background of Jewish Apocalyptic* (London: Athlone Press, 1978); P. D. Hanson, *The Dawn of Apocalyptic: The Historical and Sociological Roots of Jewish Apocalyptic Eschatology* (Philadelphia: Fortress Press, 1975), pp. 30–34; "Jewish Apocalyptic Against Its Near Eastern Environment," *Revue Biblique* 78 (1971): 31–58; J. J. Collins, "Jewish Apocalyptic Against its Hellenistic Near Eastern Environment," in *Seers, Sybils and Sages in Hellenistic-Roman Judaism* (Leiden, New York, Köln: Brill, 1997), pp. 59–74; *The Apocalyptic Vision of the Book of Daniel* (Missoula: Scholars Press, 1977), pp. 67–93; *The Apocalyptic Imagination: An Introduction to the Jewish Matrix of Christianity* (New York: Crossroad 1984), pp. 13–17.

17. On Enmeduranki and Enoch traditions see J. C. VanderKam, *Enoch and the Growth of an Apocalyptic Tradition* (Washington: The Catholic Biblical Association of America, 1984); *Enoch, A Man For All Generations: Studies on Personalities of the Old Testament* (Columbia, SC: University of South Carolina Press, 1995), pp. 1–22; Hanson, *The Dawn of Apocalyptic*, 30–34; H. S. Kvanvig, *Roots of Apocalyptic: The Mesopotamian Background of the Enoch Figure and of the Son of Man* (Neukirchen-Vluyn: Neukirchener Verlag, 1988).

18. On the presence of Mesopotamian traditions in Rabbinic sources see Y. Muffs, "Ancient Near Eastern and Rabbinic Literature," in *Love & Joy*, 139–141; J. Jacobs, "Elements of Near Eastern Mythology in Rabbinic Aggadah," *JJS* 27 (1977): 1–11; J. Tigay, "An Early Technique of Aggadic Exegesis" in *History, Historiography and Interpretation*, eds., H. Tadmor and M. Weinfeld (Jerusalem: Magnes Press, 1983), pp. 169–189; S. J. Lieberman, "A Mesopotamian Background for the So Called Aggadic "Measures" of Biblical Hermeneutics?" *HUCA* 58 (1987): 157–225.

19. On the presence of Mesopotamian traditions in Greek mythology see W. Burkert, "Oriental and Greek Mythology," in *Interpretations of Greek Mythology*, ed., J. Bremmer (London and Sydney: Croom Helm, 1987), pp. 10–40; *The Orientalizing Revolution. Near Eastern Influence on Greek Culture in the Early Archaic Age*, trans. M. E. Pinder and W. Burkert (Cambridge: Harvard University Press, 1992); M. L. West, *The East Face Helicon* (Oxford, New York: Clarendon Press, 1997); C. Penglase, *Greek Myths and Mesopotamia: Parallels and Influence in the Homeric Hymns and Hesiod* (London and New York: Routledge, 1994). On Mesopotamian sources in Greek magical and astronomical traditions see D. Pingree, "Legacies in Astronomy and Celestial Omens" in *Legacy of Mesopotamia*, ed., S. Dalley (Oxford: Oxford University Press, 1998), p. 125 ff.

20. On the concept of myth in Mesopotamian sources see T. Jacobsen, *Toward the Image of Tammuz and Other Essays on Mesopotamian History and Culture* (Cambridge, MA: Harvard University Press, 1970), pp. 39–40, 104 ff.; *Treasures of Darkness*, 3–4; Oppenheim, *Ancient Mesopotamia*, 177–178; W. G. Lambert, "Myth and Ritual as conceived by the Babylonians," *JTS* 13 (1968): 104–112; "The Cosmology of Sumer and Babylon" in *Ancient Cosmologies*, eds., C. Blacker and M. Loewe (London: George Allen and Unwin Ltd., 1975), pp. 43–45; *Babylonian Wisdom Literature*, 120–130; S. N. Kramer, *Sumerian Mythology*, rev. ed. (Philadelphia: University of Pennsylvania Press, 1972), p. 73; Kramer and Maier, *Myth of Enki*, 1–10, 174–204; G. S. Kirk, *Myth, Its Meaning and Function in Ancient and Other Cultures* (Cambridge: Cambridge University Press 1970).

21. Lambert described the unification of the Mesopotamian cultures as a "peaceful symbiosis": *Babylonian Wisdom Literature*, 2. Such a description seems to characterize appropriately the Mesopotamian mythological tradition as well.

22. Kramer and Maier, *Myth of Enki*, 154.

23. Saggs, *The Encounter with the Divine*, 8.

24. Ibid., 8–9.

25. A. Heidel, *The Babylonian Genesis: The Story of Creation*, 2d ed. (Chicago: University of Chicago Press, 1963), pp. 75–81.

26. See J. Z. Smith, "Wisdom and Apocalyptic" in *Religious Syncretism in Antiquity. Essays in Conversation with George Widengen*, ed., B. A. Pearson (Missoula: Scholars Press 1975), pp. 131–156.

27. J. Barr, "Philo of Biblos and his Phoenician History," *Bulletin of the John Rylands Library* 7 (1974): 17–68.

28. See S. Dalley and A. T. Reyes "Mesopotamian Contact and Influence in the Greek World," in *Legacy of Mesopotamia*, 85–124; D. Pingree, "Legacies in Astronomy," 125–137; A. Salvesen, "The Legacy of Babylon and Nineveh in Aramaic Sources," in *Legacy of Mesopotamia*, 139–161; S. Dalley, "The Sassanian Period and Early Islam, c. AD 224–651," in *Legacy of Mesopotamia*, 163–181; E. Gruen, "Cultural Fictions and Cultural Identity," *Transactions of the American*

Philological Association 123 (1993): 1–14; P. S. Wells, *Culture, Contact and Culture Change: Early Iron Age Europe and the Mediterranean World* (Cambridge: Cambridge University Press, 1980); V. D. Arbel, "Junction of Tradition in Edessa: Possible Interaction Between Mesopotamian Mythological and Jewish Mystical Traditions in the First Centuries CE," *Aram Periodical Journal for Syro-Mesopotamian Studies* 11/2 (2001): 335–356. For a continuity of Mesopotamian literary forms see S. Brock, "The Dispute Between Soul and Body: An Example of a Long Lived Mesopotamian Literary Genre," *Aram Periodical Journal for Syro- Mesopotamian Studies* 1 (1989): 53–64.

29. Dalley, "The Sassanian Period and Early Islam"; "Bel at Palmyra and Elsewhere in the Parthian Period," *Aram Periodical Journal for Syro-Mesopotamian Studies* 7 (1995): 137–151; "Gilgamesh in the Arabian Nights," *Journal of the Royal Asiatic Society* 1 (1991): 1–17; "The Gilgamesh Epic and Manichaean Themes, *Aram Periodical Journal for Syro-Mesopotamian Studies* 3 (1991): 23–33; "The Tale of Buluqiya and the Alexander Romance in Jewish and Sufi Mystical Circles," in *Tracing the Threads, Studies in the Vitality of Jewish Pseudepigrapha,* ed., J. C. Reeves (Atlanta: Scholars Press, 1994), pp. 239–269.

30. A. Salvesen "The Legacy of Babylon and Nineveh," 139 ff.

31. H. J. W. Drijvers, *Cults and Beliefs in Edessa* (Leiden: Brill, 1980); "The Persistence of Pagan Cults and Practices in Christian Syria," *East of Anitoch, Studies in Early Syriac Christianity,* (1982; reprint London: Variorum Reprints, 1984), 16: 35–43; R. Murray, *Symbols of Church and Kingdom, A Study in Early Syriac Tradition* (Cambridge: Cambridge University Press, 1975), pp. 4–9, 30 ff.; J. B. Segal, *Edessa: The Blessed City* (Oxford: Clarendon Press, 1970); J. Texidor, *The Pagan God. Popular Religion in the Greco-Roman Near East* (Princeton: Princeton University Press, 1977); T. M. Green, *The City of the Moon God Religious Traditions of Harran* ((Leiden, New York, Köln: Brill, 1992).

32 Green, *The City of the Moon God,* 217.

33. See discussion and references in Dalley, "The Sassanian Period and Early Islam."

34. For background, analysis, and bibliography on the *Epic of Gilgamesh* see representative studies: S. Dalley, "The Epic of Gilgamesh" in *Myth from Mesopotamia* (Oxford: Oxford University Press, 1991), 182–189; E. A. Speiser "The Epic of Gilgamesh," *ANET*: 72–99; A. Heidel, *The Gilgamesh Epic and Old Testament Parallels* (Chicago: University of Chicago Press, 1949); J. Tigay, *The Evolution of the Gilgamesh Epic.* (Philadelphia: University of Pennsylvania Press, 1982); T. Jacobsen, *The Treasures of Darkness,* 219–391.

35. Tigay, *The Evolution of the Gilgamesh Epic.*

36. S. Dalley "Occasions and Opportunities" in *Legacy of Mesopotamia,* 42; "Bel at Palmyra and Elsewhere."

37. J. T. Milik, *The Book of Enoch: Aramaic Fragments of Qumran Cave 4* (Oxford: Clarendon Press 1976), pp. 298–339.

38. J. Reeves, *Jewish Lore in Manichaean Cosmology: Studies in the Book of Giants Traditions* (Cincinnati: Hebrew Union College, 1992), 116–121; "Utnapishtim in the Book of Giants?," *JBL* 112 (1993): 110–115.

39. S. Dalley, "Gilgamesh in the Arabian Nights," 1–17; "The Gilgamesh Epic and Manichaean Themes, *Aram Periodical Journal for Syro-Mesopotamian Studies* 3 (1991): 23–33; "The Tale of Buluqiya and the Alexander Romance, 239–269.

40. For translations, background, analysis, and bibliography on *Enumah Elish* see representative studies: S. Dalley, "The Epic of Creation," in *Myth from Mesopotamia*, 233–277; Heidel, *The Babylonian Genesis*; B. R. Foster, *Before the Muses*, (Bethseda, MD: CDL Press, 1996), 351–402; Jacobsen, *Treasures of Darkness*, 167–191; E. A. Speiser "The Creation Epic," *ANET*, 60–72; W. G. Lambert and S. B. Parker, *Enumah Elish, The Cuneiform Text* (Oxford: Clarendon Press, 1966); Lambert, "The Cosmology of Sumer and Babylon," 42–62; Saggs, *The Encounter with the Divine*, 57–63.

41. On the *akitu* festival see S. A. Pallis, *The Babylonian Akitu Festival* (Copenhagen: Bianco Lunos Bogtrykkeri, 1926); W. G Lambert, "The Great Battle of the Mesopotamian Religious Year: The Conflict in the Akitu House," *Iraq* 25 (1963): 89–90; J. A. Black, "The New Year Ceremonies in Ancient Babylon: 'Taking Bel by the Hand' and a Cultic Picnic," *Religion* 11 (1981): 39–59.

42. Dalley, "Bel at Palmyra and Elsewhere," 137–151.

43. Ibid., 150–151.

44. G. Cagiran and W. G. Lambert, "The Late Babylonia *kislimu* Ritual for Esagil," *JCS* 43–45 (1991–93): 89–106. Compare a neo-Assyrian tablet, K–2892, which lists different New Year festivals for several gods: A. Livingstone, *Mystical and Mythological Explanatory Works of Assyrian and Babylonian Scholars* (Oxford: Clarendon Press, 1986), 157.

45. Dalley, "Bel at Palmyra and Elsewhere," 146.

46. Ibid., 146.

47. Ibid., 144.

48. Drijvers, *Cults and Beliefs in Edessa*. On Edessa as a paradigm see pp. 4–6; Segal, *Edessa*, 29–61; Texidor, *The Pagan God*, 146–151.

49. The text was first published and translated into English by G. Phillips, *The Doctrine of Addai, the Apostle, Now First Edited in a Complete Form in the Original Syriac* (London: Trubner and Co., 1876). It is now also available in Phillips' edition, but with a new English version, in *The Teaching of Addai*, ed., G. Howard (Chico, CA: Scholars Press, 1981), p. 23ff.

50. "He (Satan) put Apollo as an idol in Antioch and others with him. In Edessa he set up Nabu and Bel together with many others . . ." See discussion and translation in Drijvers, *Cults and Beliefs in Edessa,* 43 ff.

51. See discussion, textual examples and references in Drijvers, *Cults and Beliefs in Edessa,* 34–38, 40–75, 175–181, 195; "The Persistence of Pagan Cults," 35–38; Texidor, *The Pagan God,* 105 ff., 115 ff., 136 ff.; Segal, *Edessa,* 45, 47 ff., 79 ff.

52. See discussion and textual examples and references in Drijvers, *Cults and Beliefs in Edessa,* 43 ff., 73.

53. H. J. W. Drijvers, "Syrian Christianity and Judaism," in *History and Religion in Late Antique Syria,* Collected Studies Series (London: Variorum, 1984), pp. 128–129.

54. Drivers, *Cults and Beliefs in Edessa,* 43. (Revision of W. Wright, 's 1882 version: *The Chronicle of Joshua the Stylite, composed in Syriac, A. D. 507, with a translation into English and Notes*).

55. *The Babylonian Talmud, Avodah Zarah,* 2. b. Dalley refers to this citation: *Legacy of Mesopotamia,* 163. See also J. Neusner, *Judaism, Christianity and Zoroastrianism in Talmudic Babylonia.* (Atlanta: Scholars Press, 1990), 64.

56. See discussion and references in J. Neusner, *A History of the Jews in Babylonia,* vol. 5: *The Later Sasanian Times* (Leiden: Brill, 1969); H. J. W. Drijvers, "Jews and Christians at Edessa," *JJS* 36/1 (1985): 88–102; "The Persistence of Pagan Cults"; Murray, *Symbols of Church and Kingdom,* 4–9, 30 ff.; S. Brock, "Jewish Traditions in Syrian Sources," JJS 30 (1979): 212–232. See also Josephus, *Antiquities,* 20. 17–37, in which he attests that the kingdom of Adiabene was ruled in the first century C.E. by a dynasty that had converted to Judaism.

57. See chapter 1 above.

58. Dan, *Mysticism,* 215. See discussion 220–224.

59. Green, *Keter,* ix.

CHAPTER 4: MYSTICAL JOURNEYS IN MYTHOLOGICAL LANGUAGE

1. *Hekhalot Rabbati; Synopse,* 335.

2. On patterns of characterization see S. Chatman's conceptualization of a literary character as a "paradigm of traits": *Story and Discourse: Narrative Structure in Fiction and Film* (Ithaca, NY: Cornell University Press, 1978), pp. 116–134. See also J. Phelan, *Reading People, Reading Plot: Character, Progression and the Interpretation of Narrative* (Chicago: University of Chicago Press, 1989).

3. S. Nidtich, *A Prelude to Biblical Folklore: Underdogs and Tricksters* (Urbana, IL and Chicago: University of Illinois Press, 2000), pp. 70–92; A. Dundes, "The Hero Pattern and the Life of Jesus," in *Interpreting Folklore* (Bloomington:

Indiana University Press, 1980), p. 232 ff.; A. B. Lord, *The Singer of Tales* (Cambridge, MA: Harvard University, 1989). See their critical observations and references to former, general studies of the hero figure (such as L. Raglan, *The Hero, A Study in Tradition, Myth and Drama;* and O. Rank, *The Myth of the Birth of the Hero).*

4. For background, analysis, and bibliography on the *Epic of Gilgamesh* see representative studies: S. Dalley, "The Epic of Gilgamesh," in *Myth from Mesopotamia* (Oxford: Oxford University Press, 1991), 182–189; E. A. Speiser "The Epic of Gilgamesh," 72–99; Heidel, *The Gilgamesh Epic* Tigay, *The Evolution of the Gilgamesh Epic;* Jacobsen, *The Treasures of Darkness,* 219–391.

5. On Adapa myth see representative studies for translations, discussions and bibliographies: S. Dalley, "Adapa," in *Myth from Mesopotamia,* 184–188.; B. R. Foster, "The Adapa Story," in *Before the Muses: An Anthology of Akkadian Literature* (Bethseda, MD: CDL Press 1996), 429–436; E. A. Speiser, "Adapa," *ANET,* 101–103; S. Izre'el, *Adapa and the South Wind. Language Has the Power of Life and Death (*Winona Lake, IN: Eisenbrauns, 2001).

6. On Etana myth see representative studies for translations, discussions and bibliographies: S. Dalley, "Etana," in *Myth from Mesopotamia,* 190–204; B, R. Foster, "Etana," in *Before the Muses,* 437–460; J. V. Kinnier-Wilson, *The Legend of Etana: A New Edition* (Warminster, UK: Aris and Phillips, 1985); E. A. Speiser, "Etana," *ANET,* 114–118; W. Horowitz, "Two Notes on Etana's Flight to Heaven," *Or. NS* 59 (1990): 511–17.

7. For a discussion of the hero figure in ancient near eastern sources see S. N. Kramer, "Heroes of Sumer: A New Heroic Age in World History and Literature," *Proceedings of the American Philosophical Society* 90 (1946): 120–130. On the figure of a hero in late antiquity see M. Hadas and M. Smith, *Heroes and Gods. Spiritual Biographies in Late Antiquity* (New York: Harper and Row, 1965).

8. "Gilgamesh," I [SBV]; Dalley, *Myths,* 51.

9. "Etana," Dalley, *Myths,* 190–191.

10. "Adapa," Dalley, *Myths,* 184.

11. On heavenly ascents in the ancient world and the ancient near east see G. Widengren, *The Ascension of the Apostle and the Heavenly Book (*Uppsala: Lundequistska, 1950); Culianu, *Psychanodia I;* I. T. Abusch, "Ascent to the Stars in a Mesopotamian Ritual: Social Metaphor and Religious Experience," in *Death, Ecstasy and Other Worldly Journeys,* eds., J. J. Collins and M. Fishbane (New York: State University of New York Press, 1995), pp. 15–39; W. Horowitz, *Mesopotamian Cosmic Geography* (Winona Lake, IN: Eisenbrauns, 1988), pp. 43–66, 267.

12. Abusch, "Ascent to the Stars in a Mesopotamian Ritual."

13. "Gilgamesh and the Land of the Living," trans. Tigay, in *The Evolution of the Gilgamesh Epic,* 164.

14. S. H. Hooke, *Middle Eastern Mythology* (London: Penguin Books, 1963), pp. 49–60; Jacobsen, *Treasures of Darkness*, 215–219.

15. "Etana," Dalley, *Myths*, 189–202.

16. "Adapa," Dalley, *Myths*, 184–185.

17. "Gilgamesh," III, [SBV]; Dalley, *Myths*, 63.

18. "Gilgamesh," III, [SBV]; Dalley, *Myths*, 62. Full presentation: Gilgamesh IX–X; Dalley, *Myths*, 95–109. See discussion in R. J. Clark, "Origins: New Light on Eschatology in Gilgamesh's Mortuary Journey, " in *Gilgamesh, A Reader*, ed., J. Maier (Wauconda, IL: Bolchazy-Carducci Publishers, 1997), p. 134 ff.

19. See Dan, "The Concept of History." On lack of a formal presentation of a typical "descender to the Merkavah," and of standard requirements for eligible members of this mystical circle, see discussion in chapter 1 above.

20. See discussion in chapter 2 above.

21. Compare, for example, experiences described in 2 Baruch 21: 1 ff.; 37: 1 ff.; Daniel 10: 2 ff.; 1 Enoch 13: 7 ff. On various kinds of mystics and their encounters with the divine see J. E. Collins, *Mysticism and New Paradigm*, xv–xxi.

22. *Hekhalot Zutarti; Synopse*, 335. Compare *Synopse*, 364, 421, 564, 841. For discussion see Chernus, "The Pilgrimage," 6–7, 13–15.

23. *Hekhalot Rabbati; Synopse* 81. Compare a more passive role of various prophets who often declare "The Lord showed me." See, for example, Jeremiah 24: 1; Amos 7: 1, 4.

24. *Hekhalot Rabbati; Synopse*, 107–111. Compare Enoch's role in *3 Enoch; Synopse*, 5–19.

25. *Hekhalot Rabbati; Synopse*, 159. Compare *Synopse* 198, 220, 224.

26. *Hekhalot Rabbati; Synopse*, 199.

27. *Hekhalot Rabbati; Synopse*, 199. Compare *Synopse*, 93, 199–201, 224, 234. For discussion see Scholem, *Major Trends*, 41–42, 52–70; Gruenwald, *Apocalypticism to Merkavah*, 161 ff.; Dan, "The Secret of the World," 21–22 [Hebrew].

28. *Hekhalot Rabbati;* Synopse, 201. On the qualities of the mystics see Scholem, *Major Trends*, 41–42, 52–70; Gruenwald, Apocalypticism and Merkavah, 161 ff.

29. *3 Enoch; Synopse, 3* (compare Synopse, 884); trans. Alexander, "3 Enoch," 257.

30. *3 Enoch; Synopse, 3.*

31. See, for example, *Hekhalot Zutarti; Synopse*, 344, in which Rabbi Akiva expresses this idea, attributing his successful ascent to the pardes to his deeds.

32. *Hekhalot Rabbati; Synopse,* 163.

33. On influences of the destruction of the Second Temple on Jewish society and consciousness see M. Stone, "Reactions to the Destruction of the Second Temple," *JSJ* 12 (1981): 193–204.

34. Compare M. Smith, "Ascent to the Heavens and Deification in 4QM," in *Archeology and History in the Dead Sea Scrolls,* ed., L. H. Schiffman (Sheffield: JSOT Press 1990), p. 52.

35. *Hekhalot Rabbati; Synopse,* 201.

36. *Hekhalot Zutarti, Synopse,* 337.

37. *Hekhalot Zutarti, Synopse,* 366.

38. *Ma'aseh Merkavah; Synopse,* 580–581. See analysis: Swartz, *Mystical Prayer,* 22–23; Janowitz, *Poetics of Ascent,* 95–97.

39. *Hekhalot Rabbati; Synopse,* 225. On this incident see *Synopse,* 224–229. Compare 554. See discussion: L. H. Schiffman, "The Recall of Rabbi Nehunia ben Ha-Qanah from Ecstasy in Heikhalot Rabbati," *AJSR* 1 (1976): 269–281; S. Lieberman, "The Knowledge of Halakha by the Author (or Authors) of the Heikhaloth," Appendix 2 in I. Gruenwald, *Apocalyptic and Merkavah,* 164, 241–244.

40. *Hekhalot Rabbati; Synopse,* 227.

41. R. J. Clifford, *The Cosmic Mountain in Canaan and the Old Testament* (Cambridge, MA: Harvard University Press, 1972), p. 6.

42. *Ma'aseh Merkavah; Synopse,* 559.

43. Frankfort and Frankfort, "Myth and Reality," 20–27.

44. For suggestions of a biblical dual or triadic universe see, for example, Ps. 69: 34, 89: 9–11, 96: 11; 148: 4; Pro. 3: 19–20, 8: 28–29. See discussion in: L. Jacob, "Jewish Cosmology," in *Ancient Cosmologies,* eds., C. Blacker and M. Loewe (London: George Allen and Unwin, 1975), pp. 68–70; J. E. Wright, "Israelite Traditions" in *The Early History of Heaven,* 52ff.; O. Keel, *The Symbolism of the Biblical World: Ancient Near Eastern Iconography and the Book of Psalms,* trans. T. J. Hallett (New York: Seabury Press, 1978), p. 34ff. On Mesopotamian concepts see W. G. Lambert, "The Cosmology of Sumer and Babylon," 44 ff.; Horowitz, *Mesopotamian Cosmic Geography;* Wright, "Ancient Mesopotamian Traditions," in The Early History of Heaven, 26ff. See a pictorial representation of the Mesopotamian universe which seems to be represented by a kudurru stone, namely a boundary stone, from the twelfth century B.C.E.: Keel, *The Symbolism of the Biblical World,* 46–47.

45. Lambert, "The Cosmology," 44 ff.; Horowitz, *Mesopotamian Cosmic Geography;* F. Rochberg-Halton, "Mesopotamian Cosmology," in *Encyclopedia of Cosmology: Historical, Philosophical and Scientific Foundations of Modern Cosmology,*

ed., N. S. Hetherington (New York and London: Garland, 1993), pp. 398–407; Livingstone, *Mystical and Mythological Explanatory Works,* 82 ff. Seven and three are the most common degrees of heavenly layering.

46. See Lambert, "The Cosmology," 58. The text was published in two versions. The longer version is VAT (Vorderasiatisches Museum, Berlin) 8917, OBV. 30-rev = E. Ebeling (1931), pp. 33–34. The shorter version was published in the 1960s by E. Weidner in *Archiv für Orientforschung* 19 (1959–60): 110.

47. Horowitz, *Mesopotamian Cosmic Geography,* 209. For more examples see 210 ff.

48. On patterns of reaching heaven see Horowitz, *Mesopotamian Cosmic Geography,* 267.

49. On the gates of heaven in this text and other sources see Horowitz, *Mesopotamian Cosmic Geography,* 266 ff; W. Heimpel, "The Sun at Night and the Doors of Heaven in Babylonian Texts," *JCS* 38: 2 (1986): 127–151.

50. Kinnier-Wilson, *The Legend of Etana,* 121 [the late version].

51. "Etana," III [SBV]; Dalley, *Myths,* 197–198.

52. Dalley, *Legacy of Mesopotamia,* 41.

53. Horowitz, *Mesopotamian Cosmic Geography,* 65.

54. "Gilgamesh," IX [SBV]; Dalley, *Myths,* 99.

55. "Gilgamesh," X [SBV]; Dalley, *Myths,* 101.

56. For images of plural heavens in the Hebrew bible see additional examples, Gen. 7: 11; cf. 8: 2; Ps. 115: 15–17; I Kgs 8: 27. See discussion and references in: L. Jacob, "Jewish Cosmology," 68–70; N. M. Sarna, *Understanding Genesis: The Heritage of Biblical Israel* (New York: Schoken, 1970), p. 1 ff; N. C. Habel, "He Who Stretches Out the Heavens," *CBQ* 34 (1972): 417–430; Wright, "Israelite Traditions," in *The Early History of Heaven,* 52–97. For images of heaven as the abode of God see Exod. 20: 19; Isa. 66: 1; Ezek. 1: 1. For the concept of plural heavens, two and seven, present in rabbinic sources see Babylonian Talmud, *Hagigah* 13a; L. Ginzberg, *The Legends of the Jews,* vol. 5. trans. H. Szold (Philadelphia: The Jewish Publication Society of America, 1942), pp. 10–11. For the presence of biblical and ancient Near Eastern conception of heaven in later sources see discussion and reference Wright, "Early Jewish and Christian Traditions I: The Persistence of Biblical and Near Eastern Models," in *The Early History of Heaven,* 117–138.

57. Compare to the flood story in which the vast body of water came down through the windows of the sky which were opened: Gen. 7: 11; cf. 8: 2.

58. *3 Enoch; Synopse,* 21. Compare other lists of seven heavens as, for example, in the *Genizah* fragments. The plurality of heavens is said to derive from the plural form of the verb as presented, for example in Ezekiel 1: 1: "the

heavens were opened" For discussion of the plurality of heavens in the Hekhalot and rabbinical sources see: I. Gruenwald, "The Visions of Ezekiel: Critical Text and Commentary," in *Temirim: Text and Studies in Kabbalah and Hasidism* I, ed., I. Weinstock, (Jerusalem: Mosad Ha-Rav Kook, 1972), pp. 110–139. [Hebrew]

59. *3 Enoch; Synopse,* 21.

60. On a similar mythological concepts of space see a semiotic perspective: J, M. Lotman and B. A. . Upenskij, "Myth-Name-Culture," in *Soviet Semiotics,* ed., D. P. Lucid (Baltimore: Johns Hopkins University Press, 1977), pp. 233–259, esp. 247.

61. *3 Enoch; Synopse,* 24. On the Hekhalot mythological images of God's palaces, see discussion in chapter five below.

62. *3 Enoch; Synopse,* 1.

63. *Ma'aseh Merkavah; Synopse,* 546.

64. *Ma'aseh Merkavah; Synopse,* 559.

65. *Ma'aseh Merkavah; Synopse,* 559.

66. *Ma'aseh Merkavah; Synopse,* 558.

67. *3 Enoch; Synopse,* 10; compare *Synopse,* 891

68. *3 Enoch; Synopse,* 60.

69. *Hekhalot Rabbati; Synopse,* 231. On influences of Elijah traditions on the Hekhalot descriptions see Gruenwald, *Apocalypticism and Merkavah,* 120 ff.

70. *3 Enoch; Synopse,* 9; trans. Alexander, "3 Enoch," 262.

71. *Hekhalot Rabbati; Synopse,* 236

72. *Hekhalot Rabbati; Synopse,* 199.

73. See M. Eliade, *Images and Symbols: Studies in Religious Symbolism.* trans. P. Mairet (Princeton, NJ: Princeton University Press, 1991), pp. 50–56, 115–119.

74. See Rochberg-Halton, "Mesopotamian Cosmology," 402–403.

75. See Lambert, "Cosmology, " 62.

76. "Enumah Elish," V; Dalley, *Myths,* 259.

77. See R. George, *House Most High, The Temples of Ancient Mesopotamia* (Winona Lake, ID: Eisenbrauns, 1993), pp. 80, 87, 96, 149, 157.

78. See G. B. Gragg, "The Kesh Temple Hymn," in *The Collection of the Sumerian Temple Hymns* (Texts from Cuneiform Sources III), eds., A. W. Sjöberg, E. Bergmann, and G. B. Gragg (Locust Valley, NY: Augustin, 1969), p. 170; A. W. Sjöberg, and E. Bergmann, "The Collection of the Sumerian Temple Hymns,"

in *The Collection of the Sumerian Temple Hymns* (Texts from Cuneiform Sources III) eds., A. W. Sjöberg, E. Bergmann, E., and G. B. Gragg, (Locust Valley, (NY: Augustin: 1969), p. 17.

79. See Lambert, "Cosmology," 64 n. 16. See a detailed description in T. N. D. Mettinger "YHWH Sabaot—The Heavenly King on the Cherubim Throne," in *Studies in the Period of David and Solomon and Other Essays,* ed. T. Ishida (Tokyo: Yamakawa-Shuppansha, 1982), p. 119 ff.; M. Metzger, "Himmelische und irdische Wohnstatt Jahwes," *Ugarit Forschungen* 2 (1970): 139–158. esp 141–144.

80. T. N. D. Mettinger, *The Dethronement of Sabaoth: Studies in the Shem and Kabod Theologies* (Lund: CWK Gleerup, 1982), pp. 29–30; "YHWH Sabaot," 119 ff.

81. See H. Frankfort, *Cylinder Seals: A Documentary Essay on the Art and Religion of the Ancient Near East* (1939; reprint, London: Macmillan, 1965), p. 187, figs. 57, 59, 209; 219 figs. 66, 67; J. L. Crowley, *The Aegean and the East: An Investigation into the Transference of Artistic Motifs between the Aegean and Egypt and the Near East in the Bronze Age* (Jonsered, Sweden: Paul Aström, 1989), pp. 127, 212, figs. 64B.

82. See Fishbane, *Biblical Interpretation,* 368–369. References to pillars situated between heaven and earth occur also in several Talmudic sources. These sources alternatively describe one, seven or twelve pillars as the foundations of the cosmos on which the world rests. See Babylonian Talmud, *Hagigah* 12b. Compare *1 Enoch,* 18: 3. See also E. R. Goodenough, *Jewish Symbols in the Greco-Roman Period,* vol. 8. (New York: Bollinger Foundation, 1953), pp. 148–157; A. A. Altmann, "The Ladder of Ascension," in *Studies in Mysticism and Religion Presented to Gershom G. Scholem on his Seventieth Birthday,* eds. E. E. Urbach, R. J. Z. Werblowsky, and C. Wirszubski (Jerusalem: Magnes Press, 1967), pp. 1–31.

83. Compare Job 9: 6; 26: 1; Ps. 75: 4; 1 Sam 2: 8.

84. See discussion in G. W. Ahlström, "Heaven on Earth at Hazor and Arad" in *Religious Syncretism in Antiquity,* ed. B. A. Pearson (Missoula: Scholars Press, 1975), pp. 67–83.

85. *Hekhalot Rabbati; Synopse,* 201.

86. *Hekhalot Zutarti; Synopse,* 348. See Elior, *Hekhalot Zutarti,* 17.

87. *Genizah,* 8; compare Gruenwald, "New Passages," 356 [Hebrew].

88. *Hekhalot Rabbati;* Synopse, 98 (MS Vatican); trans. Schäfer, "3 Enoch," 12.

89. *Hekhalot Rabbati; Synopse,* 182.

90. *Hekhalot Rabbati; Synopse,* 216.

91. *Hekhalot Rabbati; Synopse,* 199.

92. *3 Enoch; Synopse,* 10; trans. Alexander, "3 Enoch," 262.

93. M. Eliade has discussed this concept in several of his works. See, for example Eliade, *Images and Symbols,* 11, 16–18, 55, 166; Critical observations on Eliade's views and attempts to universalize the religious impulse cannot be discussed in this context. References to "nostalgia for paradise" in this study are limited to specific cultures, texts, and contexts.

94. Fishbane, *Biblical Interpretation,* 369.

95. Fishbane, *Biblical Interpretation,* 369.

96. See Fishbane, *Biblical Interpretation,* 368–372, and his reference to sources such as Psalms (48: 3, 46: 5, 48: 2–4, 12–14); Ezekiel (36: 35, 47: 1–12); Joel (2: 3, 4: 18, 20: 1); Zechariah (14: 8–11); Isaiah (28: 16, 51: 3). On Eden symbolism in temple traditions see discussion and references in T. Stordalem, *Echoes of Eden, Genesis 2–3 and Symbolism of the Garden in Biblical Hebrew Literature* (Leuvern: Peeters 2000), pp. 305–321.

97. *3 Enoch; Synopse,* 7.

98. *3 Enoch; Synopse,* 8.

99. *3 Enoch; Synopse,* 8.

100. *3 Enoch; Synopse,* 10.

101. On Enoch as a model for "Yordei Merkavah" see Scholem, *Major Trends,* 47; *Merkavah,* 60; Schäfer, *Hidden and Manifest,* 134. For a detailed discussion see chapter 1 above.

102. For discussion of these texts and debates about the mythological backgrounds of Gen. 2–3 and Ezek. 28 see representative studies: U. Cassuto, *A Commentary on the Book of Genesis: From Adam to Noah,* trans. I. Abrahams (Jerusalem: Magnes Press 1961), pp. 74–84; M. H. Pope, *El in the Ugaritic Text* (Leiden: Brill, 1955), pp. 97–100.; R. R. Wilson, "The Death of the King of Tyre: The Editorial History of Ezekiel 28" in *Love & Death in the Ancient Near East, Essays in Honor of Marvin H. Pope,* eds., J. H. Marks and R. M. Good (Guilford, Conn.: Four Quarters, 1987), pp. 211–218; T. Stordalen, *Echoes of Eden,* 21–138, 394–397; D. E. Challender Jr. *Adam in Myth and History. Ancient Israelite Perspectives on the Primal Human* (Winona Lake, IN: Eisenbrauns, 2000). For parallels between Gen. 2–3, Ezek. 28 and Mesopotamian literature see discussion and references in representative studies: H. N. Wallace, *The Eden Narrative* (Atlanta: Scholars Press, 1985), pp, 71–104; 119–120; J. van Seters, *Prologue to History, The Yahwist as Historian in Genesis* (Louisville: Westminster John Knox Press, 1992), pp. 120–127. H. P. Müller, "Parallelen zu Gen. 2 und Ez. 28 aus dem Gilgamesh-Epos," *Zeitschrift für die alttestamentliche Wissenschaft* 3 (1990): 167–178.

103. See J. D. Levenson, *Creation and Persistence of Evil* (Princeton: Princeton University Press, 1994), pp. 2–78, 111–120.

104. See references in n. 102 above. See also J. Morgenstern "The Mythological Background of Psalm 82," *HUCA* 14 (1939): 111–114; H. G. May, "The

King in the Garden of Eden: A Study of Ezekiel 28: 12–19," in *Israel's Prophetic Heritage; Essays in Honor of James Muilenburg,* eds. B. Anderson and W. Harrelson (New York: Harper and Row, 1962), pp. 166–176.

105. *Ma'aseh Merkavah; Synopse* 592. Compare *Synopse,* 1, 216, 348, 405, 545, 554, 556–557, 579, 592.

106. *Hekhalot Rabbati; Synopse,* 213.

107. Heimpel, "The Sun at Night and the Doors of Heaven," 132–43; Horowitz, *Mesopotamian Cosmic Geography,* 52–53, 58–60, 114–116, 144–145, 217, 248, 265–267, 300, 359; Rochberg-Halton,"Mesopotamian Cosmology."

108. See Kinnier-Wilson, *The Legend of Etana.* See discussion in Horowitz, *Mesopotamian Cosmic Geography,* 59, 65–66. Compare descriptions in the myth "Nergal and Ereshkigal," (A, B) in B. R. Foster, *Before the Muses,* 414 ff.

109. I. Starr, *The Rituals of the Diviner* (Malibu: Undena, 1983), p. 122 ff.; Foster, *Before the Muses,* 680. 15, 662. 3–5; Heimpel, "The Sun at Night and the Doors of Heaven," 132–140.

110. Foster, *Before the Muses,* 569. 1–3. Compare *1 Enoch,* 33–36, 72–76.

111. See L. K. Handy, *Among the Host of Heaven. A Syro-Palestinian Pantheon as Bureaucracy* (Winona Lake, IN: Eisenbrauns, 1994), pp. 4–15.

112. "Gilgamesh," II, [SBV]; Dalley, *Myths,* 61.

113. "Gilgamesh," V, [SBV]; Dalley, *Myths,* 75.

114. "Gilgamesh," IX; [SBV]; Dalley, *Myths,* 96.

115. "Gilgamesh," IX; [SBV]; Dalley, *Myths,* 96.

116. Compare a similar doubt raised by divine beings in the case of Adapa: "Why did Ea to a worthless human of the heaven and of the earth the plan disclose. . . . " See "Adapa,"Dalley, *Myths,* 187.

117. "Gilgamesh," IX [SBV]; Dalley, *Myths,* 97.

118. "Etana," Dalley, *Myths,* 185.

119. On this composition see representative studies: B. R. Foster, "The Descent of Ishtar to the Netherworld," in *Before the Muses,* 402 ff.; W. G. Lambert, "A New Babylonian Descent to the Netherworld" in *Lingering Over Words: Studies in Ancient Near Eastern Literature in Honor of William L. Moran,* eds., I. T. Abusch et al., (Atlanta: Scholars Press, 1990), pp. 289–300.

120. On the two related metaphors of descent and ascent in the ancient world see Segal, "Heavenly Ascent," 1333–1343; Stroumsa, "Mystical Descent," 137–153.

121. Compare the flood narrative which presents the image of the windows of heaven: Gen 7: 11, 8: 2. For images of windows see Isa. 24: 18, Mal. 3: 10, 1 Kgs. 8: 35.

122. *Hekhalot Rabbati; Synopse,* 215.

123. Gruenwald, "Knowledge and Vision," 96–97.

124. See, for example, *3 Enoch; Synopse,* 2; trans. Alexander, "3 Enoch," 256: ". . . as soon as the princes of the chariot looked at me and the fiery seraphim fixed their gaze on me I shrank back trembling. . . ." Compare the frightful glance of the guards in *Gilgamesh Epic* mentioned above.

125. *3 Enoch; Synopse,* 9; trans. Alexander, "3 Enoch," 261. A similar angelic opposition is reported in *3 Enoch* when Metatron admits Rabbi Ishmael to the seventh heaven: "why have you allowed one born of a woman to come in and behold the chariot?" *Synopse,* 3; trans. Alexander, "3 Enoch," 257.

126. *Hekhalot Rabbati; Synopse,* 219. Rabbi Akiva mentions both the names of the seven heavenly guards and the names of their seals in *Synopse,* 229–231, 413–417.

127. See Swartz, *Scholastic Magic,* 124–126, 198–199, 210. *Synopse,* 413, 414–415, 206–237.

128. See, for example, *Synopse,* 566–568.

129. See Dalley, *Legacy of Mesopotamia,* 47–48.

130. Dalley, *Legacy of Mesopotamia,* 48. Compare "things of stone" in tablet X of the Gilgamesh Epic [OBV]. They appear to be amulets which can bring Ur-shanabi safely over the lethal waters. See Dalley, "Gilgamesh," *Myths,* 132, n. 113.

131. Dalley, *Legacy of Mesopotamia,* 140.

132. See W. W. Hallo, "'As Seal upon Thine Arm': Glyptic Metaphor in the Biblical World," in *Ancient Seals and the Bible,* eds., L. Gorelick and E. Williams-Forte (Malibu: Undena, 1983), pp. 7–17; Callender, *Adam in Myth,* 91–97. See examples of biblical references to seals as marks of identification: Gen 38 (Judah's seal) and Gen 41: 39–45 (Joseph as the bearer of Pharaoh's seal and thus his manifested representative).

133. *Hekhalot Rabbati; Synopse,* 219. Compare *Synopse,* 229–231, 413–417.

134. *Bavli Hagigah* 14b.

135. On Hero narratives see nn. 3; 7 above.

136. "Gilgamesh," XI [OBV]; Dalley, *Myths,* 116 ff.

137. "Adapa,"; Dalley, *Myths,* 187. See discussions: Jacobsen, *Treasures of Darkness,* 115–116; Hooke, *Middle Eastern Mythology,* 56–58; Izre'el, *Adapa and the South Wind,* 107ff.

138. On tests see Dan, *Mysticism,* 93–107; "At the Entrance of the Sixth Gate." *Jerusalem Studies in Jewish Thought 6: 1–2* (1987): 197–220 [Hebrew Section]; Schäfer, *Hidden and Manifest,* 37–45; Gruenwald, *Apocalypticism and Merkavah,* 146–149. On the "water test" see Morray-Jones, *Transparent Illusion,* 34–82.

139. *Hekhalot Rabbati; Synopse,* 258.

140. *3 Enoch; Synopse,* 9–15; trans. Alexander, "3 Enoch," 263–264.

141. For translation, background, and bibliography of this poem, known as *Ludlul Bel Nemeqi* ("I Will Praise the Lord of Wisdom") according to its opening words, see Lambert, *Babylonian Wisdom Literature,* 32–62; Foster, "The Poem of the Righteous Sufferer in *Before the Muses,* 306–325; R. D. Biggs, "I Will Praise the Lord of Wisdom," *ANET,* 596–600.

142. Lambert, *Babylonian Wisdom Literature,* 61.

143. See W. G. Lambert, "Enmeduranki and Related Matters," *JCS* 21 (1967): 126–138.

144. From the third to the first millennium the term "the beloved" of a specific god was often used as the epithet or title for chosen individuals, such as kings. At times it was made into a personal name. For example, "Naram-Sin," "beloved of [the god] Sin." Compare the title King Solomon received from the prophet Natan: "Yedid-Yah," "Beloved of Yah," "because the Lord loved him" in 2 Sam, 12: 24. Compare Deut. 33: 12; Ps. 60: 7. See M. Goshen-Gottstein, "Abraham—Lover or Beloved of God" in *Love and Death in the Ancient Near East,* eds. J. H. Marks and R. M. Good (Guilford: Four Quarters Publishing, 1987) pp. 101–104.

145. The order of the lines follows Lambert, "Enmeduranki and Related Matters,"132.

146. On the tablet of the gods see Oppenheim, *Ancient Mesopotamia,* 201–205; Saggs, *The Encounter with the Divine,* 70–73; W. G. Lambert, "Destiny and Divine Intervention in Babylon and Israel," *Oudtestamentische Studien* 17 (1972): 65–72; "History and the Gods: A Review Article," *Or. NS* 39 (1970): 170–77; S. Paul, "Heavenly Tablets and the Book of Life," *Journal of the Ancient Near Eastern Society of Columbia University* 5 (1973): 345–353.

147. For translation and discussion of divination/observation techniques see Lambert, "Enmeduranki and Related Matters," 126–138.

148. CAD 2. 121. On the *bārû* cult see Vanderkam, *Enoch,* 56 ff.; Oppenheim, *Ancient Mesopotamia,* 207 ff.; F. C. Cryer, *Divination in Ancient Israel and its Near Eastern Environment.* (Sheffield: JSOT Press 1994), pp. 194–205.

149. It should be noted that divination in this context is about both, uncovering secrets of the present and foretelling the future. On Mesopotamian divination see representative studies: E. Reiner, "Fortune-Telling in Mesopotamia," *JNES* 19 (1960): 23–35; I. Starr, The Ritual of the Divine; F. C. Cryer, Divination in Ancient Israel and its Near Eastern, 124–229.

150. Lambert, "Enmeduranki and Related Matters," 126–138.

151. See discussion and bibliographies in representative studies: Vanderkam, *Enoch,* 1–51; Collins, *The Apocalyptic Imagination,* 33–67; *The Apoca-*

lyptic Vision of the Book of Daniel, 27–36; *Between Athens and Jerusalem: Jewish Identity in the Hellenistic Diaspora* (New York: Crossroad, 1983), pp. 32–43; Kvanvig, *Roots of Apocalyptic,* 17–53.

152. *3 Enoch; Synopse,* 150; trans. Alexander, "3 Enoch," 264 ff.

153. *3 Enoch; Synopse,* 150; trans. Alexander, "3 Enoch," 264 ff.

154. *3 Enoch; Synopse,* 11; trans. Alexander, "3 Enoch," 262.

155. On the *pargod* see Alexander, " 3 Enoch"; Odeberg, *The Hebrew Book of Enoch,* 141; Scholem, *Major Trends,* 72; *Merkavah,* 35.

156. *3 Enoch; Synopse,* 64–65; trans. Alexander, "3 Enoch," 296

157. *3 Enoch; Synopse,* 14; trans. Alexander, "3 Enoch," 264. Compare a comparable description of the mystic's great achievements as recorded in the *gedulla* passage in *Hekhalot Rabbati, Synopse,* 83–88. For discussion and translation see chapter 2 above.

158. *3 Enoch; Synopse,* 20; trans. Alexander, "3 Enoch," 268.

159. *3 Enoch; Synopse,* 20. For discussion and references see Segal, Two Powers in Heaven, 1–147.

160. *3 Enoch; Synopse,* 64–65; trans. Alexander, "Enoch," 296.

161. *Hekhalot Rabbati; Synopse,* 411–412. Compare *Synopse,* 233, 236, 417.

CHAPTER 5: THE CONCEPT OF GOD: MYSTICAL AND MYTHOLOGICAL DIMENSIONS

1. See Chernus, *JSJ* 13 (1982): 126–129; Gruenwald, *Apocalypticism and Merkavah,* 93–97; Urbach, *Sages,* 49–50, 130–131.

2. *Ma'ashe Merkavah; Synopse,* 548.

3. See views and references in representative studies: Hendel, R. S "The Social Origin of the Anicoic Tradition in Ancient Israel, 365–382; Knohl, *The Sanctuary of Silence;* M. Weinfeld, "God the Creator in Gen. 1 and in the Prophecy of Second Isaiah," *Tarbitz* 37 (1968): 105–132 [Hebrew]; *Deuteronomy and the Deuteronomic School.* See discussion below and nn. 116–119.

4. See, for example, Zechariah 3, 14, Daniel 7. The material and issues related to biblical concepts of an anthropomorphic God are complex. See discussions and references in representative studies: Saggs, The *Encounter with the Divine,* 30 ff; Smith, *The Early History of God,* 88 ff.; T. N. D. Mettinger, *No Graven Image? Israelite Aniconism in its Ancient Near Eastern Context* (Stockholm: Almqvist and Wiksell, 1995); R. S. Hendel, "Aniconism and Anthropomorphism in Ancient Israel," in *The Image and the Book,* ed., K. van der Toorn (Leuven: Peeters, 1997), pp. 205–228; Wyatt, *Myths of Power,* 5, 342; B. Uffenheimer, "Myth and Reality in Ancient Israel," in *The Origin and Diversity*

of Axial Age Civilization, ed., S. N. Eisenstadt (Albany, NY: State University of New York Press, 1986), pp. 135–168.

5. On the image of God as king see discussion in Scholem, *Major Trends,* 54–56; Schäfer, *Hidden and Manifest,* 10 ff.

6. *Hekhalot Rabbati; Synopse,* 206.

7. See discussion and references in H. Frankfort, *Kingship and the Gods, A Study of Ancient Near Eastern Religion as the Integration of Society and Nature* (Chicago: Chicago University Press, 1978), p. 215 ff; Jacobsen, *Treasures of Darkness,* 75 ff.; L. K. Handy, *Among the Host of Heaven,* p. 111 ff.; W. Hallo, "Texts, Statues, and the Cult of the Divine King," VTSup 40 (1988): 54–66.

8. See Horowitz, *Cosmic Geography,* 244–245; M. Metzger, "Himmlische und irdische Wohnstatt Jahwes," 139–158. For Canaanite traditions see E. T. Mullen, *The Assembly of the Gods: The Divine Council in Canaanite and Early Hebrew Literature* (Chico, CA: Scholars Press, 1980), p. 128 ff.; Pope, *El in the Ugaritic Texts,* 62–72.

9. See "Enumah Elish," V; Dalley, *Myths,* 259. On building stories in Mesopotamian sources see V. Hurowitz, *I Have Built You An Exalted House: Temple Building in the Light of Mesopotamian and Northwest Semitic Writing* (Sheffield: Sheffield Academic Press, 1992), pp. 32–96.

10. Kinnier-Wilson, *The Legend of Etana,* 111.

11. See discussion and references in Pope, *El in the Ugaritic Texts,* 62–72; F. M. Cross, *Canaanite Myth and Hebrew Epic* (Cambridge, MA: Harvard University Press, 1973.), 36 ff.; Hurowitz, *I Have Built You An Exalted House,* 97–105; U. Cassuto, "The Palace of Baal in Tablet II AB of Ras Shamra." in *Biblical and Oriental Studies,* vol. 2. (Jerusalem: Magnes Press, 1975), pp. 113–139. Overlapping terminology is used to refer to both temples and royal palaces. Cassuto, thus, defines the difference between God's dwelling in heaven and his temple on earth: "The two concepts of a 'dwelling' and a 'temple' are actually interrelated and are expressed by the same terms *(b't, hkl),* but they are nonetheless clearly to be distinct from each other. The house of God, his dwelling-place in the sky, his abode proper, is one thing; the temples, which are built by men in the likeness of his dwelling in order to serve him and in which he loves to stay so as to receive the homage of human brings, is another." See "The Palace of Baal," 118.

12. See Horowitz, *Cosmic Geography,* 41, 114, 119–120, 125, 130; Metzger, "Himmlische und irdische Wohnstatt Jahwes," 141–144.

13. S. N. Kramer, "The Temple in Sumerian Literature," M. V. Fox (ed.), *Temple in Society* (Winona Lake, IN: Eisenbrauns, 1988), 1–16; Frankfort, *Kingship and the Gods,* 255–288; A. Livingstone, *Mystical and Mythological Explanatory Works,* 93; Hurowitz, *I Have Built You An Exalted House,* 32–57.

14. See "Enumah Elish," VI; Dalley, *Myths,* 262–263;

15. Jacobsen, *Treasures of Darkness,* 81 ff.

16. See discussion and examples in Jacobsen, *Treasures of Darkness,* 95 ff.; 134.

17. See, for example, S. A. Olyan, *Thousand Thousands Served Him: Exegesis and Naming of Angels in Ancient Judaism* (Tübingen: Mohr Siebeck 1993), p. 97.

18. The term 'king' (מלך) is used for God forty-seven times in the Hebrew Bible. See, for example, early biblical poetry: Exod. 15: 18, Num. 23: 21, Deut. 33: 5; Psalm 68: 25. See also Psalms 24: 7–10; 47: 9; 68: 25; 93: 1; 95: 3; 99: 1; Isa. 41: 21; 43: 15; 44: 6; 52: 7; Jer. 46: 18; 48: 15; 51: 57 and prose passages: 1 Sam. 12: 12, Dan. 4: 34. For discussion of the term 'king' and corresponding terms see M. Z. Brettler, *God is King: Understanding an Israelite Metaphor* (Sheffield: JSOT Press, 1989), 29 ff. For discussion and references to aspects of God's image as king in biblical sources see discussion and references in representative studies: Brettler, *God is King,* 145–158; L. K. Handy, "Dissenting Deities or Obedient Angels: Divine Hierarchies in Ugarit and the Bible," *Biblical Research* 35 (1990): 26 ff.

19. On etymology of the biblical word *hekhal* and its links to the akkadian term *êkallu(m)* "palace" and to the Sumerian term Ê-GAL "large-house," See CAD E, 52–61.

20. M. Haran, "Temple and Community in Ancient Israel," in *Temple in Society* ed., M. V. Fox (Winona Lake, IN: Eisenbrauns, 1988), 18.

21. See N. M. Sarna, *On the Book of Psalms: Exploring the Prayers of Ancient Israel* (New York: Schoken, 1993), 152–166.

22. On God's administrative royal bureaucracy see Brettler, *God is King,* 102 ff. For selected examples see references to: "divine assembly" Ps. 82: 1; "assembly of holy beings" Ps. 89: 6; "council" Jer. 23: 18, Amos 3: 7. Ps. 89: 8. Job 15: 8; "assembly," and "hosts" 1 Kgs. 22: 19, Isa. 24: 21, Pss. 103: 21, 148: 2; "servants" Job 4: 18, "attendants" Ps. 103: 21.

23. Scholem, *Major Trends,* 49 ff.

24. See Schäfer's definition, *Hidden and Manifest,* 97. See examples: Synopse, 153, 157, 306, 322, 403, 487, 512, 554, 555, 558, 559, 579, 655, 688.

25. *Hekhalot Rabbati; Synopse,* 206. For references to TWTRWSYY as God's name compare *Synopse,* 195, 206, 219, 414, 416, 539, 540, 590, 977.

26. *3 Enoch; Synopse,* 1; trans. Alexander, "3 Enoch," 255.

27. *Hekhalot Rabbati; Synopse,* 247.

28. On God's inner rooms see *Genizah,* 22. Compare Gruenwald, "New Passages from Hekhalot Literature." *Tarbitz* 38 (1968–69): 269 [Hebrew]. See also *Synopse,* 1, 56, 81, 97, 122, 156, 157, 403, 487, 549, 552, 554, 558, 594, 675, 694, 976.

29. *Hekhalot Rabbati; Synopse,* 201.

30. *Hekhalot Rabbati; Synopse,* 163. See descriptions of joint prayers in the lower and upper realms *Synopse,* 101, 126, 163–4, 172–4, 178–180, 527–531, 807–809. See discussion Chernus, "Pilgrimage," 3 ff. Scholem, *Major Trends,* 62; Gruenwald, "Visions,"10 ff.; Schäfer, *Hidden and Manifest,* 103 ff.

31. For descriptions of the angelic realm see, for example, *Synopse,* 28 ff., 132, 138, 151–174, 206–72 (especially 215, 224–9, 239–241), 309, 310. See discussion Elior, "Mysticism, Magic, and Angelology," 33–53; Dan, *Mysticism,* 108 ff.; Schäfer, *Hidden and Manifest,* 13 ff.

32. *3 Enoch; Synopse,* 48–50.

33. *Hekhalot Rabbati; Synopse,* 46.

34. *Hekhalot Rabbati; Synopse,* 173.

35. *3 Enoch; Synopse,* 43; trans. Alexander, "3 Enoch," 282.

36. *Hekhalot Rabbati; Synopse,* 124.

37. *3 Enoch; Synopse,* 18; trans. Alexander, "3 Enoch," 266.

38. *3 Enoch; Synopse,* 48; trans. Alexander, "3 Enoch," 285.

39. *Merkavah Rabbah; Synopse,* 821.

40. *Ma'ashe Merkavah; Synopse,* 686. Compare *Synopse,* 556.

41. See the well-known view of R. Otto, *The Idea of the Holy* (1923; reprint, London: Oxford University Press, 1973).

42. *Hekhalot Zutarti; Synopse,* 353 ff. Compare *Synopse,* 246, 353–354, 356, 368, 369, 370, 954. On description of the sacred beats see Schäfer, *Hidden and Manifest,* 64 ff.

43. Among the first scholars to point this out was A. H. Layard in 1849. After excavating ancient Nineveh he suggested that the Assyrian winged, human-headed lion figures guarding its portals inspired Ezekiel vision: A. H. Layard, *Nineveh and its Remains* (London: G. P. Putnam, 1849), 1: 69–70, 2: 464–5. For more recent studies see M. Greenberg, "Ezekiel's Vision: Literary and Iconographic Aspects" in H. Tadmor and M. Weinfeld (eds.), *History, Historiography and Interpretation* (Jerusalem: Magnes Press, 1983), pp. 159–168. For pictorial examples see J. Black, and A. Green, *Gods, Demons and Symbols of Ancient Mesopotamia, An Illustrated Dictionary* (Austin: University of Texas Press, 1992), pp. 39–40, 75, 121–122.

44. *Ma'ashe Merkavah; Synopse,* 545.

45. *Hekhalot Rabbati; Synopse,* 153.

46. See S. N. Kramer, "Hymn to Enlil the All-Beneficent," *ANET,* 573.

47. H. and H. A. Frankfort, *Intellectual Adventure,* 17.

48. See KTU 1. 4 VI 53–59. R. de Vaux, R. *The Bible and the Ancient Near East,* trans. D. McHugh (London: Darton, Longman, and Todd, 1972), pp. 150–151.

49. On the "divine aura of splendor" see discussion and examples in A. L. Oppenheim, "Akkadian pul(u)t(u) and melammu," *JAOS* 63 (1943): 31–34. E. Cassin, *La Splendeur Divine* (Paris: La Haye, 1968), pp. 65–82.

50. See Mettinger, *No Graven Image,* 45–46. See pictorial illustrations: 43, ill. 2. 2; 46, ill. 2. 6.

51. Mettinger, "YHWA Sabaoth," 115–116.

52. Ibid., 115–116.

53. Jacobsen, *Treasures of Darkness,* 82.

54. See "Anzu," tablet I in Dalley, *Myths,* 207. See discussion and translation of the OBV, the SBV, and the LV in Dalley, *Myths,* 203–227; Foster, *Before the Muses,* 461–485.

55. S. N. Kramer, "Hymn to Enlil," *ANET,* 575.

56. See discussion and references: Brettler, *God is King,* 81 ff.

57. T. N. D. Mettinger, "Israelite Aniconism: Developments and Origins" in *The Image and the Book,* ed., K. van der Toorn (Leuven: Peeters, 1997), pp. 173–204; "YHWH Sabaoth."

58. Mettiinger, *No Graven Image,* 19.

59. *Hekhalot Rabbati; Synopse,* 153. The term "because" (כי) is mentioned in MS Oxford 1531, MS München 40, MS Dropsie 436, MS Budapest 238. Compare, Synopse, 206, 245, 298, 322.

60. *Hekhalot Rabbati; Synopse,* 94. Compare *Synopse,* 154, 634, 687.

61. *Hekhalot Rabbati; Synopse,* 98.

62. *Hekhalot Rabbati; Synopse,* 99. See discussion in Schäfer, *Hidden and Manifest,* 12 ff.

63. Schäfer, *Hidden and Manifest,* 21 ff. See *Hekhalot Rabbati; Synopse,* 98–99. Compare *Synopse,* 94, 103, 153–154, 160, 167–168, 172–173, 185, 187, 189.

64. *Hekhalot Rabbati; Synopse,* 98–99.

65. *Hekhalot Rabbati; Synopse,* 162.

66. *Hekhalot Rabbati; Synopse,* 119; trans. Schäfer, *Hidden and Manifest,* 12.

67. *3 Enoch; Synopse,* 38; trans. Alexander, "3 Enoch," 309.

68. See Smith, *The Early History of God,* 116 ff.; M. Weinfeld, "'The Rider of the Clouds' and 'Gatherer of the Clouds'," *JANES* 5 (1975): 421–426; J. W. McKay, "Further Light on the Houses and Chariot of the Sun in the Jerusalem

Temple (2 Kings 23: 11)," *PEQ* 105 (1973): 167–169; M. Civil, "Isme Dagan and Enlil's Chariot," *JAOS* 88 (1986): 3–15. For iconographical examples see J. B. Pritchard, *ANEP,* 50–51, nos. 165, 166, 169; 53, no. 175; M. Klingbeil, *Yahweh Fighting from Heaven: God as Warrior and as God of heaven in the Hebrew Psalter and Ancient Near Eastern Iconography,* (Göttingen: Vandenhoeck and Rupreccht, 1999), pp. 222–240.

69. Black and Green, *Gods, Demons and Symbols,* 52. Compare O. Keel and C. Uehlinger, *Gods, Goddesses and Images of God in Ancient Israel.* trans. T. H. Trapp. (Minneapolis: Fortress Press, 1988), pp. 60–62, 82, 120, 122, 243.

70. See W. G. Lambert and A. R. Millard, *Atra-Hasis: The Babylonian Story of the Flood with Sumerian Flood Stories by M. Civil* (Oxford: Clarendon Press, 1969), p. 122. Compare, Enumah Elish tablet II. 151, IV. 50.

71. See, for example, CTA 2. 4 (KTU 1. 2 IV. 8), KTU 1. 5 V 6–11. See discussion in Weinfeld, "The Rider of the Clouds," 421–426.

72. Smith, *The Early History of God,* 50 ff.; M. Weinfeld, "'Rider of the Clouds" 421–426; J. W. McKay, "Further Light on the Houses and Chariot of the Sun in the Jerusalem Temple (2 Kings 23: 11)," *PEQ* 105 (1973): 167–169; Klingbeil, *Yahweh Fighting from Heaven,* 71–74.

73. Scholem, *Major Trends,* 40–79; Dan, *Mysticism,* 25 ff.

74. *3 Enoch; Synopse,* 37; trans. Alexander, "3 Enoch," 308.

75. *3 Enoch; Synopse,* 38; trans. Alexander, "3 Enoch," 309.

76. *3 Enoch; Synopse,* 30; trans. Alexander, "3 Enoch," 276. Compare *3 Enoch; Synopse,* 40.

77. *Ma'ashe Merkavah; Synopse,* 549.

78. See Jacobsen, *Treasures of Darkness,* 23 ff.; Mullen, *Assembly of the Gods;* Handy, *Among the Host of Heaven,* 5 ff.

79. See Handy, *Among the Host of Heaven,* 112 ff.; Mullen, *Assembly of the Gods,* 198 ff.; Dalley, *The Legacy of Mesopotamia,* 154.

80. See Foster, "To Enlil," *Before the Muses,* 562.

81. See Foster, "Great Hymn to Marduk," *Before the Muses,* 526–527.

82. M. Weinfeld, "The Heavenly Praise in Unison," in *Meqor Hajjim, Festschrift für Georg Molia zum 75. Gebürtstag* (Graz: Akademische Druck und Verlagsanstalt, 1983), pp. 427–437; S. N. Kramer and M. Weinfeld, "Sumerian Literature and the Book of Psalms, An Introduction to a Comparative Study," Part 2, *Beth Miqra* 57 (1974): 136–41 [Hebrew].

83. "Enumah Elish," tablet V; Dalley, *Myths,* 260.

84. "Enumah Elish," tablet VI; Dalley, *Myths,* 266.

85. "Enumah Elish" tablet VI; Dalley, *Myths,* 264.

86. For references to mythical depictions of God's kingship see, for example, Ex. 15: 18; Isa. 24: 23; 33: 22, 52: 7; Jer. 8: 19, Mic. 4: 7, Zeph. 13: 15, Zech. 14: 9, Ps. 10: 16, 48: 3, 68: 25, 74: 12, 84: 4, 93: 3, 96: 10, 97: 1, 99: 4, 146: 10, 149: 2.

87. On angelic powers, heavenly figures, and the boundaries of monotheistic faith in the Hebrew Bible see discussions and references representative studies: F. M. Cross, "The Council of Yahweh in Second Isaiah," *JNES* 12 (1953): 274–277; Rowland, *Open Heaven,* 79 ff.; Mullen, *The Assembly of the Gods,* 190 ff.; M. S. Smith, *The Origins of Biblical Monotheism* (New York 2002); J. H. Tigay, *You Shall Have No Other Gods: Israelite Religion in Light of Hebrew Inscriptions* (Atlanta 1986). M. Barker, *The Great Angel A Study of Israel's Second God* (Louisville, Kentucky 1992); J. G. Gammie, "The Angelology and Demonology in the Septuagint and the Book of Job," *HUCA* 56 (1985): 1–19; P. Hayman, "Monotheism—Misused Word in Jewish Studies?" *JJS* 42 (1991): 1–15; Morgenstern, "The Mythological Background of Psalm 82," 29–34.

88. Compare Deut. 33: 2–3, 8–9, 43; Exod. 15: 11.

89. See discussion in Mullen, *The Assembly of the Gods,* 207–208.

90. Compare concepts of the divine realm in late antiquity and ancient Judaism as examined in several representative studies: Segal, *Two Powers;* L. W. Hurtado, *One God, One Lord: Early Christian Devotion and Ancient Jewish Monotheism.* (Philadelphia: Fortress, 1988); L. T. Stuckenbruck, *Angel Veneration and Christology* (Tübingen: Mohr Siebeck, 1995), pp. 3–204; C. A. Gieschen, *Angelomorphic Christology: Antecedents and Early Evidence* (Leiden, Boston, Köln: Brill, 1998), 7–151; C. H. T Fletcher-Louis, *Luke, Acts: Angels, Christology and Soteriology* (Tubingen: Mohr Siebeck, 1997), p. 109 ff; Olyan, *Thousand Thousands.*

91. See Elior, "Mysticism, Magic, and Angelology," 33–53. See discussion of the developed angelic realm in Scholem, *Merkavah,* 1–5, 23–24, 31–35, 65–75; Dan, *Mysticism,* 108 ff.; Schäfer, Hidden and Manifest, 21–37, 62–65.

92. *3 Enoch; Synopse,* 13.

93. *3 Enoch; Synopse,* 4, 12–15. Many studies have examined the figure of Metatron and his divine attributes. See discussions and references in representative studies Scholem, *Merkavah,* 43–55; *Major Trends,* 67–70; J. Dan, "The Seventy Names of Metatron," *Proceedings of the Eighth World Congress of Jewish Studies, Division C* (1982): 19–23 [Hebrew]; "Anafi'el, Metatron, and the Creator, 447–457 [Hebrew]; *Mysticism,* 108 ff.; Schäfer, *Hidden and Manifest,* 29 ff., 132 ff.; Lieberman, "Metatron, the Meaning of his Name and Functions," appendix 1 in I. Gruenwald, *Apocalypticism and Merkavah,* 235–241; Deuthch, *Guardians of the Gate,* 27–77.

94. *3 Enoch;* Synopse, 26; trans. Alexander, "3 Enoch," 273. The angel's name, "Anafi'el," derives from the Hebrew term *anaf* (ענף) "a branch." See Dan, "Anafi'el, Metatron, and the Creator," 447–457 [Hebrew].

95. *Hekhalot Rabbati; Synopse,* 241.

96. *3 Enoch; Synopse,* 21; trans. Alexander, "3 Enoch," 276–277.

97. *3 Enoch; Synopse,* 33–34; trans. Alexander, "3 Enoch," 278. Compare *Synopse,* 23–35, 38–44.

98. See Dan, *Mysticism,* 129.

99. See the description of Aher's reaction when he sees Metatron in *3 Enoch:* ". . . when Aher came to behold the vision of the chariot and set his eyes upon me, he was afraid and trembled . . . when he saw me seated upon a throne like a king with ministering angels. . . . then he open his mouth and said 'There are indeed two powers in Heaven!'" *Synopse,* 20, trans. Alexander, "3 Enoch," 268. See discussion and references in Segal, *Two Powers,* 60 ff.; Liebes, *The Sin of Elisha* [Hebrew].

100. *Ma'ashe Merkavah; Synopse,* 549. Compare *Synopse,* 274 : "For [it] is the duty of all creatures to make you mighty, to adorn you, to glorify you, to praise you, to extol you, to make you great, to sanctify you, to elevate you, to embellish you, to make you exalted, to laud you, great holy king, ruler over those above and below, over the first and over the last, who out of fear and trembling sanctify you with a threefold sanctification, so as is written: 'holy, holy holy'." (Isa. 6: 3), trans. Schäfer, *Hidden and Manifest,* 15.

101. *Hekhalot Zutarti; Synopse,* 418. Compare *Synopse,* 161, 265–267, 274, 276.

102. *Hekhalot Rabbati; Synopse,* 185–186. Compare, *Synopse,* 58, 306, 334.

103. *Ma'ashe Merkavah; Synopse,* 551.

104. On gaining divine qualities in a "quasi-deification" process see Wolfson, *Through a Speculum,* 82 ff.

105. *Ma'ashe Merkavah; Synopse,* 590

106. *Hekhalot Zutarti; Synopse,* 421. Compare *Synopse,* 61, 384, 514, 598, 639.

107. *Hekhalot Zutarti; Synopse,* 484.

108. Hendel, "Aniconism and Anthropomorphism in Ancient Israel," 205–228.

109. "Enumah Elish," tablet I; Dalley, *Myths,* 235–236. On similar Near Eastern patterns of depiction see S. Smith, "Divine Form and Size in Ugarit and Pre-Exilic Israelite Religion," *Zeitschrift für die Alttestamentliche Wissenschaft* 100 (1988), 424–427; E. Bloch-Smith, "Who Is the King of Glory?" in *Bible and Archaeology in Honor of Philip J. King,* eds., M. D. Coogan, J. C. Exum, and L. E. Stager, (Louisville KY: Westminster John Knox Press, 1994), pp. 21–25.

110. See Hendel, "Aniconism and Anthropomorphism."

111. On the Gudea Cylinders see discussion and references T. W. Mann, *Divine Presence and Guidance in Israelite Traditions* (Baltimore, and London: Johns Hopkins University Press, 1977), pp. 77–83.

112. Gudea Cylinder A 5. 13, trans. A. Falkenstein and W. von Soden in *Sumerische und akkadische Hymnen und Gebete* (Zurich 1953) cited in Mann, *Divine Presence and Guidance,* 78. Compare T. Jacobsen's translation in Frankfort, *Kingship and the Gods,* 255–288.

113. Livingstone, *Mystical and Mythological,* 93.

114. See translation and discussion in Jacobsen, *Treasures of Darkness,* 235–236. Compare Foster, *Before the Muses,* 632–633; Livingstone, *Mystical and Mythological,* 101–102. Compare the related manifested/abstract depiction of Mesopotamian gods: Saggs, *The Encounter with the Divine,* 8, 99–100.

115. Hendel, "Aniconism and Anthropomorphism."

116. See, for example, Exod. 20: 2–4, Deut 4: 12, 15–16. On tendency to abstract God in biblical sources see Weinfeld, *Deuteronomy and Deuteronomistic School,* 191–209; Fishbane, *Biblical Interpretation in Ancient Israel,* 322; Hendel "The Social Origin of the Anicoic Tradition in Ancient Israel," 365–382; Knohl, *The Sanctuary of Silence.*

117. This mandate that God has no image was turned into one of the central principles of Judaism in a later period by M. Maimonides. See, for example, *Guide of the Perplexed,* 2 vols. trans. S. Pines (Chicago: University of Chicago Press, 1963), 1: 36. On the controversy between Maimonides' perspective and opposing ideas that supported anthropomorphic views see B. Septimus, *Hispano-Jewish Culture in Transition* (Cambridge MA: Harvard University Press, 1982), 75–103.

118. On biblical concepts of an anthropomorphic God see discussion and references: Smith, *The Early History of God,* 97 ff; Mettinger, *No Graven Image;* H. Eilberg-Schwartz, "The Problem of the Body for the People of the Book," in H. Eilberg-Schwartz (ed.), *People of the Body* (Albany NY: State University of New York Press, 1992), pp. 17–46.

119. See Mettinger's argument that programmatic aniconism, or the anti-iconism of the bible, was rather late, but *de facto* aniconism goes back as long way in the history of Israelite religion: Mettinger, *No Graven Image.* See opposite views claiming the existence of a cult statue of Yahweh in the pre-exilic Israel: H. Niehr, "In Search of YHWH's Cult Statue in the First Temple," in *The Image and the Book* ed., K. van der Toorn (Leuven: Peeters, 1997), pp. 73–96; B. B. Schmidt "The Aniconic Tradition. On Reading Images and Viewing Texts," in *The Triumph of Elohim: From Yahwisms to Judaism,* ed., D. Edelman (Grand Rapids: Eerdmans 1996), pp. 75–105.

120. Mettinger "Israelite Aniconism: Development and Origins," in *The Image and the Book.* ed., K. van der Toorn (Leuven: Peeters, 1997), especially p. 187 ff.

121. Hendel, "Aniconism and Anthropomorphism," 223.

122. Ibid., 223.

123. J. Barr, "Theophany and Anthropomorphism in the Old Testament," VTSup 7 (1960): 32.

124. Ibid., 34

125. Hendel, "Aniconism and Anthropomorphism," 222.

126. Compare, for example, Exod 33: 11: "Yahweh would speak to Moses face to face, as one speaks to his friend"; Deut 34. 10: "Never since has there arisen a prophet in Israel like Moses whom the Lord knew face to face." The exceptional nature of the statement in Numbers 12: 8 is all more impressive in view of the rarity of "image," *temunah,* (תמונה) as a representation of Yahweh. The artistic construction of this form is expressly forbidden in the second Commandment (Exod. 20: 4; Deut. 5: 8) and the Deuteronomistic views which repeatedly emphasizes that Yahweh's *temunah* was not seen at Sinai (Deut. 4: 12, 15–16, 23, 25). See discussion in Mann, *Divine Presence and Guidance,* 144–149.

127. Hendel, "Aniconism and Anthropomorphism," 207.

128. On God's image in Ezekiel see Kutsko, *Between Heaven and Earth,* 77–100. Although the Glory of God alludes to a wide range of meanings in Israelite and later in Jewish tradition, the focus here is on the Glory of God which is not separated from him. For a survey of scholarship on the "glory theology" see Mettinger, *Dethronement of Sabaoth,* 81–115. See Rowland's discussion on Ezek. 1: 26–28, which depicts the glory appearing on the divine throne as a man, unlike Ezek. 8: 2 which shows the glory separating from the divine throne: Rowland, *The Open Heaven,* 94–113.

129. Kutsko, *Between Heaven and Earth,* 67. On the terms "image" and "likeness" as synonymous with form, body, and glory see J. E. Fossum *The Name of God and the Angel of the Lord. The Origins of Intermediation in Gnosticism* (Tübingen: Mohr Siebeck, 1985), pp. 283–284.

130. See J. M. Miller "In the Image and Likeness of God," *JBL* 91 (1972): 291–292.

131. On *Shiur Komah* traditions, transmission, and dating see Scholem, *Major Trends,* 63–67; *Merkavah,* 36–42, *On the Mystical Shape,* 20–55; Dan, "The Concept of Knowledge," 63 ff.; Cohen, *The Shiur Qomah;* Greenfield, "Prolegomena," xxxiv; Gruenwald, *Apocalyptic and Merkavah,* 213–217, "Knowledge and Vision," 63–107; Lieberman, "Mishnat Shir ha-Shirim," appendix 1 in G. Scholem, *Jewish Gnosticism,* 118–126; Elior, "The Concept of God," 97–120; Schäfer, *The Hidden and Manifest,* 60 ff., 102 ff.; Halperin, *Faces,* 405 ff.; Wolfson, *Through a Speculum,* 85 ff.

132. For a discussion of the medieval controversies about these traditions see an account of recent scholarship in Cohen, *The Shiur Qomah,* 13–41.

133. G. Scholem has presented this position suggesting that the *Shi'ur Komah* descriptions are not concerned with the hidden essence of God but

rather elaborate upon his manifested corporeal form, the *kavod.* See Scholem, *Major Trends,* 65–66. This understanding has been shared by Gruenwald, *Apocalyptic and Merkavah,* 94; Dan, "The Concept of Knowledge," 70–71; Morray-Jones, "Transformational Mysticism, 2 ff.

134. This view has been asserted, as well, by Scholem in several of his writings. See, for example, *Major Trends,* 64; *On the Mystical Shape,* 24. It has been developed further by other scholars: Chernus,"Visions of God" 123–146; Schäfer, *Hidden and Manifest,* 150; Dan,"The Concept of Knowledge" 68–69; Elior "The Concept of God"; Morray- Jones "Transformational Mysticism, 9; Wolfson, *Through a Speculum,* 90–107. From a different perspective scholars have suggested that the subject of the *Shi'ur Komah* figurative description is not God but rather a hypostatic angel. See G. G. Stroumsa, "Form(s) of God: Some Notes on Metatron and Christ," *HTR* 76 (1983): 269–288; J. E. Fossum, *The Name of God and the Angel of the Lord. The Origin of Intermediation in Gnosticism* (Tübingen: Mohr Siebeck, 1985); Deuthch, *The Gnostic Imagination,* 99–105.

135. For a very eloquent account of such views see Deutch, *The Gnostic Imagination,* 80–153.

136. Liberman, "Mishnat Shir ha-Shirim," 118–126. This firm identification of *Shiur Komah* with Midrash *Shir ha-Shirim* has been been fully accepted by Scholem. Other scholars such as M. Cohen, and D. Boyarin have rejected this theory, which has also been called into question by Green. See Scholem, *Jewish Gnosticism,* 36–40; Cohen, *The Shi'ur Qomah,* 1, 19; D. Boyarin, "Two Introductions to the Midrash on Song of Songs," *Tarbiz* 56 (1987): 479–500 [Hebrew]; Green, *Keter,* 78–79, n. 3; "The Song of Song in Early Jewish Mysticism," *Orim: A Jewish Journal at Yale* 2 (1987): 49–63.

137. Prominent manifestations of this model are likewise found in *2 Enoch,* entitled also the *Slavonic Enoch* or *Book of the Secrets of Enoch. 2 Enoch* 22: 1–3, for example, proclaims a figurative portrayal of God's form, through which his concealed, incomprehensible nature is revealed: "And on the tenth heaven, Aravoth, I saw the view of the face of the Lord, like iron made burning hot in a fire and brought out, and it emits sparks an is incandescent. Thus, even I saw the face of the Lord. But the face of the Lord is not to be talked about, it is so very marvelous and supremely awesome and supremely frightening. And who am I to give an account of the incomprehensible being of the Lord, and his face, so extremely strange and indescribable?" See F. I. Andersen "2 (Slavonic Apocalypse of) Enoch" in J. H. Charlesworth, *The Old Testament Pseudepigrapha,* (Garden City, NY: Doubleday, 1983), 1: 136. A parallel formulation is found in *2 Enoch* 39: 1–6: " . . . the lips of the Lord are a furnace of fire . . . the face of the Lord, like iron made burning hot by a fire, emitting sparks . . . the eyes of the Lord, like rays of the shining sun and terrifying the eyes of a human being . . . I have seen the extent of the Lord without measure and without analogy, who has no end." See Andersen "2 Enoch," 163. A clear connection with the terminology and views of the *Shi'ur Komah*

speculations have been discerned by Scholem, *Kabbalah* 17; Rowland, *Open Heaven*, 85; Wolfson, *Through a Speculum*, 30–31.

138. See, for example, *Synopse* 948. cf. 356, 699. For translation and discussion see Cohen, *Shi'ur Qomah*, 47, 65–66, 90–91, 141–142.

139. *Synopse*, 948.

140. *Synopse*, 950. Compare Cohen, *Shi'ur Qomah*, 214.

141. See Cohen, *The Shi'ur Qomah*, 192–194. Compare, for example, *Synopse*, 692–704; 948–951.

142. *Synopse*, 949–950. For translation and discussion see Cohen, *Shi'ur Qomah*, 198.

143. *Synopse*, 481. Compare *Synopses* 31. On the imagery of light see Scholem, *Major Trends*, 65; Elior, "The Concept of God," 107–108, Wolfson, *Through a Speculum*, 106.

144. Wolfson, *Through a Speculum*, 86. See also 87, 106–107.

145. Scholem, *Major Trends*, 64.

146. Dan, "The Concept of Knowledge," 68.

147. Elior, "The Concept of God," 114.

148. Schäfer, *The Hidden and Manifest*, 149–50. Note Schäfer's view of God's immanence as a result of his names.

149. Wolfson, *Through a Speculum*, 91.

150. *Synopse*, 949–950. Compare Cohen, *Shi'ur Qomah*, 198. For possible explanation of the guardian angel *(sar)* associated with several parts such as the divine eye-ball see Cohen, *Shi'ur Qomah*, 211.

151. See *Synopse*, 375–386, 939–973.

152. *Synopse*, 356.

153. *Hekhalot Rabbati; Synopse*, 253. Compare, for example, *Synopse*, 102, 159, 198, 248, 407–409, 481.

154. See CAD 9–12; A. L. Oppenheim, "Akkadian pul(u)t(u) and melammu," *JAOS* 63 (1943): 31–34; *Ancient Mesopotamia*, 98–99, 176–177; Cassin, *La Splendeur Divine*, 9–12. For iconographic images of divine figures surrounded with rays see examples from the end of the Assyrian Period: E. Porada, *Corpus of Ancient Near Eastern Seals in North American Collections I, the Pierpont Morgan Library Collection* (Washington: The Bollingen Series 14, 1948), nos. 679–682, 685, 691, 698, 704–705; Pritchard *ANEP*, no. 522.

155. Oppenheim, *Ancient Mesopotamia*, 176–177.

156. H. and H. A. Frankfort, *The Intellectual Adventure*, 13; T. Jacobsen, "The Graven Image," in *Ancient Israelite Religion. Essays in Honor of Frank*

Moore Cross. eds. P. D. Miller, Jr., P. D. Hanson, S. D. McBrid (Philadelphia: Fortress Press 1987), pp. 15–32.

157. See Mettinger, *The Dethronement,* 29 ff.; Olyan, *Thousand Thousands,* 105.

158. Dalley, *Legacy of Mesopotamia,* 45 ff.

159. On the tablet of the gods see Oppenheim, Ancient Mesopotamia, 201–205; Saggs, *The Encounter with the Divine,* 70–73; Lambert, "Destiny and Divine Intervention in Babylon and Israel," 65–72; Wisdom Literature, 6; "History and the Gods: A Review Article," *Or. NS* 39 (1970): 170–77. On the influence of the Babylonian ritual on rabbinic description of the Jewish new year ceremonies in the month of Tishri see discussion and references in G. Widengren, *The Ascension of the Apostle and the Heavenly Book,* 7 ff.; Dalley, *Legacy of Mesopotamia,* 77. See also discussion in Green, *Keter,* 4 ff.

160. A. L. Oppenheim, "The Golden Garments of the Gods," *JNES* 8 (1949): 172–193.

161. "Enumah Elish," tablet V; Dalley, *Myths,* 258.

162. On the biblical formula "to see the face of God" as influenced by patterns of ancient Near Eastern ceremonies see discussion and references: M. S. Smith, "Seeing God in the Psalms: The Background to the Beatific Vision in the Hebrew Bible," *CBQ* 50 (1988): 171–183.

163. Black and Green, *Gods, Demons and Symbols,* 75.

164. CTA, 4. 5. 66; cf. 3. 5. 10.

165. KTU 1. 10 III 6; KTU 1. 4 V 3–5. On El see Cross, *Canaanite Myth,* 13–44. For the influence of ancient Mesopotamian mythological motifs on biblical description of God see, for example, Cross, *Canaanite Myth;* Collins, *The Apocalyptic Vision of the Book of Daniel,* 95 ff.

166. Jer. 7: 11, 12, 14, 30; 34: 15. On theophanies of God's name see discussion and references in R. J. Tournay, *Seeing and Hearing God with the Psalms* (Sheffield: JSOT Press, 1991), p. 99 ff.

167. Olyan, *A Thousand Thousands,* 105.

168. See Sarna, *Psalms,* 54; J. Morgenstern, "Moses with the Shining Face," *HUCA* 2 (1925): 3–4; Kutsko, *Between Heaven and Earth,* 80 ff. For rabbinical views see, for example, *Hagigah 16a.*

169. For depictions of the enthroned God see 1 Kgs 22: 19; Isa. 6: 1–8; Pss. 29: 1–2, 82: 1, 89: 5–8; Isa. 14: 13; Jer. 23: 18, 22; Zech. 3; Dan. 3: 25. On the symbol of God's crown in Jewish literary sources from ancient to medieval times see a thorough study and references in Green, *Keter.*

170. *Synopse,* 253.

171. *Ma'ashe Merkavah; Synopse,* 588. Compare *Synopse,* 71, 114, 557, 587–591, 596, 655. On the mystical and magical function of names see discussion:

Scholem, *Major Trends*, 76; *Merkavah*, 65–77, 79; Grözinger, "The Names"; Schäfer, "Jewish Magic Literature in Late Antiquity and Early Middle Ages." *JJS* 41 (1990): 75–91; *Hidden and Manifest*, 56 ff., 69 ff.

172. *Synopse*, 557. Compare *Synopse*, 391, 649, 821.

173. See for example, *Hekhalot Zutarti; Synopse*, 337.

174. *Ma'ashe Merkavah; Synopse*, 596. Compare Synopse, 549, 592, 594, 694, 853, 972.

175. See *Synopse*, 320, 389, 396, 833, 840. On seals see discussion in Green, "Crowns, Tefillin and Magic Seals," *Keter*, 49–57.

176. *Hekhalot Rabbati; Synopse*, 159. Compare *Synopse*, 407, 481, 699. On God's beard see *Synopse*, 699, 700, 949.

177. *Hekhalot Rabbati; Synopse*, 159.

178. *3 Enoch; Synopse*, 45. On God's garment see Scholem, *Major Trends*, 44–45; *Merkavah*, 57–64.

179. *Hekhalot Rabbati; Synopse*, 105. Compare *Synopse*, 267, 418. See discussion in Scholem, *Merkavah*, 61.

180. *Merkavah Rabbah, Synopse*, 699.

181. *Hekhalot Zutarti, Synopse*, 356.

182. Compare testaments of personal encounters with the divine: *Synopse*, 81, 338, 347, 421, 545, 595, 655, 688, 740, 821, 873, 947.

183. *Hekhalot Zutarti, Synopse*, 356.

184. See, for example, *Synopse*, 102, 276, 966. See full discussion in chapter two above.

185. *Hekhalot Zutarti; Synopse*, 421. Compare *Synopse*, 688.

186. *Synopse*, 699. Compare: "like the measure of the gentle breeze and like the creation of the breath of life," Schäfer, *Hidden and Manifest*, 102.

187. Fishbane, "Five Stages of Jewish Myth and Mythmaking," in *The Exegetical Imagination*, 103.

CHAPTER 6: LITERARY, PHENOMENOLOGICAL, CULTURAL, AND SOCIAL IMPLICATIONS

1. *Ma'aseh Merkavah; Synopse*, 554.
2. Dan, "The Concept of History"; "The Revelation of the Secret," 20–24.
3. Scholem, *Major Trends*, 41–47; *Merkavah*, 7–8.
4. Halperin, *Merkabah*, 3 ff., 183 ff.; *Chariot*, chaps. 1 and 9.

5. Elior, "From Earthly Temple to Heavenly Shrine"; "The Merkavah Tradition"; *Temple and Chariot* [Hebrew]. See Deutsch's parallel suggestion in *The Guardians of the Gate,* 147ff.

6. P. Schäfer, "The Aim and Purpose of Early Jewish Mysticism," in *Hekhalot-Studien,* 293; *Hidden and Manifest,* 159.

7. Cohen, *Shiur Qomah*; Alexander, "3 Enoch"; "3 Enoch and the Talmud"; Swartz, *Mystical Prayer; Scholastic Magic.*

8. Swartz, *Mystical Prayer,* 211–223; *Scholastic Magic,* 22 ff.; Davila, "The Hekhalot Literature and Shamanism," 767–789, *Descenders to the Chariot.*

9. Gimello, "Mysticism in Context," 63.

10. Katz, "The 'Conservative' Character of Mysticism," 41.

11. For familiarity with Jewish traditions and writings see, for example, *Hekhalot Rabbati,* Synopse, 234, 235. For connection to temple priestly traditions see Elior, "From Earthly Temple to Heavenly Shrine"; "The Merkavah Tradition"; *Temple and Chariot* [Hebrew].

12. Halperin, *Chariot,* 34–37, 362–363, 429–446. See also n. 8 above.

13. See Schäfer, *Hidden and Manifest,* 161–166; Elior, "The Concept of God," 99. The tradition in *3 Enoch* also seems to disagree with traditional rabbinic agenda, which did not incorporate the Enochic tradition into its teaching as the two Talmuds and the tannaitic midrashim attest. See Alexander's observations in "The Historical Setting," 169–173.

14. *Ma'aseh Merkavah; Synopse,* 580–581. Compare *Synopse,* 595, 596.

15. *3 Enoch; Synopse,* 14. See discussion chapters 2 and 4.

16. *Hekhalot Rabbati; Synopse,* 228.

17. *Hekhalot Rabbati; Synopse,* 240.

18. *Hekhalot Rabbati; Synopse,* 235.

19. *3 Enoch, Synopse,* 59.

20. *3 Enoch, Synopse,* 64.

21. *Hekhalot Rabbati; Synopse,* 81.

22. *Hekhalot Zutarti; Synopse,* 426.

23. *Hekhalot Zutarti; Synopse,* 341. See discussion Schäfer, *Hidden and Manifest,* 72 ff.

24. *Hekhalot Rabbati; Synopse,* 198.

25. *Hekhalot Rabbati; Synopse,* 201.

26. *Hekhalot Rabbati; Synopse,* 239.

27. On scribal traditions associated with ancient heroes such as Moses and Enoch see J. M. Jaffee, *Torah in the Mouth: Written and Oral Tradition in Palestinian Judaism, ca. 200 BCE–400 CE* (Oxford: Oxford University Press), pp. 23–24. On the priestly identity of Enoch and Rabbi Ishmael and the significant presence of priestly traditions in Hekhalot and Merkavah literature see Elior, *Temple and Chariot*, 241–277 [Hebrew].

28. E. J. Bickerman, "Scribes and Sages," in *The Jews in the Greek Age* (Cambridge, MA: Harvard University Press, 1988), p. 161.

29. On scribes see discussions and references in representative studies: A. Saldarini, *Pharisees, Scribes and Sadducees* (Wilmington, Delaware: Michael Glazier, 1988), pp. 241–276; C. Schams, *Jewish Scribes in the Second Temple Period* (Sheffield: Sheffield, Academic Press, 1998); R. Kalmin, *The Sage in Jewish Society of Late Antiquity* (London and New York: Routledge, 1999). M. E. Stone, "Ideal Figures and Social Context: Priest and Sage in the Early Second Temple Period," in *Ancient Israelite Religion*, eds., P. D. Miller, Jr., P. D. Hanson, and S. D. McBride (Philadelphia Fortress Press, 1988), pp. 575–586.

30. Saldarini, *Pharisees, Scribes and Sadducees*, 273.

31. Ibid., 273–275.

32. For evidence of Near Eastern and Mesopotamian traditions of scribes in the Second Temple period see Schams, *Jewish Scribes* and her references to the existence of such traditions in Persian, Hellenistic, and Roman periods, pp. 69, 97, 101, 141, 284–286, 310, 323; J. J. Collins, "Jewish Apocalypticism Against Its Hellenistic Near Eastern Environment," in *Seers, Sybils and Sages in Hellenistic-Roman Judaism* (Leiden, New York, Köln: Brill, 1997), pp. 59–74; "The Sage in Apocalyptic and Pseudepigraphic Literature," in *Seers, Sybils and Sages*, 339–350. On priests, scribes, prophets and other leaders who produced and transmitted the biblical books see Fishbane, *Biblical Interpretation*. On the scribal-priestly character of Deuteronomy see Weinfeld, *Deuteronomy*. For overlapping scribal and priestly traditions in several periods see: Bickerman, *The Jews in the Greek Age*, 162–3; Saldarini, *Pharisees, Scribes and Sadducees*, 244 ff; M. J. Jaffee, *Torah in the Mouth: Writing and Oral Tradition in Palestine Judaism 200 BCE–400 BC* (Oxford 2001), pp. 20ff. For critical discussions and references to the connection and identification of scribes and priests in principal studies see Schams, *Jewish Scribes*, 24–35, 309–324. On "sons of zadok" see Elior, *Temple and Chariot*, 202–211.

33. See nn. 28, 29, 32.

34. See R. Murphy, "The Hebrew Sage and Openness to the World," in *Christian Action and Openness to the World*, ed., J. Pipin (Villanova PA: Villanova University Press, 1970), pp. 219–244.

35. For discussion of this portrait of a scholar-sage see P. W. Shehan and A. A. Di Lella, *The Wisdom of Ben Sira* (New York: Doubleday, 1987), pp. 48–50.

36. Gammie, "The Sage in Sirach," 361.

37. For translation and background information see R. J. H. Shutt, "Letter of Aristeas," in *The Old Testament Pseudepigrapha*, 2: 5–34; G. W. E. Nickelsbeurg,

Jewish Literature Between the Bible and the Mishnah. A Historical and Literary Introduction (Philadelphia: Fortress, 1981), pp. 165–169.

38. Schams, *Jewish Scribes*, 102.

39. Ibid., 322

40. See discussion in R. F. G. Sweet, "The Sage in Mesopotamian Palaces and Royal Courts," in *The Sage in Israel and the Ancient Near East*, eds., J. G. Gammie and L. G. Perdue (Winona Lake, IN: Eisenbrauns, 1990.), pp. 99–107; "The Sage in Akkadian Literature: A Philological Study," *The Sage in Israel and the Ancient Near East*, 45–65.

41. Sweet, "The Sage in Akkadian Literature," 55.

42. Ibid., 57.

43. Ibid., 105–106.

44. See chapter 3.

45. See J. J. Collins, "Jewish Apocalypticism Against Its Hellenistic Near Eastern Environment," 59–74.

46. Vanderkam, *Enoch*, 1–51; Collins, *The Apocalyptic Imagination*, 33–67; *The Book of Daniel*, 27–36.

47. Collins, "The Sage in Apocalyptic and Pseudepigraphic Literature," 346.

48. Ibid., 343.

49. On *1 Enoch*, its different versions and writings, dates, historical background and significant themes see discussion and references in E. Isaac, "1 Enoch," in *The Old Testament Pseudepigrapha*, 1: 5–12; Collins, "The Early Enoch Literature," in *The Apocalyptic* Imagination, 33–67.

50. See E. Isaac, "1 Enoch," 73. Compare Vanderkam, *Enoch*, 173; Collins,"The Sage in Apocalyptic and Pseudepigraphic Literature," 344–345.

51. Compare 93: 2, 106: 19. See Vanderkam, *Enoch*, 135–140, 148–151.

52. On the Book of Daniel, dates, background, and significant themes see Collins, *The Book of Daniel; The Apocalyptic Imagination*, 68–92.

53. On the *maskil* see discussion and references in Collins,"The Sage in Apocalyptic and Pseudepigraphic Literature," 349–351; C. A. Newsom, "The Sage in the Literature of Qumran: The Functions of the Maskil," in *The Sage in Israel and the Ancient Near East*, 373–382.

54. See M. Fishbane, "From Scrbalism to Rabbinism," 487–495, especially 445; *Biblical Interpretation*, 487–495.

55. Fishbane emphasizes this notion of interpreting hidden meaning: "Those in possession of the special exegetical illumination are called knowers . . . who understand . . . the true application of the prophecies . . . the illuminates of Prophecy are also divinely guided into the "hidden and sealed"

meaning of ancient revelation (Dan 12: 9). It is this special understanding that functions for them as a mode of divine sustenance in the awesome and wondrous . . . times of the end." See Fishbane, "From Scrbalism to Rabbinism,"445.

56. See M. Z Segal, *Sepher Ben Sira ha-Shalem* (Jerusalem: Bialik Institute 1972), pp. 17–18 [Hebrew]; Gruenwald, *Apocalyptic and Merkavah,* 18.

57. Compare, *Genesis Rabbah* 8: 2. See Fishbane, *Biblical Interpretation,* 539–540; Halperin, *Chariot,* 47.

58. On *4 Ezra,* dates, background, and significant themes see J. J. Collins, "After the Fall: 4 Ezra, 2 Baruch, and the Apocalypse of Abraham," in *The Apocalyptic Imagination,* 156–169.

59. On 2 Baruch, dates, background, and significant themes see J. J. Collins, "After the Fall: 4 Ezra, 2 Baruch, and the Apocalypse of Abraham," in *The Apocalyptic Imagination,* 170–180.

60. Examined by Schams, *Jewish Scribes in the Second Temple Period,* 140–143.

61. Newsom, "The Sage in the Literature of Qumran," n. 3, p. 374.

62. Collins, *The Apocalyptic Imagination,* 120.

63. On the term *pesher* and the affinity with the notion of interpretation in Daniel 9 see Collins, *The Apocalyptic Imagination,* 120–121; "Prophecy and Fulfillment in the Qumran Scrolls," in *Seers, Sybils and Sages,* 301–314.

64. G. Vermes, *The Dead Sea scrolls in English.* 2nd. ed. (Harmondsworth: Penguin 1975), p. 92.

65. Newsom emphasizes: "The superior gift of knowledge that God had given to the maskil made him also the one who could guide the members of his community into the experience of wonders of the heavenly realm and even show them how much knowledge might be used to protect themselves against the powers of evil." See Newsom, "The Sage in the Literature of Qumran," 382.

66. See discussion on "inspired exegesis" Fishbane, *Biblical Interpretation,* 447ff. See Wolfson's observation regarding the strong interconnection between exegesis and prophetic or visionary states of consciousness; Wolfson, *Through a Speculum,* 119–124.

67. *Hekhalot Zutarti; Synopse,* 335.

68. *Ma'aseh Merkavah; Synopse,* 554.

Bibliography

PRIMARY SOURCES AND REFERENCE WORKS

Alexander, P. S. "3 (Hebrew Apocalypse of) Enoch." In *The Old Testament Pseudepigrapha.* vol. 1. Edited by I. J. Charlesworth, 223–315. New York: Doubleday, 1983.

Andersen F. I. "2 (Slavonic Apocalypse of) Enoch" In *The Old Testament Pseudepigrapha.* vol. 1. Edited by J. Charlesworth, 191–221. Garden City, NY: Doubleday, 1983.

Cohen, M. S. *The Shiur Qomah: Texts and Recensions.* Tübingen: Mohr Siebeck, 1985.

Dalley, S. *Myth from Mesopotamia.* Oxford: Oxford University Press, 1991.

Dietrich, M. Loretz, O. and J. Samartin, J. *Die Keilaphabetischen Texte aus Ugarit.* Kevelaer: Verlag Butzon & Bercker; Neukirchen-Vluyn: Neukirchener, 1976.

Elior, R. *Hekhalot Zutarti.* Jerusalem Studies in Jewish Thought Supplement 1; Jerusalem: Magnes Press, 1982.

Foster, B. R. *Before the Muses: An Anthology of Akkadian Literature.* Bethseda, MD: CDL Press 1996.

Ginzberg, L. *The Legends of the Jews.* vol. 5. Translated by H. Szold. Philadelphia: The Jewish Publication Society of America, 1942.

Gruenwald, I. "New Passages from Hekhalot Literature." *Tarbitz* 38 (1968–69): 354–372. [Hebrew]

——— "Remarks on the Article New Passages from Hekhalot Literature," *Tarbitz* 39 (1970): 216–217. [Hebrew]

——— "The Visions of Ezekiel: Critical Text and Commentary." In *Temirim: Text and Studies in Kabbalah and Hasidism.* vol. 1. Edited by I. Weinstock, 110–139. Jerusalem: Mosad Ha-Rav Kook, 1972. [Hebrew]

Herdner, A. *Corpus des tablettes en cunéiformes alphabétiques déscouvertes à Ras Shamra-Ugarit de 1929 à 1939.* Paris: Imprimerie Nationale, 1963.

Herrman, K. *Massekhet Hekhalot: Traktat von den himmlischen Palästen. Edition, Übersetzung, und Kommentar.* Tübingen: Mohr Siebeck, 1994.

Isaac, E. "1 (Ethiopic Apocalype of) Enoch" In *The Old Testament Pseudepigrapha.* vol. 1. Edited by J. Charlesworth, 5–12. Garden City, NY: Doubleday, 1983.

Jellinek, A. *Bet ha-Midrasch, Sammlung kleiner Midraschim und vermischter Abhandlungen aus der ältern Jüdischen Literatur.* 6 vols. Leipzig 1873–78. Reprint; 2nd ed. 6 vols. Jerusalem: Wahrman Books, 1967.

Kinnier-Wilson, J. V. *The Legend of Etana: A New Edition.* Warminster, UK: Aris and Phillips, 1985.

Lambert, W. G. *Babylonian Wisdom Literature.* Oxford: Clarendon Press, 1960.

Lambert, W. G. and Millard, A. R. *Atra-Hasis: The Babylonian Story of the Flood with Sumerian Flood Stories by M. Civil.* Oxford: Clarendon Press, 1969.

Lambert, W. G. and Parker, S. B. *Enumah Elish, The Cuneiform Text.* Oxford: Clarendon Press, 1966.

Lewin, B. M. *Otzar Ha-Geonim: Thesaurus of the Gaonic Responsa and Commentaries: Tractae Jom-Tow, Chagiga and Maschkin,* vol. 4. Haifa and Jerusalem: Hebrew University Press, 1931.

Margaliot, M. *Sefer ha-Razim.* Jerusalem: American Academy for Jewish Research, 1966. [Hebrew]

Milik, J. T. and Black, M. *The Book of Enoch: Aramaic Fragments of Qumran Cave 4.* Oxford: Clarendon Press, 1976.

Musajoff, S. *Merkavah Shelemah.* Jerusalem: Diffus Solomon, 1921.

Odeberg, H. *The Hebrew Book of Enoch or Third Enoch* 2nd ed. with Prolegomenon by J. C. Greenfield. 1928. Reprint, New York: Ktav, 1973.

Pritchard, J. B. *Ancient Near Eastern Texts,* 3rd. ed. Princeton, NJ: Princeton University Press, 1969.

Schäfer, P. *Synopse zur Hekhalot Literatur.* In collaboration with M. Schlüter and H. G. von Mutius. Tübingen: Mohr Siebeck, 1981.

——— *Geniza Fragmente zur Hekhalot Literatur.* Tübingen: Mohr Siebeck, 1984.

Scholem, G. "Ma'aseh Merkavah," appendix 3. In *Jewish Gnosticism, Merkabah Mysticism and Talmudic Tradition,* 103–136. New York: Jewish Theological Seminary of America, 1965.

Sjöberg, A. W. Bergmann, E. , and Gragg, G. B. *The Collection of the Sumerian Temple Hymns* (Texts from Cuneiform Sources, III). New York: Augustin: 1969.

Shutt, R. J. H. "Letter of Aristeas." In *The Old Testament Pseudepigrapha.* vol. 2. Edited by J. Charlesworth, 5–34. Garden City, NY: Doubleday, 1985.

Vermes, G. *The Dead Sea scrolls in English.* 2nd ed. Harmondsworth: Penguin 1975.

Wertheimer, A. J. *Batei Midrashot.* 2 vols. Jerusalem: HaRav Kook, 1950–53. Reprint, Jerusalem: Katav-yad ve-Sepher, 1989. [Hebrew]

SELECTED SECONDARY LITERATURE

Abusch, I. T. "Ascent to the Stars in a Mesopotamian Ritual: Social Metaphor and Religious Experience." In *Death, Ecstasy and Other Worldly Journeys.* Edited by J. J. Collins and M. Fishbane, 15–39. New York: State University of New York Press, 1995.

Ackerman, S. "Myth." In *The Oxford Companion to the Bible.* Edited by B. M. Metzger and M. D. Coogan, 539–541. New York: Oxford University Press, 1993.

Ahlström, G. W. "Heaven on Earth at Hazor and Arad." In *Religious Syncretism in Antiquity.* Edited by B. A. Pearson, 67–83. Missoula: Scholars Press, 1975.

Alexander, P. S. "The Historical Setting of the Hebrew Book of Enoch." *JJS* 28 (1977): 156–180.

——— "Synopses zur Hekhalot-Literatur." *JJS* 34 (1983): 102–106.

——— "Comparing Merkavah Mysticism and Gnosticism, An Essay in Methods." *JJS* 35 (1984): 1–18.

——— "3 Enoch and the Talmud." *JSJ* 18 (1987): 40–68.

Altmann, A. "The Gnostic Background of the Rabbinic Adam Legends." *JQR* 35 (1944): 371–389.

——— " 'Kedusha' Songs in Ancient Hekhalot Literature." *Melilah* 2 (1946): 1–24. [Hebrew]

——— "The Ladder of Ascension." In *Studies in Mysticism and Religion Presented to Gershom G. Scholem on his Seventieth Birthday,* Edited by E. E. Urbach, R. J. Z. Werblowsky and C. Wirszubski, 1–31. Jerusalem: Magnes Press, 1967.

Arbel, V. D. "Understanding of the Heart—Mystical Experiences in the Hekhalot Literature." *JSJ* 6/4 (1999): 319–344.

———"Junction of Tradition in Edessa: Possible Interaction Between Mesopotamian Mythological and Jewish Mystical Traditions in the First Centuries CE." *Aram Periodical Journal for Syro-Mesopotamian Studies* 11/2 (2001): 335–356.

Bar-Ilan, M. *The Mysteries of Jewish Prayer and Hekhalot.* Ramat Gan: Bar-Ilan University Press, 1987. [Hebrew]

Barker, M. , *The Great Angel A Study of Israel's Second God.* Louisville, KY: Westminster John Knox Press, 1992.

Barr, J. "Philo of Biblos and his Phoenician History." *Bulletin of the John Rylands Library* 7 (1974): 17–68.

Batto, B. *Slaying the Dragon; Mythmaking in the Biblical Tradition.* Louisville, KY: Westminster John Knox Press, 1992.

Baumgarten, J. M. "The Qumran Sabbath Shirot and Rabbinic Merkabah Tradition." *Revue de Qumran* 13 (1988): 199–213;

Bell, C. *Ritual: Perspectives and Dimensions.* New York: Oxford University Press, 1997.

Bianchi, U. *The Greek Mysteries.* Leiden: Brill, 1967.

Bickerman, E. J. *The Jews in the Greek Age.* Cambridge, MA: Harvard University Press, 1988.

Black, J. A. "The New Year Ceremonies in Ancient Babylon: 'Taking Bel by the Hand' and a Cultic Picnic." *Religion* 11 (1981): 39–59.

Black, J. and Green, A. *Gods, Demons and Symbols of Ancient Mesopotamia, An Illustrated Dictionary.* Austin: University of Texas Press, 1992.

Bloch, P. "Die Yordei Merkawa, die Mystiker der Gaonenzeit und ihr Einfluss auf die Liturgie." *MGWJ* 37 n. s. 1 (1893): 18–311.

Bloch-Smith, E. "Who is the King of Glory?" In *Solomon's Temple and its Symbolism. Scripture and Other Artifacts: Essays on the Bible and Archeology in Honor of Philip J. King.* Edited by M. D. Coogan, J. C. Exum and L. E. Stager, 18–31. Louisville, KY: Westminster John Knox Press, 1994.

Bodi, D. *The Book of Ezekiel and the Poem of Erra.* Freiburg and Göttingen: Vandenhoeck Reprecht, 1991.

Bousset, W. "Die Himmelsrise der Seele." *Archiv für Religionswissenschaft* 4 (1901): 136–169, 229–273.

Boyarin, D. "Two Introductions to the Midrash on Song of Songs." *Tarbiz* 56 (1987): 479–500 [Hebrew]

Brettler, S. M. Z. *God is King. Understanding an Israelite Metaphor.* Sheffield: JSOT Press, 1989.

Brock, S. "Jewish Traditions in Syrian Sources." *JJS* 30 (1979): 212–232.

——— "The Dispute Between Soul and Body: An Example of a Long Lived Mesopotamian Literary Genre." *Aram Periodical Journal for Syro-Mesopotamian Studies* 1 (1989): 53–64.

Buber, M. *Kingship of God.* Translated by R. Scheimann. New York: Harper and Row, 1967.

——— "Myth in Judaism." In *On Judaism.* Edited by N. N. Glatzer, 95–107. New York : Schocken, 1967.

Burkert, W. *Greek Religion.* Translated by J. Raffan. 1977; Reprint Cambridge, MA: Harvard University Press, 1985.

——— "Oriental and Greek Mythology: The Meeting of Parallels." In *Interpretations of Greek Mythology.* Edited by J. Bremmer, 10–40. London and Sydney: Croom Helm, 1987.

——— *Ancient Mystery Cults.* Cambridge, MA: Harvard University Press, 1987.

——— *The Orientalizing Revolution. Near Eastern Influence on Greek Culture in the Early Archaic Age.* Translated by M. E. Pinder and W. Burkert. Cambridge: Harvard University Press, 1992.

Cagiran G. and Lambert, W. G. "The Late Babylonian *kislimu* Ritual for Esagil." *JCS* 43–45 (1991–93): 89–106.

Cassin, E. *La Splendeur Divine.* Paris: La Haye, 1968.

Cassuto, U. *A Commentary on the Book of Genesis: From Adam to Noah.* Translated by I. Abrahams. Jerusalem: Magnes Press, 1961.

——— *Biblical and Oriental Studies.* 2 vols. Jerusalem: Magnes Press, 1973, 1975.

Challender Jr. D. E. *Adam in Myth and History. Ancient Israelite Perspectives on the Primal Human.* Winona Lake, IN: Eisenbrauns, 2000.

Chatman, S. *Story and Discourse: Narrative Structure in Fiction and Film.* Ithaca, NY: Cornell University Press, 1978.

Chernus, I. "Individual and Community in the Reduction of the Hekhalot Literature." *HUCA* 52 (1981): 253–257.

——— *Mysticism in Rabbinic Judaism.* Berlin and New York: de Gruyter, 1982.

——— "Visions of God in Merkabah Mysticism." *JSJ* 13 (1982): 123–146.

——— "The Pilgrimage to the Merkavah: An Interpretation of Early Jewish Mysticism." *Jerusalem Studies in Jewish Thought* 6: 1–2 (1987): 1–36. [English Section]

Civil, M. "Isme Dagan and Enlil's Chariot." *JAOS* 88 (1986): 3–15.

Clark, R. J. "Origins: New Light on Eschatology in Gilgamesh's Mortuary Journey." In *Gilgamesh, A Reader* Edited by J. Maier, 131–145. Wauconda, IL: Bolchazy-Carducci Publishers, 1997.

Clements, R. E. *God and Temple.* Oxford: Blackwell, 1965.

Clifford, R. J. *The Cosmic Mountain in Canaan and the Old Testament.* Cambridge, MA: Harvard University Press, 1972.

Cohen, M. *The Shiur Qomah: Liturgy and Theurgy in Pre-Kabbalistic Jewish Mysticism.* Lanham, MD: University Press of America, 1983.

Collins, J. J. *The Apocalyptic Vision of the Book of Daniel.* Missoula: Scholars Press, 1977.

——— *Between Athens and Jerusalem: Jewish Identity in the Hellenistic Diaspora.* New York: Crossroad, 1983.

——— *The Apocalyptic Imagination: An Introduction to the Jewish Matrix of Christianity.* New York: Crossroad 1984.

——— "Jewish Apocalypticism Against Its Hellenistic Near Eastern Environment" in *Seers, Sybils and Sages in Hellenistic-Roman Judaism,* Edited by J. J. Collins, 59–74. Leiden, New York, Köln: Brill, 1997.

——— "The Sage in Apocalyptic and Pseudepigraphic Literature." In *The Sage in Israel and the Ancient Near East.* Edited by J. G. Gammie and L. G. Perdue, 339–350. Winona Lake, IN: Eisenbrauns, 1990.

Collins, J. J. and Nickelsburg, G. W. E. eds. *Ideal Figures in Ancient Judaism.* Chico: Scholars Press, 1980.

Collins J. E. *Mysticism and New Paradigm Psychology.* Savage, MD: Rowman & Littlefield, 1991.

Cooper, A. "Psalm 24. 7–10: Mythology and Exegesis." *JBL* 102 (1983): 37–60.

Cross, F. M. "The Council of Yahweh in Second Isaiah." *JNES* 12 (1953): 274–277.

——— *Canaanite Myth and Hebrew Epic.* Cambridge, MA: Harvard University Press, 1973.

——— "New Direction in the Study of Apocalyptic." *JTC* 6 (1969): 175–165.

Crowley, J. L. *The Aegean and the East. An Investigation into the Transference of Artistic Motifs Between the Aegean and Egypt and the Near East in the Bronze Age.* Jonsered, Sweden: Paul Aström, 1989.

Cryer, F. C. *Divination in Ancient Israel and its Near Eastern Environment.* Sheffield: JSOT Press, 1994.

Culianu, I. P. *Psychanodia I—A Survey of the Evidence concerning the Ascension of the Soul and its Relevance.* Leiden: Brill, 1983.

Dalley, S. "Gilgamesh in the Arabian Nights." *Journal of the Royal Asiatic Society* 1 (1991): 1–17.

——— "The Gilgamesh Epic and Manichaean Themes." *Aram Periodical Journal for Syro-Mesopotamian Studies* 3 (1991): 23–33.

——— "The Tale of Buluqiya and the Alexander Romance in Jewish and Sufi Mystical Circles." In *Tracing the Threads, Studies in the Vitality of Jewish Pseudepigrapha.* Edited by J. C. Reeves, 239–269. Atlanta: Scholars Press, 1994.

——— "Bel at Palmyra and Elsewhere in the Parthian Period." *Aram Periodical Journal for Syro-Mesopotamian Studies* 7 (1995): 137–151.

——— *The Legacy of Mesopotamia*. Oxford: Oxford University Press, 1998.

Dalley, S. and Reyes, A. T. "Mesopotamian Contact and Influence in the Greek World." In *Legacy of Mesopotamia*, Edited by S. Dalley, 85–124. Oxford: Oxford University Press, 1998).

Dan, J. "The Concept of Knowledge in the Shi'ur Qomah." In *Studies in Jewish Religious and Intellectual History Presented to Alexander Altmann*. Edited by S. Stein and R. Loewe, 67–73. Alabama: University of Alabama Press, 1979.

——— "The Seventy Names of Metatron." *Proceedings of the Eighth World Congress of Jewish Studies, Division C* (1982): 19–23. [Hebrew]

——— "Anafi'el, Metatron, and the Creator." *Tarbitz* 52 (1982–83): 447–457. [Hebrew]

——— *Three Types of Jewish Mysticism*. Cincinnati: University of Cincinnati Press, 1984.

——— "The Religious Experience of the Merkavah." In *Jewish Spirituality: From the Bible Through the Middle Ages*. Edited by A. Green, 289–307. New York: Crossroad, 1986.

———"At the Entrance of the Sixth Gate." *Jerusalem Studies in Jewish Thought 6: 1–2* (1987): 197–220. [Hebrew Section]

——— "In Quest of a Historical Definition of Mysticism." *Studies in Spirituality 3* (1993): 58–90.

——— *The Ancient Jewish Mysticism*. Tel Aviv: MOD Books, 1993.

——— "The Revelation of the Secret of the World." In *On Sanctity: Religious, Ethics and Mysticism in Judaism and Other Religions*, 179–201. Jerusalem: Magnes Press, 1997. [Hebrew]

Davies, G. H. "An Approach to the Problem of Old Testament Mythology." *PEQ* 88 (1956): 83–91.

Davila, J. R. "The Hekhalot Literature and Shamanism." *Society of Biblical Literature Seminar Papers* 33 (1994): 767–789.

——— "The Hodayot Hymnist and the Four who Entered Paradise." *Revue de Qumran* 17 (1996): 457–478.

——— "Prolegomena to a Critical Edition of the Hekhalot Rabbati." *JJS* 45 (1994): 208–226.

——— "Of Methodology, Monotheism, and Metatron: Introductory reflections on Divine Mediators and the Origins of the Worship of Jesus." In *The Jewish Roots of Christological Monotheism. Papers from the St. Andrews*

Conference on the Historical Origin of the Worship of Jesus. Edited by C. C. Newman, J. R. Davila, and G. S. Lewis, 3–18. Leiden: Brill, 1999.

———. *Descenders to the Chariot. The People behind the Hekhalot Literature.* Leiden, Boston, Köln: Brill, 2001.

Day, J. *God's Conflict with the Dragon and the Sea. Echoes of a Canaanite Myth in the Old Testament.* Cambridge: Cambridge University Press, 1985.

Deutsch, N. *The Gnostic Imagination.* Leiden, New York, Köln: Brill, 1985.

——— *Guardians of the Gate, Angelic Vice Regency in Late Antiquity.* Leiden, Boston, Köln: Brill, 1999.

Doniger, W. *Other Peoples' Myths.* New York, London: Macmillan, 1988.

Drijvers, H. J. W. Cults and Beliefs at Edessa. Leiden: Brill, 1980.

——— "The Persistence of Pagan Cults and Practices in Christian Syria." In *East of Anitoch, Studies in Early Syriac Christianity,* 35–43. London: Variorum Reprints 1984.

——— "Syrian Christianity and Judaism" in *History and Religion in Late Antique Syria,* Collected Studies Series, 128–129. London: Variorum, 1984.

——— "Jews and Christians at Edessa." *JJS* 36/1 (1985): 88–102.

Dundes, A. *Interpreting Folklore.* Bloomington: Indiana University Press, 1980.

——— *Sacred Narratives, Readings in the Theory of Myth* Berkeley: University of California Press, 1984.

Eilberg-Schwartz, H. "The Problem of the Body for the People of the Book." In *People of the Body.* Edited by H. Eilberg-Schwartz, 17–46. Albany, NY: State University of New York Press, 1992.

Eliade, M. *Birth and Rebirth: The Religious Meanings of Initiation in Human Culture.* Translated by W. R. Trask. New York: Harper and Row, 1958.

——— *Images and Symbols: Studies in Religious Symbolism.* Translated by P. Mairet. Princeton, NJ: Princeton University Press, 1991.

Elior, R. "Schäfer's Synopse zur Hekhalot-Literatur." *JQR* 77 (1986/87): 213–217.

——— "The Concept of God in Hekhalot Mysticism." In *Binah, Studies in Jewish Thought II.* Edited by J. Dan, 97–120. New York, Westport, Conneticut, London: Praeger, 1989.

——— "Merkabah Mysticism. A Critical Review." *Numen* 73 (1990): 233–249.

——— "Mysticism, Magic, and Angelology: The Perception of Angels in Hekhalot Literature." *JSQ* 1 (1993/94): 3–53.

——— "From Earthly Temple to Heavenly Shrine: Prayer and Sacred Song in the Hekhalot Literature and Its Relation to Temple Traditions." *JSQ* 4 (1997): 217–267.

——— "The Merkavah Tradition and the Emergence of Jewish Mysticism: From Temple to Merkavah from Hekhal to Hekhalot from Priestly Opposition to Gazing upon the Merkavah." In *Sino–Judaica: Jews and Chinese in Historical Dialogue*. Edited by A. Oppenheimer, 101–158. Tel Aviv: Tel Aviv University Press, 1999.

——— *Temple and Chariot, Priests and Angels, Sanctuary and Heavenly Sanctuaries in Early Jewish Mysticism*. Jerusalem: Magnes Press, 2002. [Hebrew]

Eskola, T. *Messiah and the Throne: Jewish Merkabah Mysticism and Early Christian Exaltation Discourse*. Tübingen: Mohr Siebeck, 2001.

Festugière, A. J. *Personal Religion Among the Greeks*. 1954. Reprint, Berkeley: University of California Press, 1960.

Fishbane, M. *Biblical Interpretation in Ancient Israel*. Oxford and New York: Oxford University Press, 1985.

——— *The Garments of the Torah, Essays in Biblical Hermeneutics*. Bloomington, IN: Indiana University Press, 1989.

——— *The Exegetical Imagination, On Jewish Thought and Theology*. Cambridge, MA: Harvard University Press, 1998.

——— "From Scribalism o Rabbinism: Perspectives on the Emergence of Classical Judaism." In *The Sage in Israel and the Ancient Near East*. Edited by J. G. Gammie and G. Perdue, 439–456. Winona Lake, IN: Eisenbrauns, 1990.

Fletcher-Louis, C. H. T. *Luke Acts: Angels, Christology and Soteriology*. Tübingen: Mohr Siebeck, 1997.

Flusser, D. "Scholem's Recent Book on Merkabah Literature." *JJS* 11 (1960): 59–68.

Fossum, J. E. *The Name of God and the Angel of the Lord. The Origin of Intermediation in Gnosticism*. Tübingen: Mohr Siebeck, 1985.

——— *The Image of the Invisible God: Essays on the Influence of Jewish Mysticism on Early Christology*. Göttingen: Vandenhoeck and Ruprecht, 1995.

Foster, B. R. "Wisdom and the Gods in Ancient Mesopotamia." *Orientalia* 43 (1974): 344–354.

Frankfort, H. *Cylinder Seals: A Documentary Essay on the Art and Religion of the Ancient Near East*. 1939. Reprint, London: Macmillan, 1965.

——— *Kingship and the Gods, A Study of Ancient Near Eastern Religion as the Integration of Society and Nature*, Chicago: Chicago University Press, 1978.

Frankfort, H. and Frankfort, H. A. "Myth and Reality." In *The Intellectual Adventure of the Ancient Man: An Essay on Speculative Thought in the Ancient Near East*. Edited by H. Frankfort, H. A. Frankfort, J. A. Wilson, T. Jabobsen, and W. A. Irwin. 3–27. 1946. Reprint, Chicago and London: Chicago University Press, 1977.

Freedman, D. N. " 'Who is Like Thee Among The Gods?' The Religion of Early Israel." In *Ancient Israelite Religion. Essays in Honor of Frank Moore Cross.* Edited by P. D. Miller, Jr. , P. D. Hanson, S. D. McBride, 315–335. Philadelphia: Fortress Press, 1987.

Gammie J. G. , "The Sage in Sirach." In *The Sage in Israel and the Ancient Near East.* Edited by J. G. Gammie and L. G. Perdue, 355–372. Winona Lake, IN: Eisenbrauns, 1990.

Garland, R. *The Greek Way of Death.* London: Duckworth, 1985.

Garside, B. "Language and the Interpretation of Mystical Experience." *International Journal for Philosophy of Religion* 3 (1972): 93–102.

Gaster, M. *Studies and Texts in Folklore, Magic, Medieval Romance, Hebrew Apocrypha and Samaritan Archaeology.* London: Maggs Bros. 1925–1928.

van Gennep, A. *The Rites of Passage.* Translated by M. B. Vizedom and G. L. Caffe. Chicago: University of Chicago Press, 1960.

George, A. R. *House Most High: The Temples of Ancient Mesopotamia.* Winona Lake, IN: Eisenbrauns, 1983.

Gimello, R. M. "Mysticism in Context." In *Mysticism and Religious Traditions.* Edited by S. Katz, 61–88. New York: Oxford University Press 1983.

Gieschen, C. A. *Angelomorphic Christology: Antecedents and Early Evidence.* Leiden, Boston, Köln: Brill, 1998.

Goodenough, E. R. *Jewish Symbols in the Greco-Roman Period.* vol. 8. New York: Bollinger Foundation, 1953.

Goshen-Gottstein, M. "Abraham—Lover or Beloved of God." In *Love and Death in the Ancient Near East.* Edited by J. H. Marks and R. M. Good, 101–104. Guilford: Four Quarters Publishing, 1987.

Graetz, H. H. "Die mystische Literatur in der gaonäischen Epoche." *MGWJ* 8 (1859): 67–153.

Gragg, G. B. "The Kesh Temple Hymn." In *The Collection of the Sumerian Temple Hymns. Texts from Cuneiform Sources, 3.* Edited by A. W. Sjöberg, E. Bergmann, and G. B. Gragg, 155–189. Locust Valley, NY: Augustin, 1969.

Grant, F. C. *Roman Hellenism and the New testament.* Edinburg and London: Oliver and Boyd, 1962.

Grant, R. M. *Gods and the One God.* Philadelphia: Westminster Press, 1986.

Green, A. *Keter: The Crown of God in Early Jewish Mysticism.* Princeton, NJ: Princeton University Press, 1997.

——— "The Song of Song in Early Jewish Mysticism." *Orim: A Jewish Journal at Yale* 2 (1987): 49–63.

Green, A. "Ancient Mesopotamian Religious Iconography." In *Civilizations of the Ancient Near East*. Edited by J. M. Sasson, 1837–1855. New York: Macmillan Library Reference, 1995.

Green, T. M. *The City of the Moon God Religious Traditions of Harran*. Leiden, New York, Köln: Brill, 1992.

Greenberg, M. "Ezekiel's Vision: Literary and Iconographic Aspects." In *History, Historiography and Interpretation*. Edited by H. Tadmor and M. Weinfeld, 159–168. Jerusalem: Magnes Press, 1983.

Greenfield, J. C. "Prolegomena" In *3 Enoch or The Hebrew Book of Enoch*. Edited by H. Odeberg. 1982. Reprint, New York: Ktav, 1973.

Greenfield, J. C. and Stone, M. E. "The Enochic Pentateuch and the Date of the Similitudes." *HTR* 70 (1977): 51–65.

Grözinger, K. E. "The Names of God and the Celestial Powers: Their Function and Meaning in the Hekhalot Literature." *Jerusalem Studies in Jewish Thought 6: 1–2* (1987): 53–69. [English Section]

——— *Musik und Gesang in der Theologie der fruehen juedischen Literatur.* Tübingen: Mohr Siebeck, 1982.

Gruen, E. "Cultural Fictions and Cultural Identity." *Transactions of the American Philological Association* 123 (1993): 1–14.

Gruenwald, I. "Knowledge and Vision: Towards a Clarification of Two "Gnostic" Concepts in the Light of their Alleged Origin." *Israel Oriental Studies* 3 (1973): 63–107.

——— "The Impact of Priestly Traditions on the Creation of Merkavah Mysticism and the Shiur Komah." *Jerusalem Studies in Jewish Thought* 6: 1–2 (1987): 65–120. [Hebrew Section]

——— *Apocalyptic and Merkavah Mysticism*. Leiden: Brill, 1980.

——— *From Apocalypticism to Gnosticism*. Frankfurt: Peter Lang, 1988.

Gunkel, H. *Schöpfung und Chaos in Endzeit Und Urzeit*. Göttingen: Vandenhoeck and Ruprecht, 1895.

Habel, N. C. "He Who Stretches Out the Heavens." *CBQ* 34 (1972): 417–430.

Hadas, M. and Smith, M. *Heroes and Gods. Spiritual Biographies in Late Antiquity*. New York: Harper and Row, 1965.

Hallo, W. W. "Akkadian Apocalypses." *Israel Exploration Journal* 16 (1966): 231–242.

——- "'As Seal upon Thine Arm: Glyptic Metaphor in the Biblical World." In *Ancient Seals and the Bible*. Edited by L. Gorelick and E. Williams-Forte, 7–17. Malibu: Undena, 1983.

——— "Texts, Statues, and the Cult of the Divine King." *Congress Volume VTSup* 40 (1988): 54–66.

Hallo, W. W. et al. eds. *The Bible in Light of Cuneiform Literature.* Lewiston, NY: Edwin Mellen Press, 1990.

Halperin, D. J. "Ascension or Invasion: Implication of the Heavenly Journey in Ancient Judaism." *Religion* 18 (1988): 47–67.

——— *The Faces of the Chariot: Early Jewish Responses to Ezekiel's Vision.* Tübingen: Mohr Siebeck, 1988.

——— *The Merkabah in Rabbinic Literature.* New Haven: American Oriental Society, 1980.

——— "A New Edition of the Hekhalot Literature." *JAOS* 104 (1984): 543–552.

Handy, L. K. *Among the Host of Heaven. A Syro-Palestinian Pantheon as Bureaucracy.* Winona Lake, IN: Eisenbrauns, 1994.

——— "Dissenting Deities or Obedient Angels: Divine Hierarchies in Ugarit and the Bible," *Biblical Research* 35 (1990): 18–35.

Hanson, P. D. *The Dawn of Apocalyptic: The Historical and Sociological Roots of Jewish Apocalyptic Eschatology.* Philadelphia: Fortress Press, 1975.

——— "Jewish Apocalyptic Against Its Near Eastern Environment." *Revue Biblique* 78 (1971): 31–58.

Haran, M. "The Ark and the Cherubim: Their Symbolic Significance in Biblical Ritual." *Israel Exploration Journal* 9 (1959): 30–38, 89–94.

——— "Temple and Community in Ancient Israel." In *Temple in Society.* Edited by M. V. Fox, 17–25. Winona Lake, IN: Eisenbrauns, 1988.

Hayman, P. "Monotheism—Misused Word in Jewish Studies?" *JJS* 42 (1991): 1–15.

Heidel, A. *The Gilgamesh Epic and Old Testament Parallels.* Chicago: University of Chicago Press, 1949.

——— *The Babylonian Genesis: The Story of Creation.* 2d ed. Chicago: University of Chicago Press, 1963.

Heimpel, W. "The Sun at Night and the Doors of Heaven in Babylonian Texts." *JCS* 38: 2 (1986): 27–151.

Hendel, R. S. "The Social Origin of the Anicoic Tradition in Ancient Israel." *Classical Biblical Quarterly* 50 (1988): 365–382.

——— "Aniconism and Anthropomorphism in Ancient Israel." In *The Image and the Book.* Edited by K. van der Toorn, 205–228. Leuven: Peeters, 1997.

Herrmann, K. "Text und Fiktion. Zur Textüberlieferung des Shiur Qoma." *Frankfurter Judaistische Beiträge* 16 (1988): 89–142.

Himmelfarb, M. *The Ascent to Heaven in Jewish and Christian Apocalypses.* New York and Oxford: Oxford University Press, 1993.

——— "The Practice of Ascent in the Ancient Mediterranean World." In *Death, Ecstasy and Other Worldly Journeys.* Edited by J. Collins and M. Fishbane, 123 –137. Albany, NY: State University of New York Press, 1995.

Hooke, S. H. *Middle Eastern Mythology.* London: Penguin Books, 1963.

Horowitz, W. *Mesopotamian Cosmic Geography.* Winona Lake, IN: Eisenbrauns, 1988.

——— "Two Notes on Etana's Flight to Heaven." *Or. NS* 59 (1990): 511–17.

Howard G. ed. *The Teaching of Addai.* Chico, CA: Scholars Press, 1981.

Hurowitz, V. *I Have Built You An Exalted House: Temple Building in the Light of Mesopotamian and Northwest Semitic Writing.* Sheffield: Sheffield Academic Press, 1992.

Hurtado, L. W. *One God, One Lord: Early Christian Devotion and Ancient Jewish Monotheism.* Philadelphia: Fortress Press, 1988.

Idel, M. "The Concept of Torah in Hekhalot Literature and Its Metamorphosis in Kabbalah." *Jerusalem Studies in Jewish Thought 1* (1981): 23–84. [Hebrew]

——— "Hitbodedut as Concentration in Jewish Philosophy." *Da'at* 14 (1985): 35–82; 15 (1986): 117–120. [Hebrew]

——— "Enoch is Metatron." *Jerusalem Studies in Jewish Thought* 6: 1–2 (1987): 151–170. [Hebrew Section]

——— *Kabbalah, New Perspectives.* New Haven: Yale University Press, 1988.

——— "Franz Rosenzweig and the Kabbalah." In *The Philosophy of Franz Rosenzweig.* Edited by P. Mendes-Flohr, 162–71. Hanover and London: University of New England Press, 1988.

Izre'el, S. *Adapa and the South Wind. Language Has the Power of Life and Death.* Winona Lake, IN: Eisenbrauns, 2001.

Jacob, L. "Jewish Cosmology." In *Ancient Cosmologies.* Edited by C. Blacker and M. Loewe, 68–70. London: George Allen and Unwin, 1975.

Jacobs, J. "Elements of Near Eastern Mythology in Rabbinic Aggadah." *JJS* 27 (1977): 1–11.

Jacobsen, T. *Toward the Image of Tammuz and Other Essays on Mesopotamian History and Culture.* Cambridge, MA: Harvard University Press, 1970.

——— *The Treasures of Darkness: A History of Mesopotamian Religion.* New Haven: Yale University Press, 1976.

——— "The Graven Image." In *Ancient Israelite Religion. Essays in Honor of Frank Moore Cross.* Edited by P. D. Miller, Jr. , P. D. Hanson, S. D. McBride, 15–32. Philadelphia: Fortress Press, 1987.

Jaffee, M. J. *Torah in the Mouth: Writing and Oral Tradition in Palestine Judaism 200 BCE–400 BC*. Oxford: Oxford University Press, 2001.

Janowitz, N. *The Poetics of Ascent: Theories of Language in a Rabbinic Ascent Text*. Albany, NY: State University of New York Press, 1989.

Jonas, H. "Myth and Mysticism: A Study of Objectification and Interiorization in Religious Thought." *The Journal of Religion* 49 (1969): 315–329.

Kalmin, R. *The Sage in Jewish Society of Late Antiquity*. London and New York. Routledge, 1999.

Kapelrud, A. S. "Temple Building, A Task for Gods and Men." *Orientalia* 32 (1963): 56–62.

Katz, S. T. "Models, Modeling, and Mystical Training," *Religion* 12 (1982): 247–275.

——— "The 'Conservative' Character of Mysticism." In *Mysticism and Religious Traditions*. Edited by S. T. Katz, 3–60. New York: Oxford University Press, 1983.

——— "Language, Epistemology and Mysticism." In *Mysticism and Philosophical Analysis*. Edited by S. T. Katz, 22–24. London and New York: Sheldon 1978.

——— "Mystical Speech and Mystical Meaning." In *Mysticism and Language*. New York: Oxford University Press, 1992.

Kaufmann, Y. *History of the Religion of Israel*. New York: KTAV, 1977.

Keel, O. *The Symbolism of the Biblical World: Ancient Near Eastern Iconography and the Book of Psalms*. Translated by T. J. Hallett. New York: Seabury Press, 1978.

Keel, O. and Uehlinger, C. *Gods, Goddesses and Images of God in Ancient Israel*. Translated by T. H. Trapp. Minneapolis: Fortress Press, 1988.

Keller, C. "Mystical Literature." In *Mysticism and Philosophical Analysis*. Edited by S. Katz, 75–99. London and New York: Sheldon, 1978.

Klingbeil, M. *Yahweh Fighting from Heaven: God as Warrior and as God of Heaven in the Hebrew Psalter and Ancient Near Eastern Iconography*. Göttingen: Vandenhoeck and Ruprecht, 1999.

Kirk, G. S. *Myth, Its Meaning and Function in Ancient and Other Cultures*. Cambridge: Cambridge University Press, 1970.

Kloos, C. *Yhwh's Combat with the Sea*. Leiden: Brill, 1986.

Knohl, I. *The Sanctuary of Silence: The Priestly Torah and the Holiness School*. Minneapolis: Fortress Press, 1995.

Kramer, S. N. "Heroes of Sumer: A New Heroic Age in World History and Literature." *Proceedings of the American Philosophical Society* 90 (1946): 120–130.

——— *Sumerian Mythology,* Rev. ed. Philadelphia: University of Pennsylvania Press, 1972.

——— "The Temple in Sumerian Literature." In *Temple in Society.* Edited by M. V. Fox, 1–16. Winona Lake, IN: Eisenbrauns, 1988.

——— "The Sage in Sumerian Literature: A Composite Portrait." In *The Sage in Israel and the Ancient Near East.* Edited by J. G. Gammie and. G. Perdue, 31–44. Winona Lake, IN: Eisenbrauns, 1990.

Kramer, S. N. and Maier J. *Myths of Enki, The Crafty God.* New York and Oxford: Oxford University Press, 1989.

Kramer, S. N. and Weinfeld, M. "The Sumerian Literature and the Psalms: An Introduction to a Comparative Study." *Beth Miqra* 56–57 (1963): 8–25; 136–160. [Hebrew]

Kuhrt A. and Sherwin-White (eds.) *Hellenism in the East: The Interaction of Greek and non-Greek Civilizations from Syria to Central Asia after Alexander.* London: Duckworth, 1987.

Kutsko J. F. *Between Heaven and Earth. Divine Presence in the Book of Ezekiel.* Winona Lake, IN: Eisenbrauns, 2000.

Kuyt, A. "Once again Yarad in Hekhalot Literature." *Frankfurter Judaistische Beiträge* 18 (1990): 45–69.

——— *The "Descent" to the Chariot: Towards a Description of the Terminology, Place, Function and Nature of the Yeridah in Hekhalot Literature.* Tübingen: Mohr Siebeck, 1995.

Kvanvig, H. S. *Roots of Apocalyptic: The Mesopotamian Background of the Enoch Figure and of the Son of Man.* Neukirchen-Vluyn: Neukirchener Verlag, 1988.

Lambert, W. G. 'The Great Battle of the Mesopotamian Religious Year: The Conflict in the *Akitu* House', *Iraq* 25 (1963): 189–90

——— "Enmeduranki and Related Matters." *JCS* 21 (1967): 126–138.

——— "Myth and Ritual as conceived by the Babylonians." *JTS* 13 (1968): 104–112.

——— "History and the Gods: A Review Article." *Or. NS* 39 (1970) 170–77.

——— "Destiny and Divine Intervention in Babylon and Israel." *Oudtestamentische Studien* 17 (1972) 65–72;

——— *The Background of Jewish Apocalyptic.* London: Athlone Press, 1978.

——— "The Cosmology of Sumer and Babylon." In *Ancient Cosmologies.* Edited by C. Blacker and M. Loewe. 41–62. London: George Allen and Unwin Ltd. , 1975.

——- "A New Babylonian Descent to the Netherworld." In *Lingering Over Words: Studies in Ancient Near Eastern Literature in Honor of William L. Moran.* Edited by I. T. Abusch et al, 289–300. Atlanta: Scholars Press, 1990.

Lesses, R. M. *Ritual Practices to Gain Power: Angels, Incantation, and Revelation in Early Jewish Mysticism.* Harrisburg, PA: Trinity, 1998.

Levenson, J. D. *Creation and Persistence of Evil.* Princeton, NJ: Princeton University Press, 1994

Lieberman, S. "How Much Greek in Jewish Palestine." In *Biblical and Other Studies.* Edited by A. Altmann, 123–141. Cambridge, MA: Harvard University Press, 1963.

——— "The Knowledge of Halakha by the Author (or Authors) of the Heikhaloth." In *Apocalyptic and Merkavah Mysticism.* Appendix 2. I. Gruenwald, 241–244. Leiden: Brill, 1980.

——— "Metatron, The Meaning of his Name and his Function." In *Apocalyptic and Merkavah Mysticism.* Appendix 1. I. Gruenwald, 235–244. Leiden: Brill, 1980.

——— "Song of Songs." In *Jewish Gnosticism, Merkabah Mysticism and Talmudic Tradition.* Appendix 4. G. Scholem, 118–126. New York: Jewish Theological Seminary of America, 1965.

Lieberman, S. J. "A Mesopotamian Background for the So Called Aggadic "Measures" of Biblical Hermeneutics?" *HUCA* 58 (1987): 157–225.

Liebes, Y. "De Natura Dei: On the Development of the Jewish Myth." In *Studies in Jewish Myth and Jewish Messianism.* Translated by B. Stein, 1–64. Albany, NY: State University of New York Press, 1993.

——— *The Sin of Elisha: The Four Who Entered Paradise and the Nature of Talmudic Mysticism.* Jerusalem: Akademon, 1990. [Hebrew]

Liebeschurtz, J. H. W. *Continuity and Change in Roman Religion.* Oxford: Oxford University Press, 1979.

Livingstone, A. *Mystical and Mythological Explanatory Works of Assyrian and Babylonian Scholars.* Oxford: Clarendon Press, 1986.

Lord, A. B. *The Singer of Tales.* Cambridge, MA: Harvard University, 1989.

Lotman, J. M. and Upenskij, B. A. "Myth-Name-Culture." In *Soviet Semiotics.* Edited by D. P. Lucid, 233–259. Baltimore: Johns Hopkins University Press, 1977.

MacMullen, R. *Paganism in the Roman Empire.* New Haven, CT: Yale University Press, 1981.

Mann, T. W. *Divine Presence and Guidance in Israelite Traditions.* Baltimore, and London: Johns Hopkins University Press, 1977.

Marmorstein, A. *Essays in Anthropomorphism.* vol. 2. 1937; Reprint New York: Ktav, 1968.

May, H. G. "The King in the Garden of Eden: A Study of Ezekiel 28: 12–19." In *Israel's Prophetic Heritage; Essays in Honor of James Muilenburg,* Edited by B. Anderson and W. Harrelson, 166–176. New York: Harper and Row, 1962.

McGinn, B. *The Foundations of Mysticism.* vol. 1. New York: Crossroad, 1991.

McKay, J. W. "Further Light on the Houses and Chariot of the Sun in the Jerusalem Temple (2 Kings 23: 11)." *PEQ* 105 (1973), 167–169.

Merkur, D. "Unitive Experiences and the State of Trance." In *Mystical Union and Monotheistic Faith: An Ecumenical Dialogue.* Edited by M. Idel and B. McGinn, 125–153. New York: Continuum, 1989.

——— *Gnosis: An Esoteric Tradition of Mystical Visions and Unions.* Albany, NY: State University of New York Press, 1993.

——— *Mystical Moments and Unitive Thinking.* Albany, NY: State University of New York Press, 1999.

Mettinger, T. N. D. *The Dethronement of Sabaoth: Studies in the Shem and Kavod Theologies.* Lund: CWK Gleerup, 1982.

——— "YHWH Sabaoth—The Heavenly King on the Cherubim Throne." In *Studies in the Period of David and Solomon and Other Essays.* Edited by T. Ishida, 109–138. Tokyo: Yamakawa-Shuppansha, 1982.

——— *No Graven Image? Israelite Aniconism in its Ancient Near Eastern Context.* Stockholm: Almqvist and Wiksell, 1995.

——— "Israelite Aniconism: Development and Origins." In *The Image and the Book.* Edited by K. van der Toorn, 173–204. Leuven: Peeters, 1997.

Metzger, B. M." Considerations of Methodology in the Study of the Mystery Religions and Early Christianity." *HTR* 48 (1955): 1–20.

——— "A Classified Bibliography of the Greco-Roman Mystery Religions 1924–1973 with a Supplement 1974–77." In *Aufstieg und Niedergang der römischen Welt.* Edited by H. Temporini and W. Haase, Band II. 17. 3, 1259–1423. Berlin: Walter de Gruyter, 1984.

Metzger, M. "Himmelische und irdische Wohnstatt Jahwes." *UF* 2 (1970): 139–158.

Meyer M. W. ed. *The Ancient Mysteries, A Source Book.* New York: Harper, 1987.

Miller, J. M. "In the Image and Likeness of God." *JBL* 91 (1972): 291–292.

Moore, P. "Mystical Experience, Mystical Doctrine, Mystical Technique." In *Mysticism and Philosophical Analysis.* Edited by S. T. Katz, 101–131. London and New York: Oxford University Press, 1978.

Morgenstern, J. "Moses with the Shining Face." *HUCA* 2 (1925): 1–27.

——— "The Mythological Background of Psalm 82," *HUCA* 14 (1939): 111–114.

Morray-Jones, C. R. A. "Hekhalot Literature and Talmudic Tradition: Alexander's Three Test Cases." *JSJ* 22 (1991): 1–39.

——— "Paradise Revisited: The Jewish Mystical Background of Paul's Apostolate, Part 1: The Jewish Sources." *HTR* 86 (1993): 177–217.

——— "Paradise Revisited: The Jewish Mystical Background of Paul's Apostolate, Part 2: Paul's Heavenly Accent and Its Significance." *HTR* 86 (1993): 265–92.

——— "Transformational Mysticism in the Apocalyptic-Merkabah Tradition." *JJS* 43 (1992): 1–31.

———. *Transparent Illusion. The Dangerous Vision of Water in Hekhalot Mysticism. A Source-Critical and Tradition-Historical Inquiry.* Leiden, Boston, Köln: Brill, 2002.

Muffs, Y. *Love & Joy. Law, Language and Religion in Ancient Israel.* New York: Jewish Theological Seminary of America, 1992.

Mullen, E. T. *The Assembly of the Gods. The Divine Council in Canaanite and Early Hebrew Literature.* Chico, CA: Scholars Press, 1980.

Müller, H. P. "Parallelen zu Gen. 2 und Ez. 28 aus dem Gilgamesh-Epos." *Zeitschrift für die alttestamentliche Wissenschaft* 3 (1990): 167–178.

Murphy, R. "The Hebrew Sage and Openness to the World." In *Christian Action and Openness to the World,* Edited by J. Pipin, 219–244. Villanova, PA: Villanova University Press, 1970.

Murray, R. *Symbols of Church and Kingdom, A Study in Early Syriac Tradition.* Cambridge: Cambridge University Press, 1975.

Mylonas, *G. E. Eleusis and the Eleusinian Mysteries.* Princeton, NJ: Princeton University Press, 1961.

Nemoy, L. *Karaite Anthology.* New Haven, CN: Yale University Press, 1952.

Neusner, J. *A History of the Jews in Babylonia.* vol. 5. *Late Sasanian Time.* Leiden: Brill, 1970.

——— "The Development of the Merkavah Tradition." *JSJ* 11 (1971): 59–82.

——— *Judaism, Christianity and Zoroastrianism in Talmudic Babylonia.* Atlanta: Scholars Press, 1990.

Newsom, C. "Merkabah Exegesis in the Qumran Sabbath Shirot." JJS 38 (1987): 11–30.

——— "The Sage in the Literature of Qumran: The Functions of the Maskil." In *The Sage in Israel and the Ancient Near East.* Edited by G. Gammie and L. G. Perdue, 373–382. Winona Lake, IN: Eisenbrauns, 1990.

Nickelsburg, G. W. E. and Stone, M. *Faith and Piety in Early Judaism: Texts and Documents.* Philadelphia: Fortress Press, 1983.

Nickelsburg, G. W. E *Jewish Literature between the Bible and the Mishnah.* Philadelphia: Fortress Press, 1981.

Niditch, S. *A Prelude to Biblical Folklore: Underdogs and Tricksters.* Urbana, IL and Chicago: University of Illinois Press, 2000.

Niehr, H. "In Search of YHWH's Cult Statue in the First Temple." In *The Image and the Book* Edited by K. van der Toorn, 73–96. Leuven: Peeters, 1997.

Nock, A. D. *Conversion: The Old and the New in Religion from Alexander the Great to Augustine of Hippo.* Oxford: Oxford University Press, 1933.

Olyan, S. A *Thousand Thousands Served Him: Exegesis and Naming of Angels in Ancient Judaism.* Tübingen: Mohr Siebeck, 1993.

Oppenheim, A. L. "Akkadian pul(u)t(u) and melammu." *JAOS* 63 (1943): 31–34.

——— "The Golden Garments of the Gods." *JNES* 8 (1949), 172–193.

——— *Ancient Mesopotamia: Portrait of a Dead Civilization.* Chicago: University of Chicago Press, 1964.

Otto, O. *The Idea of the Holy* 1923. Reprint, London: Oxford University Press, 1973.

Pallis, S. A. *The Babylonian* Akitu *Festival.* Copenhagen: Bianco Lunos Bogtrykkeri, 1926.

Paul, S. "Heavenly Tablets and the Book of Life." *Journal of the Ancient Near Eastern Society of Columbia University* 5 (1973): 345–353.

Pearson, B. A. ed. *Religious Syncretism in Antiquity:* Essays in Conversation with Geo Widengren Missoula: Scholars Prress, 1975.

Penglase, C. *Greek Myths and Mesopotamia: Parallels and Influence in the Homeric Hymns and Hesiod.* London and New York: Routledge, 1994.

Phelan, J. *Reading People, Reading Plot: Character, Progression and the Interpretation of Narrative.* Chicago: University of Chicago Press, 1989.

Pingree, D. "Legacies in Astronomy and Celestial Omens" In *Legacy of Mesopotamia,* Edited by S. Dalley 125–137. Oxford: Oxford University Press, 1998.

Pope, M. H. *El in the Ugaritic Text.* Leiden: Brill, 1955.

Porada, E. *Corpus of Ancient Near Eastern Seals in North American Collections I, the Pierpont Morgan Library Collection.* Washington: The Bollingen Series, vol. 14, 1948.

von Rad, G. *The Old Testament Theology,* 2 vols. New York: Harper & Row, 1962, 1965.

Reeves, J. *Jewish Lore in Manichaean Cosmology: Studies in the Book of Giants Traditions.* Cincinnati: Hebrew Union College, 1992.

——— "Ut-napishtim in the Book of Giants?" *JBL* 112 (1993): 110–115.

Reiner, E. "Fortune-Telling in Mesopotamia." *JNES* 19 (1960): 23–35.

Rochberg-Halton, F. "Mesopotamian Cosmology." In *Encyclopedia of Cosmology: Historical, Philosophical and Scientific Foundations of Modern Cosmology.* Edited by N. S. Hetherington, 398–407. New York and London: Garland, 1993.

Rowland, C. *The Open Heaven: A Study in Apocalypticism in Judaism and Early Christianity.* New York: Crossroad, 1982.

Rudolph, K. "Mystery Religions." In *The Encyclopedia of Religion.* Edited by M. Eliade, 10: 230–239. New York: Macmillan, 1987.

Russell, D. S. *The Methods and Message of Jewish Apocalyptic.* Philadelphia: Westminster, 1964.

Saggs, H. W. F. *The Encounter with the Divine in Mesopotamia and Israel.* London: Athlone Press, 1978.

Saldarini, A. J. *Pharisees, Scribes and Sadduccees in Palestinian Society: A Sociological Approach.* Wilmington, DE: Michael Glazier, 1988.

Salvesen, A." The Legacy of Babylon and Nineveh in Aramaic Sources." In *Legacy of Mesopotamia.* Edited by S. Dalley, 139–161. Oxford: Oxford University Press, 1998.

Sarna, N. M. *Understanding Genesis: The Heritage of Biblical Israel.* New York: Schoken, 1970.

——— *On the Book of Psalms. Exploring the Prayers o Ancient Israel.* New York: Schoken, 1993.

Schäfer, P. "Tradition and Redaction in Hekhalot Literature." *JSJ* 14 (1983): 172–181.

——— "New Testament and Hekhalot Literature: The Journey into Heaven in Paul and in Merkavah Mysticism." *JJS* 35 (1984): 19–35.

——— "Redactional Identity of 'Hekhalot Rabbati'." *Jerusalem Studies in Jewish Thought* 6: 1–2 (1987): 1–12. [Hebrew Section]

——— *Hekhalot-Studien,* Texte und Studien zum antiken Judentum 19. Tübingen: Mohr Siebeck, 1988.

——— "The Aim and Purpose of Early Jewish Mysticism." In *Hekhalot-Studien,* 277–295. Tübingen: Mohr Siebeck, 1988.

——— "Jewish Magic Literature in Late Antiquity and Early Middle Ages." *JJS* 41 (1990): 75–91.

——— *The Hidden and Manifest God: Some Major Themes in Early Jewish Mysticism.* Translated by A. Pomererance. Albany, NY: State University of New York Press, 1992.

——— "Magic and Religion in Ancient Judaism." In *Envisioning Magic: A Princeton Seminar and Symposium.* Edited by P. Schäfer and H. G. Kippenberg, 19–43. Leiden: Brill, 1997.

Schams, C. *Jewish Scribes in the Second Temple Period.* Sheffield: Sheffield Academic Press, 1998.

Schiffman, L. H. "The Recall of Rabbi Nehunia ben Ha-Qanah from Ecstasy in Heikhalot Rabbati." *AJSR* 1 (1976): 269–281.

———"Merkavah Speculations at Qumran: The 4Q Serekh Shirot Olat ha-Shabbat." In *Mystics, Philosophers, and Politicians: Essays in Jewish Intellectual History in Honor of Alexander Altmann.* Edited by J. Reinharz and D. Swetschinski, 15–45. Durham: Duke University Press, 1982.

Schiffman, L. H. and Swartz, M. D. *Hebrew and Aramaic Incantation Texts from the Cairo Genizah: Selected Texts from Taylor-Schechter K-1.* Sheffield: Sheffield Academic Press, 1992.

Schmidt, B. B. "The Aniconic Tradition. On Reading Images and Viewing Texts." In *The Triumph of Elohim: From Yahwisms to Judaism.* Edited by D. Edelman, 75–105. Grand Rapids: Eerdmans, 1996.

Scholem, G. *Major Trends in Jewish Mysticism.* 3d ed. New York: Schoken, 1954.

——— *Jewish Gnosticism, Merkabah Mysticism and Talmudic Tradition.* 2d ed. New York: Jewish Theological Seminary of America, 1965.

——— *Kabbalah.* Jerusalem: Keter, 1974.

——— *On the Mystical Shape of the Godhead: Basic Concepts in the Kabbalah.* Translated by J. Neugroschel. New York: Schoken, 1991.

Schultz, J. P. "Angelic Opposition to the Ascension of Moses and the Revelation of the Law." *JQR* 61 (1970–71): 282–307.

Schürer, E. *The History of the Jewish People in the Age of Jesus Christ.* Revised and edited by G. Vermes, F. Millar, and M. Black. Edinburgh: T&T Clark, 1979.

Sebeok, T. S. *Myth, A Symposium.* Bloomington: Indiana University Press, 1986.

Segal, A. F. *Two Powers in Heaven: Early Rabbinic Reports about Christianity and Gnosticism.* Leiden: Brill, 1977.

——— "Heavenly Ascent in Hellenistic Judaism, Early Christianity, and their Environment." *Aufstieg und Niedergang der Römischen Welt* II. 23. 2 (1980): 1333–1394.

——— *Paul, the Convert: The Apostolate and Apostsasy of Saul of the Pharisee.* New Haven and London: Yale University Press, 1990.

Segal, M. Z. *Sepher Ben Sira ha-Shalem* (Jerusalem: Bialik Institute 1972. [Hebrew]

——— *Edessa 'The Blessed City'.* Oxford: Clarendon Press, 1970.

van Seters, J. *Prologue to History: The Yahwist as Historian in Genesis.* Louisville: Westminster John Knox Press, 1992.

Shehan P. W. and Di Lella, A. A. *The Wisdom of Ben Sira.* New York: Doubleday, 1987.

Sjöberg, A, W. and Bergmann, E. "The Collection of the Sumerian Temple Hymns." In *The Collection of the Sumerian Temple Hymns* (Texts from Cuneiform Sources, III). Edited by A. W. Sjöberg, E. Bergmann, E. , and G. B. Gragg, 3–154. Locust Valley, NY: Augustin: 1969.

Smith, J. Z. "Wisdom and Apocalyptic." In *Religious Syncretism in Antiquity. Essays in Conversation with Geo Widengren.* Edited by B. A. Pearson, 131–156. Missoula: Scholars Press, 1975.

Smith, M. "Some Observations on Hekhalot Rabbati." In *Biblical and Other Studies.* Edited by A. Altmann, 149–156. Cambridge, MA: Harvard University Press, 1963.

——— "Ascent to the Heavens and Deification in 4QM." In *Archeology and History in the Dead Sea Scrolls.* Edited by L. H. Schiffman, 181–188. Sheffield: JSOT Press, 1990.

Smith, M. S. "Divine Form and Size in Ugaritic and Pre-Exilic Israelite Religion." *Zeitschrift für die Alttestamentliche Wissenschaft* 100 (1988): 424–427.

——— "Seeing God in the Psalms. The Background to the Beatific Vision in the Hebrew Bible." *CBQ* 50 (1988): 171–183.

——— *The Early History of God. Yahweh and the Other Deities in Ancient Israel.* San Francisco: Harper and Row, 1990.

——— "The Near Eastern Background of Solar Language for Yahweh." *JBL* 109 (1990): 29–39.

——— *The Origins of Biblical Monotheism: Israel's Polytheistic Background and the Ugaritic Texts.* New York: Oxford University Press, 2001.

Snaith, N. H. *The Jewish New Year Festival: Its Origin and Development.* London: SPCK, 1947.

Starr, I. *The Rituals of the Diviner.* Malibu: Undena, 1983.

Stevenson-Smith, W. *Interconnections in the Ancient Near East.* New Haven and London, 1965.

Stone, M. E. "Reactions to the Destruction of the Second Temple." *JSJ* 12 (1981): 193–204.

——— "Ideal Figures and Social Context: Priest and Sage in the Early Second Temple Period." In *Ancient Israelite Religion.* Edited by P. D. Miller, Jr. , P. D. Hanson, and S. D. McBride, 575–586. Philadelphia Fortress Press, 1988.

Strommenger, E. *5000 Years of the Art of Mesopotamia.* New York: H. N. Abrams, 1964.

Stordalem, T. *Echoes of Eden, Genesis 2–3 and Symbolism of the Garden in Biblical Hebrew Literature.* Leuven: Peeters, 2000.

Streng, F. J. "Language and Mystical Awareness." In *Mysticism and Philosophical Analysis.* Edited by S. Katz, 141–169. London and New York: Sheldon, 1978.

Stroumsa, G. G. "Aher: A Gnostic." In *The Rediscovery of Gnosticism,* II. Edited by B. Layton Bentley, 808–818. Leiden: Brill, 1981.

——— "Form(s) of God: Some Notes on Metatron and Christ." *HTR* 76 (1983): 269–288.

——— "Mystical Descent" In *Death, Ecstasy and Other Worldly Journeys.* Edited by J. J. Collins and M. Fishbane, 137–53 (New York: State University of New York Press, 1995.

Strugnell, J. "The Angelic Liturgy At Qumran—4Q Serekh Sirot Olat Hassabbat." Congress VTSup 7 (1960): 318–345.

Stuckenbruck, L. T. *Angel Veneration and Christology.* Tübingen: Mohr Siebeck, 1995.

Swartz, M. D. *Mystical Prayer in Early Judaism: An Analysis of Ma'aseh Merkavah.* Tübingen: Mohr Siebeck, 1992.

———. *Scholastic Magic. Ritual and Revelation in Early Jewish Mysticism.* Princeton, NJ: Princeton University Press, 1996.

Sweet, R. F. G. "The Sage in Mesopotamian Palaces and Royal Courts." In *The Sage in Israel and the Ancient Near East.* Edited by J. G. Gammie and L. G. Perdue, 99–107. Winona Lake, IN: Eisenbrauns, 1990.

——— "The Sage in Akkadian Literature: A Philological Study." In *The Sage in Israel and the Ancient Near East.* Edited by J. G. Gammie and L. G. Perdue, 45–65. Winona Lake, IN: Eisenbrauns, 1990.

Tabor, J. D. *Things Unutterable: Paul's Ascent to Paradise in its Greco-Roman, Judaic, and Early Christian Contexts.* Lamham, MD: University Press of America, 1986.

Tadmor, H. "Autobiographical Apology in the Royal Assyrian Literature." In *History, Historiography and Interpretation.* Edited by H. Tadmor and M. Weinfeld, 36–57. Jerusalem: Magnes Press, 1983.

Talbert, C. H. "The Concept of Immortals in Mediterranean Antiquity." *JBL* 94 (1975): 419–439.

Texidor, J. *The Pagan God. Popular Religion in the Greco-Roman Near East.* Princeton, NJ: Princeton University Press, 1977.

Tiggay, J. *The Evolution of the Gilgamesh Epic.* Philadelphia: University of Pennnsylvania Press, 1982.

——— "An Early Technique of Aggadic Exegesis." In *History, Historiography and Interpretation.* Edited by H. Tadmor and M. Weinfeld. Jerusalem: Magnes Press, 1983.

——— *You Shall Have No Other Gods: Israelite Religion in Light of Hebrew Inscriptions.* Atlanta: Scholars Press, 1986.

Tournay, R. J. *Seeing and Hearing God with the Psalms, The Prophetic Liturgy of the Second Temple in Jerusalem.* Sheffield: JSOT Press, 1991.

Turner, V. *The Ritual Process: Structure and Anti-Structure.* London: Routledge and Kegan, 1969.

Uffenheimer, B. "Myth and Reality in Ancient Israel." In *The Origin and Diversity of Axial Age Civilization.* Edited by S. N. Eisenstadt, 135–168. Albany, NY: State University of New York Press, 1986.

Underhill, E. *Mysticism, A Study in the Nature and Development of Man's Spirituality.* 1911. Reprint, New York and Ontario: Meridian, 1974.

Urbach, E. E. *The Sages, Their Concepts and Beliefs.* Translated by I. Abrahams. Jerusalem: Magnes Press, 1975.

———. "The Traditions about Merkavah Mysticism in the Tannaitic Period." In *Studies in Mysticism and Religion Presented to Gershom G. Scholem on his Seventieth Birthday.* Edited by E. E. Urbach, R. J. Z. Weblowsky and H. Wirshuvski, 1–28. Jerusalem: Magnes Press, 1967. [Hebrew Section]

VanderKam, J. C. *Enoch and the Growth of an Apocalyptic Tradition.* Washington, DC: The Catholic Biblical Association of America, 1984.

———. *Enoch, A Man For All Generations: Studies on Personalities of the Old Testament.* Columbia, SC: University of South Carolina Press, 1995.

de Vaux, R. *The Bible and the Ancient Near East.* Translated by D. McHugh. London: Darton, Longman, and Todd, 1972.

Vermes, G. "Biblical and Midrash: Early Old Testament Exegesis." In *The Cambridge History of the Bible. From the Beginning to Jerome.* Edited by P. R. Ackroyd and C. F. Evans, 199–231. Cambridge: Cambridge University Press, 1970.

Wallace, H. N. *The Eden Narrative.* Atlanta: Scholars Press, 1985.

Waujman, K. "Mysticism from the Perspective of the Jewish-Christian Tradition." *Studies in Spirituality* 2 (1992): 5–50.

——— "Towards a Phenomenological Definition of Spirituality." *Studies in Spirituality* 3 (1993): 5–57.

Wedderburn, A. J. M. *Baptism and Resurrection. Studies in Pauline Theology Against its Graeco-Roman Background.* Tübingen: Mohr Siebeck, 1987.

Weinfeld, M. "God the Creator in Gen. 1 and in the Prophecy of Second Isaiah." *Tarbitz* 37 (1968): 105–132. [Hebrew]

——— *Deuteronomy and the Deuteronomic School.* Oxford: Clarendon Press, 1972.

——— "'Rider of the Clouds' and 'Gatherer of the Clouds'." *JNES* 5 (1975): 421–426.

——— "Sabbath, Temple Building and the Enthronement of the Lord" *Beth Miqra* 69 (1977): 188–193. [Hebrew]

——— "The Heavenly Praise in Unison." in *Meqor Hajjim, Festschrift fur Georg Molia zum 75. Gebürtstag.* 427–433. Graz: Akademische Druck und Verlagsanstalt, 1983.

Weisberg, D. B. "Some Observations on Late Babylonian Texts and Rabbinic Literature." *HUCA* 39 (1968): 71–80.

Wells, P. S. *Culture, Contact, and Culture Change: Early Iron Age Europe and the Mediterranean World.* Cambridge: Cambridge University Press, 1980.

Werblowsky, R. J. Z. "Mystical and Magical Contemplation." *History of Religions* 1 (1961): 9–36.

——— "On the Mystical Rejection of Mystical Illuminations." *Religious Studies* 1 (1965/6): 177–184.

West, M. L. *The East Face Helicon.* Oxford, New York: Clarendon Press, 1997.

Widengren, G. *The Ascension of the Apostle and the Heavenly Book.* Uppsala: Lundequistska, 1950.

Wilson, R. R. "The Death of the King of Tyre: The Editorial History of Ezekiel 28." In *Love and Death in the Ancient Near East, Essays in Honor of Marvin H. Pope.* Edited by J. H. Marks and R. M. Good, 211–218. Guilford, CN: Four Quarters, 1987.

Wolfson, E. R. "Halperin's The Faces of the Chariot." *JQR* 81 (1991): 498–499.

——— "Yerida la -Merkavah: Typology of Ecstasy and Enthronement in Ancient Jewish Mysticism." In *Mystics of the Book-Themes, Topics and Typologies.* Edited by R. A. Herrera, 13–45. New York: Peter Lang, 1993.

——— *Through a Speculum that Shines. Visions and Imagination in Medieval Jewish Mysticism.* Princeton, NJ: Princeton University Press, 1994, pp. 74–124.

Wright, J. E. *The Early History of Heaven.* Oxford, New York: Oxford University Press, 2000.

Wyatt, N. *Myths of Power: A Study of Royal Myth and Ideology in Ugarit and Biblical Tradition.* Münster: Ugarit-Verlag, 1996.

Index of Passages Discussed

CLASSICAL RABBINIC LITERATURE

GREEK, GNOSTIC, EARLY CHRISTIAN SOURCES

HEKHALOT AND MERKAVAH LITERATURE

CAIRO GENIZAH

Index of Authors

General Index